The Mulatto Republic

D1564059

UNIVERSITY PRESS OF FLORIDA

Florida A&M University, Tallahassee
Florida Atlantic University, Boca Raton
Florida Gulf Coast University, Ft. Myers
Florida International University, Miami
Florida State University, Tallahassee
New College of Florida, Sarasota
University of Central Florida, Orlando
University of Florida, Gainesville
University of North Florida, Jacksonville
University of South Florida, Tampa
University of West Florida, Pensacola

THE MULATTO REPUBLIC

Class, Race, and Dominican National Identity

APRIL J. MAYES

University Press of Florida

Gainesville/Tallahassee/Tampa/Boca Raton

Pensacola/Orlando/Miami/Jacksonville/Ft. Myers/Sarasota

This book may be available in an electronic edition.

First cloth printing, 2014
First paperback printing, 2015

Library of Congress Cataloging-in-Publication Data
Mayes, April J., author.
The Mulatto Republic : class, race, and Dominican national identity / April J. Mayes.
pages cm
Includes bibliographical references and index.
ISBN 978-0-8130-4919-9 (cloth)
ISBN 978-0-8130-6196-2 (pbk.)
1. Ethnicity—Dominican Republic. 2. Racially mixed people—Race identity—Dominican Republic. 3. National characteristics, Dominican. 4. Racism—Dominican Republic. 5. Race awareness—Dominican Republic. 6. Social classes—Dominican Republic. 7. Dominican Republic—Race relations. I. Title.
F1941.A1M39 2014
305.80097293—dc23   2013038957

University Press of Florida
15 Northwest 15th Street
Gainesville, FL 32611-2079
http://www.upf.com

For Mom, Miriam, and Nayeem

CONTENTS

ILLUSTRATIONS

Figures

Maps

TABLES

ACKNOWLEDGMENTS

Quiero, primero, reconocer a mi familia y todos los sacrificios que se han hecho por mi. A un padre ausente, a una mamá por naturaleza y a una mamá de crianza; tanto en Estados Unidos como en la República Dominicana, doy gracias por su confort, su apoyo y su fe en mi. Dedico estas palabras a mis tías, Blanca y María; a mis primas, que son mis hermanas, Betsaida y Hortensia; y mi primito Lilo. Gracias también a Fanny Ramírez Aracenas, nuestra querida Mama Nelly, por cuidar a mis chiquillos mientras trabajaba. Dedico este libro a ellos, Miriam y Nayeem, por tener que sacrificar tanto tan joven.

I want to thank, first, my family, spread across the United States and into the Caribbean. To my mother who raised me, Margaret, and the woman who birthed me, Shirley—thank you for your love. Sabrina, thank you for help on so many occasions. And to the circle of *abuelos*—grandmothers, grandfathers, aunts, and uncles who care for me from above—thank you.

I am especially indebted to Sueann Caulfield, Rebecca J. Scott, Frances Aparicio, Jesse Hoffnung-Garskoff, Richard Turits, and María Montoya. My thanks to a great cohort of friends—José Amador, Adrian Burgos, John McKiernan González, Frank Guridy, Lourdes Gutiérrez, Kate Masur, Aims McGuinness, Ellen Moodie, Millery Polyné, Lara Putnam, Mario Ruiz, and David Salmonson. I am particularly grateful to Barbara Berglund for her friendship, emotional support, intellectual companionship, and willingness to engage in retail therapy. Barb, you are a gift. Heartfelt thanks also to colleagues who helped me at Virginia Tech—Terry Kershaw, Marian Mollin, Amy Nelson, Helen Schneider, and Dan Thorp.

In the Dominican Republic Dr. Frank Moya Pons provided institutional and personal support while I conducted research. He was instrumental in introducing me to the community of scholars and historians in San Pedro de Macorís that included Dr. Jorge Hazim and Don José Horacio Ramírez. I am particularly grateful to Dr. Fermín Álvarez Santana for allowing me to use his vast library of primary and secondary sources related to San Pedro de Macorís, which includes bound copies of *El Cable*, photographs, papers from El Ateneo, genealogies, and local histories.

Dr. Jorge Hazim narrated a literary history of San Pedro and gave me a volume of Gastón Deligne's poetry that I treasure. Artist and community activist Nadal Walcott gave me a valuable walking tour of Ingenio Consuelo and a radical interpretation of San Pedro's history. I am also grateful to another local historian, who wished to remain anonymous, who allowed me to sit in her home and read volumes of *Renacimiento*.

Miguel Phipps Cueto, Benjamín Silva, and Don Bello were also helpful in guiding me through Consuelo's and San Pedro's shared past and their present circumstances. I am honored to have been part of their efforts to write a multi-ethnic history of San Pedro. I am also grateful to Orlando Inoa and his family's hospitality while I pored through his personal collection of material related to many aspects of Dominican history.

Important sections of this book would not have been possible without the valuable collaboration of Anglican Bishop Telésforo Isaac, Doña Estrella Cooks de Pérez, Doña Martha Williamson viuda González, Don Emille Washington, Doña Ruth Washington, Uncle John Walcott, and the entire San Esteban Episcopal Church community, especially the Reverend Mercedes Julián. Gracias por todo y que Dios siga bendeciéndoles. Over the years, too, numerous students have assisted this project—Saraí Jiménez, Julia Kramer, Jessica Lewis, and Nancy Quiñones. I am also grateful to my *hermanas* especially, Lisette García and Cicely Washington.

I am thankful to the tremendous staff at the Dominican National Archives. I extend my heartfelt gratitude to Edy Jáquez. In recent years, leadership of the Dominican National Archives has changed and the transformation, under Roberto Cassá's direction, has benefited all those interested in Dominican social history. I am grateful for his leadership and for many long conversations with Raymundo González and Quisqueya Lora Hugi. They challenged my thinking about Dominican history. I am also thankful for the faculty and staff at the Instituto Pedro Francisco Bonó, especially Anne Beltre and Pablo Mella, S.J. Gracias por todo. Finally, many thanks to archivists and staffs at the National Archives and Records Administration in Washington, D.C. and in College Park, Maryland; the Moorland Spingarn Research Center at Howard University, D.C.; the Naval Historical Center; the Public Record Office in Kew Gardens, England; the Centro de Investigación Histórica at the University of Puerto Rico, Río Piedras; and the Centro de Estudios Hostosianos at the University of Puerto Rico.

Back in the United States, a community of *dominicanistas* has offered me tremendous support. Mil abrazos y agradecimientos a Sarah Aponte, Emelio Betances, Bruce Calder, Rosario Espinal, Julie Franks, Ramona Hernández, and Silvio Torres Saillant. I am so happy that over the years Ginetta Candelario, Carlos Decena, Robin (Lauren) Derby, María Filomena González, Elizabeth Manley, and Kimberly Simmons have become close and faithful friends. *Besos* especially to Alicia Sangro Blasco! An honorary member of this cohort, Catherine LeGrand, read an early version of chapter 5. Teresita Martínez-Vergne read this manuscript with a fine-tooth comb and helped me improve it in important ways.

Many thanks to Amy Gorelick and the anonymous reviewers at the University Press of Florida for their patience and for helping me make this book a reality.

I am forever grateful to the cohort of Fulbright scholars (2009–2010) who shared in this manuscript process and who also became close friends and *cómplices*: Lesley Bartlett, Tanya Golash-Boza, Sarita Jackson, Kiran Jayaram, and Yolanda Martín. I remember our lunches at Villar Hermanos fondly. Yoli, it was an honor to share the struggles of motherhood and research with you! Kiran, ya tú sabes. Gracias por todo. Samir Nadkarni, thank you for your friendship. Thanks to Bridget Wooding and the staff at OBMICA (Observatorio Migrantes del Caribe/Caribbean Migrants' Observatory) for providing us a space to meet. With Yolanda, Kiran, Carlos, and Yveline Alexis, we formed the Transnational Hispaniola Collective. Our conversations and the conferences we organized have challenged me profoundly.

Finally, I am thankful to my friends and colleagues at Pomona College. The Minority Scholars in Residence Fellowship at Pomona College, subsequent research grants, and the Steele Leave, complemented with a Fulbright Scholar grant, allowed me to make significant progress on the manuscript. I am grateful for colleagues in my department, especially Sidney Lemelle, Victor Silverman, Miguel Tinker Salas, and Robert Woods. Friends at Pomona have been a very important part of this process. Thank you, Cecilia Conrad, Evelyn Khalili, Pardis Mahdavi, Erin Runions, Val Thomas, Kyla Tompkins, and Eva Valle. All my love.

INTRODUCTION

In November 2009 Sammy Sosa, the Dominican-born Chicago Cub who competed with Mark McGwire, of the St. Louis Cardinals, in the home run race of 1998, once again made national and international headlines. Sosa was born in Consuelo, a sugar estate located on the outskirts of San Pedro de Macorís, a town famous for producing a critical mass of Dominicans who play Major League Baseball in the United States. During his baseball career, Sosa achieved a level of success, fame, and socioeconomic mobility that many young men from Consuelo and other sugar-mill towns grow up dreaming about. Now retired, Sosa made an appearance at the 2009 Latin Grammys that shocked reporters and baseball fans alike: Sosa, formerly a dark-skinned man (what some Dominicans may refer to as "*indio-oscuro*"), had a white face and white hands as a result of using bleaching creams. By using light-colored contact lenses, Sosa had transformed socioeconomic whitening (*blanqueamiento*) into a physical fact.[1]

Sammy Sosa admitted to using a "rejuvenating" skin cream: "I apply [it] before going to bed and [it] whitens my skin."[2] For Dominicans of a certain age, Sosa's ritual probably resonated with the personal habits of General Rafael Leonidas Trujillo, the dictator who controlled the Dominican Republic from 1930 until 1961. Although a much lighter-skinned man than Sosa, he faithfully applied powder to his face to whiten his appearance.

In the United States Sosa's admission appeared to confirm representations of Dominicans as a racist people who deny their African ancestry. An article published in the *Miami Herald* claimed that Dominicans of African descent, long told that they were white Hispanics, suffered from a psychosis rooted in antiblack racism, anti-Haitian xenophobia, and the desire to whiten and distance themselves from their African past.[3] How was it possible, some asked, for millions of similarly hued Sammy Sosas to think of themselves as white and Hispanic?

It is true that for much of the twentieth century, official state nationalism in the Dominican Republic privileged European ancestry and Hispanic cultural norms such as the Spanish language and Catholicism. It is also the case that twentieth-century iterations of this national identity—*hispanidad*—achieved their most brutal expression during General Trujillo's dictatorship. The architects of antiblack, anti-Haitian *hispanidad* in the 1930s and 1940s in effect transformed a racist conceptualization of the Dominican nation—as a collective unified by its rejection of blackness, vodoun, and Kreyòl—held by a small group of intellectual and bureaucratic elites into an ideology that has since permeated Dominican society and culture.[4]

The pervasiveness of antiblack, anti-Haitian nationalism among elites and nonelites alike raises questions: Is contemporary Dominican national identity simply a persistent legacy of the Trujillato (Trujillo regime)? Or does Dominican *hispanidad* represent a nationalism unique to an island divided between two countries long engaged with each other in sometimes cooperative and, at other times, conflicted ways?

The present study makes three arguments to answer these questions. First, I will show that while *hispanicismo*, the elevation of cultural norms and values associated with Spain and Spanish colonialism, was present in all currents of nationalist thought elaborated in the late nineteenth century, not all conceptualizations of Dominican national identity were antiblack or anti-Haitian. I then argue that although *hispanicismo* had been, since the 1880s, a key element in intellectual conversations about *dominicanidad* (Dominicanness), its significance became more pronounced in towns such as San Pedro de Macorís as native-born elites expanded their ranks to include wealthy white immigrants from Cuba, Puerto Rico, and Spain. Finally, I demonstrate that while the path from *hispanicismo* toward official *hispanidad* was never linear, a patriarchal, racist, and authoritarian representation of the Dominican nation became viable and acceptable among modernizing elites by the 1920s. As a result, I conclude, Trujillo-era nationalism was an ideological invention unique to the dictatorship that drew on long-held ideas that national unity derived from Dominicans' culturally pure Hispanic tradition. Proponents of *hispanidad* nationalism, however, injected *hispanicismo* with a profound pessimism about the Dominican nation's future and complemented this bleary outlook with a virulent antiblack rhetoric that resonated with Negrophobic intellectual traditions but was more vitriolic in its application.

The origins of anti-Haitian and antiblack nationalist ideologies in the Dominican Republic have long been central to debates among Dominican historians, political scientists, and journalists concerning the relationship between popular expressions of Dominican identity and official nationalism. For example, as Franklin Franco Pichardo and Ernesto Sagás argue, Dominican intellectual and political elites invented anti-Haitian xenophobia and antiblack racism in Dominican national discourse. Particularly since the Trujillo era, these scholars insist, Dominican elites have imposed their racist, authoritarian nationalism onto the general public, manipulating racism at politically opportune moments in order to secure the domination of their class and direct attention away from their exploitation of Dominicans in general.[5]

How (or whether) Dominican elites have managed to impose their ideology beyond their class has made the pervasiveness of anti-Haitian xenophobia and antiblack racism among working-class and lower-middle-class Dominicans another topic of great debate. Anthropologists such as David Howard and Kimberly Simmons, as well as political scientist Mark Sawyer and sociologist Ginetta Candelario, have shown that while Dominicans accept that they are a racially mixed people, they adhere to idealizations of *dominicanidad* defined by its distance from blackness and its rejection of anything associated with Haiti and Haitians.[6]

To make the argument that *hispanidad* nationalism has a history presents a methodological challenge for the historian and can be a political minefield. The most prolific Trujillo-era ideologues, such as Manuel Arturo Peña Batlle (1902–1954), who served as ambassador to Haiti and secretary of state, and Joaquín Balaguer (1906–2002), poet and essayist who served as vice president during the Trujillo regime, insisted that Dominicans forged a collective identity as *criollos* (creoles) as early as the seventeenth century. However, their cohesion as a nation had been continually threatened by French and, later, Haitian incursions into Dominican territory. According to them, anti-Haitian sentiment became even more ingrained among Dominicans in the wake of the Haitian invasion and occupation of Santo Domingo from 1822 until 1844.[7] They also argued that in the latter part of the nineteenth century, exiled Puerto Rican philosopher Eugenio María de Hostos (1839–1903) introduced secular pedagogy to the Dominican Republic, and this direct challenge to the Catholic Church's teachings further undermined the Dominican nation's attachment to Spain.[8] For these intellectuals, General Trujillo (1891–1961), as "Padre de la Patria" (father of the nation), represented the best hope Dominicans had to fulfill their collective historical destiny as a Hispanic nation, free from the threats represented by Haitians, blackness, and secularism.

Claims that *hispanidad* nationalism has historical roots may appear to give credence to the conclusions drawn by Peña Batlle and Balaguer. However, the intellectual opening occasioned by the end of the dictatorship in 1961 and the struggle for democracy in the 1960s and 1970s provided a generation of scholars in the 1980s opportunities to challenge Trujillo–era narratives. Branded the "*nueva ola*" (new wave), Dominican historians such as Roberto Cassá, Frank Moya Pons, Franklin Franco Pichardo, Orlando Inoa, Raymundo González, Carlos Doré Cabral, Rubén Silié, José Chez Checo, María Filomena González, and Emilio Cordero Michel used social history methodologies to reinterpret the Dominican past "from below" in order to refute Peña Batlle's and Balaguer's historical interpretations as ideological fictions invented to justify authoritarianism.[9]

With specific reference to the origins of Dominican national identity and the historical roots of *hispanidad*, these scholars made five important arguments that inform this study. Franklin Franco Pichardo rejected the idea that anti-Haitian nationalism sprang from the popular classes and insisted on *hispanidad* as an ideological manipulation meant to buttress elite hegemony. Raymundo González and Frank Moya Pons showed that while the Dominican Republic's colonial history bequeathed it the unique legacy of having led to the development of an autonomous peasant society by the eighteenth century, claims that Dominicans across class and color expressed a unified identity oriented around a connection with Spain prior to the nineteenth century were not supported by available evidence. González and Moya Pons also demonstrated that Haitian governance over Santo Domingo, from 1822 to 1844, was not simply the result of Haitians' imperialist machinations; rather, Haitian rule proved both repressive and significantly progressive for various sectors of Dominican society. Building on this reinterpretation of Haitian rule, Emilio Cordero Michel and José Chez Checo argued that Dominican racial democracy emerged not as a result of Spanish benevolence; rather, it emerged from the cross-class, cross-racial mobilization that defeated Spanish reannexation (1861–1865) during the War of Restoration (1863–1865). The national project, in their view, began after 1865, not in the wake of separation from Haiti in 1844 and certainly not during the colonial period.[10] Together, these historians and their new interpretations of the past complicated Dominicans' historical relationships with Spain and Haiti and therefore challenged the centrality of antiblack Hispanophilia to Dominican national identity, especially among the rural majority.

Finally, Roberto Cassá and Orlando Inoa questioned the idea that Trujillo-era anti-Haitianism was simply a manifestation of fears and anxieties about Haitians and Haiti that dated back to the Haitian revolution. Roberto Cassá argued that while racism had long served as an important ideological glue that unified an otherwise divided Dominican elite, manifestations of racist nationalism occurred at specific historical moments. One such key period was the U.S. occupation, which, according to Cassá, provoked a conservative reaction among elites, who responded to U.S. imperialism with a notion of Hispanic moral superiority in contrast to North American Anglo-Saxonism. Orlando Inoa and Michiel Baud, a Netherlands-based historian, argue that Trujillo-era anti-Haitian discourse was more directly the product of the state's need to justify its exploitative treatment of Haitian migrant workers in Dominican cane fields. Therefore, while twentieth-century anti-Haitianism drew on older forms of racism, it also represented a unique articulation of a modernizing, industrializing state.[11] *The Mulatto Republic* builds on the scholarship of the *nueva ola*, which forces us to explain the origins of official anti-Haitianism through empirical research that joins intellectual with social history, cultural with political analysis.

This study has also been influenced by recent research produced outside the Dominican Republic, mainly by scholars based in the United States. In conversations with the Dominican *nueva ola* generation, these scholars have also focused on anti-Haitianism in Dominican national ideology and have attempted to trace the origins of antiblack nationalism among elites and nonelites alike. For example, Robin (Lauren) Derby and Richard Turits's nuanced study of the Haiti-Dominican border finds that, as Franco Pichardo argued, the rural Dominican masses were not inherently anti-Haitian. Dominicans living in the border region became anti-Haitian when the Trujillo regime violently imposed a state-building program on the border. The Matanza, or Haitian Massacre, of 1937, followed state–driven Dominicanization. In their work, modern anti-Haitianism is a feature of state consolidation and the imposition of a modern regime onto an area traditionally regarded as neither Dominican nor Haitian.[12]

Lauren Derby and Christian Krohn-Hansen, in particular, inspire new ways of considering Dominican anti-Haitianism as a result of their innovative research. Derby's study of Haitians in the Dominican popular imagination, for instance, questions the simple linkage between blackness and Haitianness as the basis of Dominican prejudice against Haitians. In contrast, she argues that as the Dominican-Haitian border joined the global economy, "Haitians came to be seen as the very embodiment of money magic," but once the border region became incorporated into the national state beginning in the 1910s, Haitians were viewed as a threat to the national body. This shift in local meanings of race and nation helped Dominicans who had worked with Haitians and, in some instances, had Haitian kin make sense of a massacre that was itself a brutal response to a problem extraneous to border realities. Similarly, Krohn-Hansen has argued that Dominicans living along the border differentiate themselves from Haitians "through the symbolic construction of the devil's money"—meaning, they conceive of national identities through the logic of good and evil. Dominicans associate Haitians with the magical power to make money or think of them as people who have a relationship with money, conceived of as an evil force that destroys otherwise equal social relations.[13]

For Ginetta Candelario, too, Dominican anti-Haitianism is a narrative of difference and a practice of differentiation that responds to shifts in regional and global power. Candelario argues that Dominican national identity took form in a triangular relationship, articulated against Haiti but also engaged with nineteenth-century U.S. imperialism in the Caribbean. In some instances, Dominican politicians and intellectuals insisted on Dominicans' whiteness in their support of U.S. intervention; at other moments, the argument that Dominicans were racially mixed and not pure blacks like Haitians was also used to defend Dominican sovereignty in the face of European and U.S. interventions.[14]

The research of the Dominican *nueva ola* and U.S.-based scholars has emphasized the substantial divergence and distance between official state anti-Haitianism and the quotidian, lived experiences of ethnic and racial difference among nonelite Dominicans. Dominican and U.S. scholars have also explained how political elites manipulate anti-Haitianism at specific moments to create a crisis or to forward a national agenda that, in the end, harms poor Dominicans and Haitians alike. Finally, by teasing apart the relationship between anti-blackness and anti-Haitianism, these scholars have taken the significant step of questioning presumptions about Dominicans' relationship to blackness.

Building on this rich scholarship, I analyze the period between 1870 and 1940 to argue that a racist, patriarchal, and authoritarian state emerged in the 1940s as a result of exclusionary governing practices that disenfranchised rural Dominicans, reactions to black labor, and U.S. military intervention. I show that the monopolization of political power by a Hispanic-identified group of elites, the conservative reaction against U.S. imperialism, and anti-black policing prepared the groundwork for *hispanidad* nationalism in two ways. First, the period between 1870 and 1940 witnessed the emergence of a regional, modernizing elite that increasingly defined itself in exclusive, racial terms and governed accordingly. Second, and related to the first, the political significance of race changed as a result of Afro-Antillean immigration and the country's integration into the U.S. sphere of influence. I argue, then, that Trujillo-era nationalism, like nationalist projects across Latin America, was a product of historical processes and represented a distinct break from the past. This study responds specifically to Silvio Torres-Saillant's acerbic critique of popular and scholarly representations of Dominican racial identity that "exaggerate the exceptionality of Negrophobia in the ethno-racial constructions of the Dominican nation . . . [and fail] to consider the Dominican case in a comparative perspective."[15]

The analysis presented here also moves the scholarship in new directions. For example, by focusing on San Pedro de Macorís, heart of the eastern sugar-growing region, *The Mulatto Republic* removes both Santo Domingo and the border as the *kilómetro zero* (ground zero) of debates over Dominican national identity and constructions of Dominican anti-Haitianism. Taking a cue from Derby, Turits, and Krohn-Hansen, in this book I draw attention to another, porous, space defined by trade, commercial relations, and the movement of Afro-Antillean people from the circum-Caribbean. Focusing on Afro-Antilleans in this story adds another dimension to the analysis of Dominican antiblackness, suggesting that antiblack racism emerged as a reaction against Haitians *and* Afro-Antilleans. Moreover, although San Pedro was not the historical center of the country, the city achieved notoriety for its cultural production and contribution to advances in education. An intellectual and bourgeois cultural life flourished in San Pedro. Meanwhile, its busy streets were populated by Afro-Antillean workers; in sugarcane fields, Afro-Antilleans and Haitians labored in horrendous conditions; and in noisy sugar mills, British West Indian, Puerto Rican, Cuban, and U.S. managers, accountants, and engineers literally forged a new economy. These contrasting spheres make possible an examination of race, class, and nation at various levels of Dominican society and among historical actors differentiated significantly by ethnicity, race, class, and migratory status.

This study begins in the 1870s in the decades after the War of Restoration fought against Spain's annexation of Santo Domingo (1863–1865) and just as the United States became a more influential actor in Dominican foreign affairs. In chapter 1, I argue that intellectuals and politicians such as Pedro Francisco Bonó (1828–1906), considered the Dominican Republic's first sociologist, Gregorio Luperón (1839–1897), who briefly served as president (1879–1880), and Eugenio María de Hostos (1839–1903) crafted inclusive and forward-looking national projects that were neither anti-Haitian nor antiblack. According to Bonó and some commentators in the United States, the Dominican Republic was a mulatto nation between the blackness of Haiti and the whiteness of the United States and Europe. During the 1880s, as Roberto Cassá and Teresita Martínez-Vergne have argued, debates over citizenship, governance, and the development of a modern civil society motivated conversations about *dominicanidad*.[16] These debates, while conceived in racial terms, were not always inherently racist. Gregorio Luperón and Eugenio María de Hostos, in particular, struggled explicitly with the problem of black political leadership in a historical moment saturated with antiblack racism and fear of black political power.

These intellectuals/politicians also grappled with the social and economic conflicts that emerged with the development of large-scale sugar production. In the 1860s and early 1870s San Pedro de Macorís was just a fishing village located on the banks of the Higuamo River in the eastern part of the island. Then, in 1876 Juan Amechazurra, who fled Cuba during the Ten Years' War (1868–1878), built San Pedro's first steam-driven sugar mill. By 1907 the Dominican Republic's largest and most productive sugar mills operated around San Pedro de Macorís. As a result, San Pedro evolved into a major city, a provincial capital, and a microcosm of a nation dealing with the social and political consequences of an economy increasingly dependent on sugar exports and tied to the United States.[17]

Although San Pedro de Macorís was the center of sugar production between 1870 and 1940 and home to a diverse population comprising white immigrants from Europe, Cuba, and Puerto Rico and black migrants from Puerto Rico, Haiti, and the Anglophone Caribbean, the city has received little attention from historians as a site for examining the origins of twentieth-century *hispanidad* nationalism. In contrast, scholars have focused on San Pedro's hinterlands, because sugar estates relied heavily on exploitable migrant labor. In their analyses, the region around San Pedro emerges as an important site to test the degree to which anti-Haitianism operated as a tool of labor management and control. As Samuel Martínez argues, in contrast to what occurred in Central America and other Caribbean locations, from the late nineteenth century into the twentieth, the Dominican state took more control over labor, producing a "government managed system of semicoerced exploitation."[18] Dividing the working classes along ethnic and racial lines, Patrick Bryan argues, was a key element in this government-managed system. According to Bryan, working-class Dominicans learned to disparage Haitians and black migrants as workers whose low wages threatened the value of Dominican labor.[19] Anti-Haitianism, then, was a convenient strategy exploited by estate administrators and local government officials to divide the laboring classes; antiblack racism and anti-Haitian xenophobia complemented the state's increasing control over migrant labor for sugar production.

These studies do not explain, however, how provincial or city authorities, in addition to estate managers, understood themselves and their economic and political interests in racially exclusive terms. Nor does available documentation permit us to determine if antiblack and anti-Haitian sentiments bubbled up from below or even how they were disseminated from elites to popular classes. Local records do show how the governing practices of local elites became exclusive and, over time, racialized and racist with regard to black migrants. Chapter 2 describes how a regional elite came into being and became politically powerful in San Pedro in the 1890s and early 1900s. This group included Dominicans with long-standing ties to the region and wealthy white immigrants. Some Dominican landowners and newly arrived immigrants cultivated cane for nearby sugar estates and became contracted sugar producers (*colonos*); others opened commercial enterprises such as import-export stores, pharmacies, and schools. At the same time, and thanks to General Ulises "Lilís" Heureaux's dictatorship (1888–1899), local governance became more vertically incorporated into his patronage system sustained by currency flows provided by foreign loans. State patronage excluded the rural masses from provincial and national politics. Not surprisingly, peasants who once assisted in the birth of the Dominican nation as it freed itself from Spain in the 1860s became viewed as a political problem in this new environment.

My examination of San Pedro's social history concurs with Roberto Cassá's argument that racist ideas were not always explicit in dominant elites' thinking about the Dominican nation or in their political ideology. Yet, as Cassá also notes, dominant elites remained concerned with racial purity and racial improvement through whitening (*blanqueamiento*) and justified their socioeconomic privileges as a function of their European ancestry. In chapter 3 I focus on San Pedro's intellectual and cultural elites—educated men and women who founded libraries and hosted literary gatherings. These men and women made up San Pedro's dominant classes and crafted an identity for themselves oriented around Hispanic cultural norms. Their investment in a robust Hispanic ideal of the nation intensified as they welcomed white immigrants into their social networks. In other words, an ideal of racial superiority, rooted in a shared appreciation of Hispanic cultural norms, became the foundation of an expanded local elite, now comprising native Dominicans and foreign-born white immigrants.

This group held a monopoly over municipal and provincial power in San Pedro. Chapter 4 demonstrates that as the city council enforced laws in the 1890s and early 1900s, the exercise of power adopted a racial cast. San Pedro's black and white immigrant populations experienced a process of racialization in which ascribed characteristics of distinct ethnic communities increasingly attached to phenotype. This chapter also shows that sexualized racism, the use of sexual stereotypes to construct racial differences, fueled antiblack racism. Policing sex work was especially important in assigning black immigrants (particularly working-class female migrants) a lower status.[20]

The period between Ulises Heureaux's assassination in 1899 and U.S. military invasion in 1916 was marred by political instability, regional insurgency, and increased U.S. intervention. Heureaux's policies had left the county in financial ruin, a point noted by Edward Reed, head of the U.S. legation in Haiti: "the external debt," he calculated, "is around $22,000,000." Around $5,000,000 in worthless paper money circulated.[21]

Ramón Cáceres's selection as president (1905–1911) ended a six-year national dilemma during which time six men occupied the presidency; in the wake of disputed elections, the secretaries of state managed affairs. Yet Cáceres's administration could not easily rewind the clock and undo Heureaux's errors. During his presidency, the United States took over the Dominican Customs House in 1907 as a way to ensure the timely payment of debts and to manage the national budget. As with Heureaux, whom Cáceres assassinated, foreign incursion proved a destabilizing force. Cáceres's death at the hands of political rivals years later prompted yet another series of revolts, presidents, and advisory groups until the U.S. invasion in 1916.[22]

The U.S. occupation (1916–1924) left a deep imprint on Dominican society. Thanks to the military government, infrastructure improvements unified the national territory; investments in public services such as health and education provided services to Dominicans who, until that time, lacked complete access to any government resources.[23] U.S. military governance also profoundly influenced racialization in the Dominican Republic.

As Bruce Calder notes, Dominican elites resented their treatment as second-class citizens by U.S. military officials, who tended to view most Dominicans, even those who were white according to Dominican standards, as tinged with African ancestry. Elites also protested policies that allowed more Haitian and Afro-Antillean laborers to work on sugar estates across the nation.[24] In chapter 5 I show that a new nationalist discourse began to cohere in response to the racist politics of the occupation. I further demonstrate that Dominican antioccupation activists embraced a robust identity as a Latin people; *latinidad* privileged whiteness as a reaction, in part, to black political mobilization in San Pedro.

Indeed, *hispanidad* nationalism has rightly been understood as a racist, racializing ideology. Ernesto Sagás puts it most succinctly: "antihaitianismo ideology created the myth of Haitians and Dominicans belonging to different races."[25] The story told here recalibrates this argument to consider anti-Haitian ideology not only as creating differences within blackness but as central to inventing Dominican whiteness. My analysis also breaks new ground in thinking about the relationship between *hispanidad* nationalism and gender. Robin Derby, for example, insists that the U.S. occupation provoked a crisis of masculinity among political elites, and General Trujillo appealed to the majority of Dominican men because he embodied the dangerous masculinity of the streetwise male—the Dominican *tíguere*.[26] In her study of contemporary Dominican identity in the United States, Ginetta Candelario has shown that the Indo-Hispanic somatic ideal—in which straight hair is highly valued—places a greater burden on Dominican women to embody this image.[27]

My analysis further reveals, to borrow Steve Stern's phrasing, the "secret history of gender" in the formulation and dispersal of *hispanidad* nationalism. The U.S. occupation forced Dominican men active in the antioccupation campaign to redefine their ideal of masculine citizenship for a new era. In the 1920s San Pedro's elites rejected martial masculinity as a source of political legitimacy and embraced, instead, an ideal of virtuous, refined manhood oriented around patriarchal authority. Concurring with their male counterparts, some female social reformers and self-identified feminists lent supportive voices to new ways of imagining the Dominican nation in the wake of occupation. Chapter 6 analyzes how Dominican women's struggles to maintain a space for their political activity made them susceptible to accepting a racist and racially limiting ideal of the nation.

In response to the question posed by Samuel Martínez about "why and when anti-Haitianism became so important" in the state's twentieth-century iterations of Dominican national identity,[28] this work places Trujillo-era nationalism in historical context—as a product of earnest debates about the Dominican national character in the late nineteenth century and exclusionary governing practices in the early decades of the twentieth. Modern *hispanidad*, like other formulations of national identity throughout the Americas, was also a response to the particular needs of a modernizing state. Negrophobic and anti-Haitian rhetoric became politically viable once the criterion of national belonging privileged Latin Dominicans. San Pedro de Macorís is central to explaining how the past prepared the groundwork for official *hispanidad* nationalism in the twentieth century. As Sammy Sosa's skin-lightening episode reveals, too, residents of San Pedro de Macorís (*petromacorisanos*) continue to influence debates about race and Dominican national identity.

A Note on Nomenclature

This study makes use of many terms and concepts that require some discussion. For instance, economic class is a tricky issue in Dominican history, and "elite" is a problematic term in a country where, as Juan Bosch argued, a modern bourgeoisie emerged only in the twentieth century. In this study, I use "elite" and "*gente de primera*" to refer to members of the traditional landowning oligarchy (in San Pedro, this would include the Richiez and Isambert families, among the region's first residents); to white, wealthy immigrants who owned or administered sugar estates (Bass, Kelly, Vicini, Serrallés); to landowning *colonos* who cultivated cane for sugar estates; to immigrants and Dominicans who owned substantial commercial enterprises in the city and real estate, or who financed these activities (Amechazurra, Zayas Bazán, Hazim, Armenteros); and to intellectuals and municipal bureaucrats who viewed themselves as a cultured, governing class but who were not necessarily wealthy. The last group was still considered *gente de primera*—they enjoyed social standing and held political appointments—but many of them worked or lived on income generated from rental properties. They are differentiated from the working classes and the poor in general because they did not labor for someone else in San Pedro's streets or in the region's cane fields.

Although "race" is the English translation of the Spanish word "*raza*," the translation does not convey the same meaning. In the Dominican Republic, as across Latin America, "*raza*" denotes "nation" or "people"; its meaning is probably closer to how English speakers define ethnicity. In the Anglophone world, in contrast, "race" refers to the privileging of skin color as the primary marker of difference and differentiated status within a socioeconomic hierarchy. As Richard Turits argues, however, the Dominican Republic may be unique for the way in which antiblack prejudice coexists with measurable integration and mobility for people of African descent.[29] Francisco Moscoso Puello (1885–1959), a medical doctor and social commentator, captured this tension in *Cartas a Evelina*, published in 1941. In one essay, originally published in 1913, Moscoso Puello proclaims, "We are a mulatto majority, tropical mulattos, of a type unique to the human species" and then later cautions, "but . . . we Dominicans are also constitutionally white."[30] Dominicans, according to Moscoso, were racially mixed—a mulatto people—but as a *raza*, they were defined by their political and ideological whiteness.

Color categories employed in official state documents and in quotidian, popular speech highlight the racial diversity and mixedness of the Dominican *raza*. For example, colonial records from the 1492 to 1822 period include the category "*blancos de* [or *que da*] *la tierra*," usually translated as "whites of the land" or "whites the land gives." This term appears to have referred to rural people who had achieved the same protections as those deemed legally white; their precise color or racial identities remain unknown. In other documents produced during the same period, one might find "*morenos*," "*pardos*," "*mulatos*," "*blancos*," or "*negros*," as one would throughout Spanish America. And, as across colonial and republican Latin America during slavery, these categories say less about phenotype and more about free or enslaved status. Late-nineteenth and early twentieth-century documents also contain a rich array of color categories, including *"trigueño"* (wheat-colored), *"amarillo"* (yellow, sometimes used for Asians), *"indio"* (Indian), and *"mestizo"* (mixed race, of color).[31] The Dominican state currently recognizes six colors for its national identity card: *blanco, amarillo, mestizo, indio, mulato,* and *negro.* Even though some activists celebrate the inclusion of *mulato* and *negro* as acknowledgment of Dominicans' African heritage, these color categories do not correspond to collective identities grounded in a specific racial consciousness. Racial mixture is still framed by the unity of the Dominican *raza* and it remains to be seen whether this official change will alter the exalted appreciation of light skin and straight—or "good"—hair.[32]

Analysis of how historical actors understood and used these terms in time and space is sorely needed. Silvio Torres-Saillant has suggested that "the tragedy of the construction of creoleness in the Dominican Republic is that the process ultimately implied a refusal of social blackness that could provide no defense against the intellectual Negrophobia the Dominican elite would subsequently promulgate to control the lower classes."[33] This may be the case, but I do not focus here on the meanings of blackness for the masses or among elites; rather, I describe another kind of creolization process, one that involved wealthy foreign whites becoming Dominican and the terms under which they were received as equals among Dominican elites. In this study, I use terms as they appear in the historical documentation, although I have not always been able to label important figures in San Pedro's history by color. Nor does such labeling matter: Dominican whites did not monopolize the elevation of whitening and Hispanic cultural norms as key components of Dominican national identity; Dominicans of color also participated in this process. I have, though, made some specific choices. Unless otherwise noted, I refer to immigrants and labor migrants from the British, Dutch, French, and Danish West Indies as "black" and "Afro-Antilleans" because they were perceived as black in the Dominican context.

Finally, although it appears that until the 1940s the national state and Dominicans preferred using *"mestizo"* to refer to other Dominicans who were between black and white, I chose to title this work *The Mulatto Republic,* in part, to avoid confusion for readers in the United States who might assume that *"mestizo"* means indigenous/European, as it does in Mexico. As Mimi Sheller reminds us, however, "mulatto" is a particularly vexatious term, fraught with ideological and cultural significance. For centuries, European government officials, writers, and travelers worried that racial mixture between whites and blacks would lead to "decadence." The mulatto, then, represented a process of creolization that would end up harming whites unless they remained physically and biologically distant from blacks.[34] Francisco Moscoso Puello spoke to this idea when he acknowledged that all Dominicans were mulattos, but this concept was derided as a national problem to be resolved through immigration and whitening.[35] Even more troubling, as I discuss in chapters 1 and 5, many U.S. observers received Dominicans as racially mixed "mulattos" even as they completely rejected Haitians as "pure" blacks. Dominicans, they believed, were racially superior to Haitians because the majority of them had some European ancestry.

The historical baggage associated with "mulatto" may hinder us from creative uses of the term. Luckily, invention is not necessary: Pedro Francisco Bonó once wrote that both Haitians and Dominicans made important contributions to building a future for blacks and mulattos across the Americas. Bonó's idea represents an alternative way to imagine the Dominican political and historical community that puts him, among others, "at the forefront of the struggle for black liberation in the modern world."[36] His view resonated with the political aspirations of many within the African diaspora. My goal, then, is to suggest that Dominican narratives of racial mixture may carry within them the possibilities of undoing antiblack Hispanic nationalism.

1

DEBATING *DOMINICANIDAD* IN THE NINETEENTH CENTURY

In October of 1882 Sarah Marinda Loguen Fraser took a steamship from Philadelphia to Puerto Plata, bringing along with her a trousseau, some furniture, and sturdy shoes—the moveable property of many nineteenth-century brides. She also carried one item that differentiated her from many women, whether white or African-descended: a medical bag. A practicing physician, Sarah Fraser was among the first African Americans to graduate with a medical degree and become a licensed doctor. She traveled with her new husband, Charles Fraser, a St. Thomas–born pharmacist who lived in the Dominican Republic.

The newlyweds owed their relationship, in part, to Frederick Douglass and his son, Charles. Frederick Douglass had visited the Dominican Republic in 1871 as assistant secretary to the Senate Commission of Inquiry into the Annexation of Santo Domingo. Afterward, and probably as a result of his father's influence, Charles Douglass served as the U.S. vice-consul in Puerto Plata, where he became friends with Charles Fraser and with Ulises Heureaux and Gregorio Luperón, heroes of the War of Restoration and political elites. As a close family friend, Charles Douglass encouraged Sarah to correspond with Fraser, and, after an exchange of letters, Fraser visited the Philadelphia World's Fair in 1876, where he met Sarah. They were engaged in 1881.

According to family papers, Frederick Douglass encouraged Sarah Loguen to marry Charles Fraser and live in the Dominican Republic. Just a decade earlier, in the 1870s, Douglass had been one of the leading proponents of annexing the Dominican Republic to the United States. He believed that in Haiti and Santo Domingo blacks and whites from the United States could seek their fortune on an equal footing. As he once wrote, Santo Domingo was where "you feel your full stature of manhood."[1] The nation's reputation as a biracial paradise was, for Douglass, the product of its history; it was the island that witnessed the birth of white Christian civilization in the New World, African slavery, and resistance to slavery and colonialism. This history inspired him to suggest that the annexation of Santo Domingo to the United States could help promote racial unity in both countries.

The same year Sarah and Charles Fraser met, Juan Amechazurra built the first steam-powered sugar mill outside San Pedro de Macorís, an otherwise forgettable small town located on the banks of the Higuamo River in the eastern part of the island. Amechazurra, who had fled Cuba during the Ten Years' War, brought with him the managerial and technical skills necessary to build his estate, Ingenio Angelina. Many regional elites believed Amechazurra and industrialized sugar production brought modernity to the country as a whole.[2]

We know much about the structure of labor in the eastern sugar zone and the important role played by Puerto Plata's political elites, such as Luperón and Heureaux, in the elaboration of a national project in the 1870s and 1880s. Yet, the Fraser and Amechazurra stories suggest new questions about the ways in which foreign investment and intervention shaped ideas about race and nation; about whether the idea of Dominican racial harmony and racial unity was farce or real; about the role that racial and gender ideologies—the quest to "feel [the] full stature of manhood"—played in making sense of international and regional power structures and emerging economic orders.

The last quarter of the nineteenth century was an especially transformative moment in Dominican history. In the 1880s and 1890s, the Dominican Republic's economy consolidated around tobacco, sugar, and cacao production. Foreign merchants resident in the country, particularly in Puerto Plata and, increasingly, in San Pedro de Macorís, linked the Dominican Republic with commercial networks that spanned the Atlantic and the circum-Caribbean.[3] Some of these commercial ties brought expatriates and investors from the United States, who began to press their government to pay closer attention to Santo Domingo, as it was also known, either through commercial investment or with the establishment of a coaling station for the U.S. Navy on the Samaná peninsula. These early interactions would culminate with an effort to annex Santo Domingo to the United States in the 1870s.[4]

The Dominican War of Restoration, fought to end Spanish annexation of Santo Domingo (1861–1865), inspired independence movements in Cuba and Puerto Rico, Spain's remaining American colonies. Veterans of the war, such as Generals Gregorio Luperón, Ulises Heureaux, and Máximo Gómez, lent material support for these efforts; Gómez even fought in the Cuban Army. The unsatisfactory end of Cuba's Ten Years' War forced some of its leaders into exile in the Dominican Republic, where they joined their Puerto Rican counterparts. Independence leaders such as Antonio Maceo from Cuba and

Ramón Emeterio Betances from Puerto Rico lived in Puerto Plata and from there built a transnational movement against Spanish colonialism.[5]

The economic change that swept across the country in the 1870s and 1880s, the U.S. intervention in the 1870s, and anticolonial activism in the 1890s occasioned an opportunity for intellectuals and politicians (often one and the same) to reflect on *dominicanidad*. I argue in this chapter that neither anti-blackness nor anti-Haitianism was a central concept in competing ideas about *dominicanidad* that emerged in the works of men such as Pedro Francisco Bonó, Gregorio Luperón, and Eugenio María de Hostos. Anti-Haitianism was, however, present in Manuel de Jesús Galván's (1834–1910) more pessimistic reflections on the national question produced during the same period. Anti-Haitian rhetoric correlated directly with support for authoritarianism while Bonó's, Luperón's, and de Hostos's arguments complemented the optimistic, democratic, and anti-imperialist impulses of men who had long been critical of Spanish colonialism and growing U.S. power in the region.

Appearing at the very moment when the Dominican Republic's and the United States' economies were becoming more integrated, there was much at stake in these debates. Complementing the question about who the Dominicans were as a nation (*raza*) was another: What was the relationship between sovereignty, governance, and race? As a *raza*, Bonó, Luperón, and Hostos argued, Dominicans were a culturally Hispanic people. Yet, their *hispanicismo* was not inherently antiblack. I argue that by the early decades of the twentieth century, *hispanicismo* had become more racially exclusive. At the end of the nineteenth century, however, a debate still raged over *raza* and race in the Dominican Republic.

· · ·

On July 25, 1865, the last Spanish troops left Santo Domingo after a disastrous defeat by an insurgency that united elites and peasants in an effort to end Spanish rule. The rebellion against the Spanish regime had been fueled by failed economic policies and, some historians have argued, the contempt with which Spaniards treated Dominicans. Although Spanish officials respected the 1821 slave emancipation decree, they forbade Dominican military personnel from wearing Spanish uniforms, replaced Dominican officers with Spaniards, and appointed Spanish bureaucrats to administer government institutions. Additionally, they imposed the *bagaje*, a system of forced labor and tribute, on rural populations. Peasants were hit particularly hard by these policies; as a result, just two years into the occupation, an organized insurgency for Dominican self-determination erupted.[6]

Afterward, the War of Restoration became a touchstone for Dominicans. Documents produced long after the war ended often begin, "In the year of the Restoration of the Republic." Letters, reports, and municipal documents express a pervasive sense of equality and social leveling through the language of citizenship. Officials and nonofficials alike addressed each other as "Ciudadano" ("Citizen").

Local archives reveal, however, that victory over Spain also engendered internal conflict, especially for local authorities intent on creating governing institutions and wielding power over their jurisdictions. First, like independence wars throughout the Americas, the War of Restoration appears to have enlarged the power of regional strongmen-turned-generals (*caudillos*) and their mobilized, armed militias. These regional leaders plunged the country into incessant warfare for the duration of the Second Republic (1865–1882).[7] In January of 1867, for example, the *caudillo* Pedro Guillermo sacked the eastern town of Hato Mayor. Days later, General Marcos Evangelista and Colonel Ciriaco Reyna raised an army of 150 "notable persons and soldiers from [Hato Mayor] and from the *común* [parish] of Higüey for the reestablishment of order."[8]

In addition to destabilizing local authority, incessant conflicts did much to undermine faith in Dominican sovereignty. In 1871 residents of Higüey threatened annexation to the United States and sent notice of their pro-U.S. sentiments to Santo Domingo as officials there debated the possibility of creating a U.S. protectorate. Governor Andrés Pérez reported to the minister of the interior, police, and agriculture that troops in the eastern army had announced their support for annexation to the United States, "bringing along the star-spangled flag, [waving it] in victory [in honor] of the president of this republic and the American [republic]." He reported that "the population rose up so spontaneously that I conceded to their desires as they are also mine"—a likely response from a besieged official.[9]

Spain's defeat helped cultivate a sense of national destiny but also unleashed power struggles that threatened national unity. Educated elites writing about the Dominican nation were faced with a difficult task: how, in the face of these conflicts and divisions, to cultivate a sense of common purpose? With an eye toward the imperialist machinations of the United States, commentators also wondered how to make the argument for Dominican sovereignty for a racially mixed people.

As happened with their counterparts throughout the Americas, the answers to these questions came through conversations about Dominicans as a unified *raza* (i.e., a collective of people who shared culture, history, and lineage) and about Dominicans' race (i.e., whether the mixture of European, indigenous, and African blood provided the necessary characteristics for nation build-ing). Beginning in the 1790s, the idea that Americans made up a *raza* in which differences of class and color warranted no special attention became a po-litical weapon that proindependence colonial elites in Nueva Granada (New Granada, present-day Colombia, Ecuador, and Venezuela) used to question the legitimacy of Spanish imperial rule. The idea that Americans, as a new *raza*, were unified despite the hierarchies that Spanish colonialism had imposed on them blanketed over the significant ideological fissures that threatened to break apart independence movements. Claims of American racial harmony also si-lenced demands for racial justice by the enslaved or free people of color.[10]

Long after independence, in the 1850s, Justo Arosemena and José María Torres Caicedo, from Colombia's Panama Province, began to speak in terms of a "Latin American interest" to counter U.S. Manifest Destiny, an idea of progress that motivated the conquest and settlement of the U.S. West. They described a Latin *raza* comprising "'spiritual,' 'heroic,' 'chivalrous,' 'noble,' and 'sentimental'" people.[11] Then, in the 1880s and 1890s, European- and African-descended Cuban nationalists equated Spanish colonialism with social, eco-nomic, and political discrimination on the basis of race. In contrast, Cuban nationalists insisted that war against Spain had sealed a unique and durable bond between black and white men in the common goal of creating a republic where all men, regardless of race, could enjoy the fullness of their civil and po-litical liberties. As a result of the wars, Cubans became a single *raza* that shared a collective identity based on their struggle against Spain, their commitment to ending slavery, and devotion to racial unity.[12]

While Colombians, Cubans, and other Latin Americans insisted on racial unity and the dignity of the Latin *raza*, U.S. foreign policy elites emphasized racial inferiority to justify U.S. intervention throughout the region. As early as the 1850s, debates about Dominicans' race influenced U.S. interactions with the country. At that time, articles that advocated annexation represented Do-minicans as a white nation on the verge of annihilation by Haiti. The African American newspaper the *National Era* noted that John C. Calhoun, former U.S. secretary of state, made much of the "White Republic of St. Domingo, the per-secution it endured from the Blacks, the duty of [the United States] to affiliate with it, and sustain it in its struggle against the Haitian Government."[13] Then, in the 1860s and 1870s, U.S. foreign policy elites who clamored for annexation of the Dominican Republic also argued that Dominicans were white enough to protect the economic interests of U.S. citizens, but they also insisted that the country was a racial paradise that could offer a haven for recently freed African Americans. President Ulysses S. Grant's annexation apologia, "Reasons Why

Santo Domingo Should Be Annexed to the United States," published in 1869, made this point explicitly: "The colored man cannot be spared until his place is supplied, but with a refuge like Santo Domingo his worth here would soon be discovered, and he would soon receive such recognition as to induce him to stay: or if Providence designed that the two races should not live together he would find a home in the Antillas."[14]

Frederick Douglass, who served as secretary of the Senate Commission of Inquiry sent to investigate the possibility of U.S. annexation, echoed Grant's arguments and made the case for U.S. intervention as a positive force in Dominican affairs. Douglass believed that Haiti and Santo Domingo were nations where blacks and whites from the United States could seek their fortunes on equal footing, and this belief inspired him to embrace the radical idea that the annexation of Santo Domingo to the United States could help promote racial unity in both countries. He understood racial unity as a universal good that the United States could nurture and protect with the strength of its institutions and laws. For example, Douglass argued that "the true cure for [the] spirit of caste, in our country and Santo Domingo, has been found in the Fifteenth Amendment of the Constitution of the United States," the one that guarantees color-blind citizenship.[15] In an anonymous unpublished manuscript, the author (whom I believe to be Frederick Douglass) argues for annexation in these stark terms:

> Were I a citizen of Santo Domingo I would hold up both hands from the rising till the going down of the sun if need be, in favor of the annexation of that country to the United States, for I see no better way to improve the fortunes and promote the highest interests of that country. In coming into the American union, in renouncing separate nationality, Santo Domingo takes no step backward. She simply swaps impotence for power, civil strife and revolution, for security and peace, stagnation and decay, for activity and growth. She parts with danger for safety, isolation and weakness for union and strength.[16]

Most important, although Douglass's proannexation arguments echoed those made by white interlocutors, Douglass additionally believed that the Dominican Republic and the United States had a great deal to teach each other about racial democracy and color-blind citizenship. He even admitted that his support of U.S. expansion in the Caribbean surprised many: "there was a time when I was opposed to all schemes of extension of territory to our national domain. That was the time when extension meant more slavery." Now that the post–Civil War federal government proved itself inclined toward racial democracy, Douglass argued, "extension now means freedom, knowledge, and progress." Rejecting arguments that Dominican racial inferiority made it ripe for U.S. colonization, Douglass insisted the island nation be welcomed into the United States "not as an inferior, not as a vassal, not by the window or the backdoor, but . . . as an equal."[17] The United States, with its fledgling (and ultimately short-lived) racial democracy, was "the hope of freedom throughout the world."[18]

Douglass's musings about the Dominican Republic and his arguments favoring annexation underscore the multiple ways that U.S. foreign policy and political elites perceived and debated Dominicans' race as they pondered the relationship between race, nation, and interhemispheric relations. In either case, whether they regarded the Dominican Republic as a white nation or as a paragon of racial harmony, U.S. observers viewed it as ripe for intervention.

For the most part, U.S. hegemony was explained as having derived its legitimacy from the racial superiority of Anglo Saxons over Latin Americans. As a result, from the 1850s until the end of the nineteenth century iterations of Latin American notions of *raza*, a unity born out of struggle against Spain or promoted through a shared sense of "Latin" culture, collided with emerging U.S. power in the region. With the United States as an increasingly important actor in the region in the nineteenth century, race—the idea that people have distinct biologically derived attributes given their ancestry or blood—became an important measure of economic development, political stability, and relations among states in the international arena.

These broader discussions of *raza* and race informed Dominican conversations about *dominicanidad*, particularly in the 1880s and 1890s. The idea that Dominicans were racially harmonious may have started with Juan Pablo Duarte (1813–1876), a founding leader of the Dominican revolt against President Jean Pierre Boyer in 1844. As he once wrote, "Whites, blacks / Browns, Mixed-Bloods / Marching peacefully / United and brave. / Let's save the fatherland / From vile tyrants, / And show the world / That we are brothers."[19] In this instance, Duarte rallies support among Dominicans, regardless of their color, against tyranny, not against Haitians. Given that Haitians, too, were in revolt against the government makes Duarte's message less anti-Haitian than strategic and pragmatic. Nevertheless, conceptualizations of the Dominican nation that were hostile to Haiti and posed Haitians as a singular threat to the nation were propagated by some elites, who, at the same time, argued that Dominicans were incapable of self-rule because the rural masses were ignorant. Worse yet, the majority of Dominicans were not white. In other words, the anti-Haitian writers of the nineteenth century tended to be the most supportive of efforts to annex the Dominican Republic to a stronger power, usually Spain or another European country. Thus, at the root of racist imaginings of *raza* was a profound pessimism about whether the Dominican Republic could be an independent country.

Manuel de Jesús Galván exemplified this pessimism. A novelist, politician, and essayist, Galván initiated his career under Pedro Santana, a *caudillo* who made possible Spanish annexation in 1861. Even after the end of Spanish rule, Galván moved to Puerto Rico, where he continued to serve the Crown. He favored annexation to Spain because he did not believe that Dominicans were ready for nationhood. When the country was reannexed to Spain, he wrote, "Today we are what God created us: Spaniards."[20] Whereas Haitian newspapers dismissed President Pedro Santana's desire for annexation as produced by a desire "for . . . vain titles, and to be named captain general," Galván insisted that Spanish annexation would have material, moral, and political benefits. It would "increase the grand Spanish family, raising its profile among the other nations, reestablishing respect for its name on other seas."[21] Through annexation, Galván believed, "Dominicans returned to Spain, invoking those sacred ties that [united] the two peoples, the titles of fraternity, origin, language, religion, and customs, the memories of the glorious loyalty for which our fathers many times spilled their blood over this island to protect it under Spanish dominion."[22]

Throughout 1863 Galván excoriated the insurgency against Spanish rule, raising the specter of Haitian incursion. In one article he caricatured the rebellion as "a column of infantry and cavalry, under the leadership of a bizarre commander of a squadron of African lancers." He apparently could not believe that the rebels were Dominicans, insisting in his reporting that the insurgent groups "departed from the Haitian border." He argued that only as Spaniards could Dominicans claim a "respectable nationality" and lampooned the movement's leaders, among the most prominent of whom were men of African descent like Gregorio Luperón and Ulises Heureaux, as ambitious *caudillos* and rural bandits.[23]

Galván's love of Spain made it impossible for him to look at the War of Restoration as a pivotal moment in Dominican history, so he turned to the colonial period. Published in 1882, Galván's novel, *Enriquillo*, is a fictional account of the War of Bahoruco, an actual rebellion against Spanish rule that lasted from 1519 to 1533. In the novel, as in historical fact, Enriquillo, a Taíno born into a noble family yet educated by Franciscan friars, fights against evil Spaniards and allies himself with good ones. Allegorized in this way, Enriquillo's struggle was not a revolt against Spain; rather, it was a rebellion against those whose evil actions besmirched Spain's benevolent rule. Enriquillo, in other words, was the defender of Hispanic cultural and religious purity. The story represents the actual conflicts over Indian souls and labor that emerged between priests from religious orders such as Dominicans and Franciscans and Spanish settlers. Las Casas negotiates the end of Enriquillo's rebellion; he is also a key go-between mediating the interests of a dying Taíno nobility and Spanish colonial order. For this reason, Doris Sommer argues, the novel "reconcile[s] the colonizer's identity...with that of the colonized."[24] Or as Pedro Henríquez Ureña wrote in 1935, "the good and the bad, the prayer and the scream unite to come together in harmony, where Spaniards and Indians arrive at peace and abandon themselves to faith and hope."[25]

According to Sommer, as a "foundational fiction" that erased the violence of the conquest, Enriquillo, the noble Indian, reconciled Dominicans to Spain and gave Dominicans an "ideological shelter against the imputation of African (that is, Haitian) identity in a country of dark people."[26] Africans played no part in this story. Instead, Enriquillo, as Ginetta Candelario argues, "represented... [a] new ethno-racial archetype: the culturally Hispanic and Catholic Indio who bested Spanish Catholics and Taínos alike."[27] From Galván's anti-Haitian, pro-Spanish musings emerged what Candelario calls the Indo-Hispano as an archetype of *dominicanidad*. The Indo-Hispano is ethnically Taíno but has acculturated to the Hispanic cultural norms. As such, Dominicans may be ethnically different, but they share a fundamental connection to Spain.

Galván represented one side of the nationalist continuum. He argued against the possibility of Dominican nationhood without Spain and touted Haiti as the republic's main threat. Galván's *Enriquillo* places the Dominican Republic squarely within Latin American reflections about *mestizaje* and *indigenismo*, mythic celebrations of the noble Indian in the nineteenth century. Galván's writings, however, also reflect the Dominican Republic's unique position as an island nation that borders another. Haiti and the identified need to distance Dominicans from their neighbors left a deep impression on Galván's nationalist musings.

For Pedro Francisco Bonó, the Dominican historical narrative held different lessons. An intellectual and politician, Bonó celebrated Dominican racial unity in the wake of U.S. expansion into the Caribbean. He was born in 1828 to a merchant family in Santiago and held various government posts during the War of Restoration. His essays suggest that this experience impressed him deeply and motivated his keen interest in how governing institutions should be structured.[28]

For Bonó, as for Galván, Spanish cultural norms unified Dominicans as a *raza*, but Bonó judged the Spanish colonial legacy as both negative and positive. For example, he blamed Spanish indolence, sustained by an economy based on ranching and illegal trade with neighboring St. Domingue, for the colony's failure to develop its natural resources and improve the material conditions of its residents. According to him, the colonial elites, satisfied with their rents and the proceeds from the sale of their cattle and prohibited by colonial policy from trading with other islands, left their slaves to herd while they resided in the "depopulated and uninhabited Dominican cities . . . [and led] superstitious, lazy, and brutish [lives]."[29]

At the same time, Bonó viewed Spanish colonial rule in romantic terms. In *Apuntes sobre las clases trabajadoras dominicanas*, published in 1881, he writes, "Spanish charity made the slave a member of the family . . . [and while] in the cities it was indecent to dance with whites at the high society dances and ally with them, in the countryside . . . it was permitted."[30] For nearly 300 years, he insisted, social conditions, combined with Spanish benevolence, "facilitated the mixture of races" and made "racial warfare" impossible. In sharp contrast to St. Domingue, where slavery had cultivated deep hatred between blacks and whites, the Spanish side of the island conferred on Dominicans a degree of "cosmopolitanism"—a racial flexibility and openness to Europe, its ideas, and peoples.

Bonó's assessment of Spanish colonialism led him to make the remarkable claim that Haiti's development as a nation-state was based on racial exclusion and race-based violence. As he wrote, "in its grand revolution at the end of the last century, [St. Domingue] showed the world what was in the heart of its blacks and of its whites with the hateful regimen of the enslavement of the first." For Bonó, blacks and whites in St. Domingue suffered from "hate and contempt." This, according to him, contrasted sharply with the historical experience of Dominicans who were open to other races and cultures (albeit with a preference for Europeans). Whereas the brutal slave regime of colonial St. Domingue led to rigid racial hierarchies and, in the end, black revolt against whites, Santo Domingo's residents enjoyed the freedom of social interaction between blacks and whites.[31]

In this argument Bonó was not alone; in fact, it is possible that he read and borrowed the concept from another Dominican intellectual, Alejandro Angulo Guridi. In 1854 Angulo Guridi published an essay, "Exclusion and Brotherhood among Countries," in which he discussed the idea of a Dominican cosmopolitanism. For him, the lack of social and economic progress among countries as diverse as Haiti, China, Russia, and Mexico was the result of their exclusionary—this could also be translated as nativist or protectionist—policies, which made trade and interaction with other countries virtually impossible. Fore-shadowing contemporary debates over globalization and free-market capital-ism, Angulo Guridi insisted on openness and tolerance as the foundation of relations among nation-states. Haiti, he argued, "is exclusivist and therefore does not partake in the progress [being made] by other modern countries." In particular, "its hateful caste distinctions isolate it [and] its restrictive laws for foreigners impoverish it." In contrast, Dominicans were cosmopolitan in their outlook and as a result of their mixed-race heritage. For Angulo Guridi, racial mixture was a positive feature for any nation because it optimized the ethnic-racial characteristics of two races in one person and made tolerance and openness to other cultures possible. In other words, rather than view Domini-can *mestizaje* in negative terms, Dominicans, as a *raza* born from European, Amerindian, and African influences, were a race singularly prepared by their genetic makeup to cultivate universal norms such as cosmopolitanism.[32]

Bonó seems to have built on Angulo Guridi's insights and articulated a *do-minicanidad* that was not anti-Haitian, just critical of policy choices made by Haitians in power. For instance, even though Bonó regarded Haitian foreign policy as shortsighted and racist, he never argued that Haitians were racially distinct from Dominicans or inferior. In one letter, he makes the interesting observation that had President Jean Pierre Boyer only "established the union of the two nations on a more equitable and favorable basis [in 1822]," Domini-cans and Haitians "would be more at peace, happier, and more civilized" be-cause "diverse elements of the two nations . . . would have competed to main-tain the equilibrium between the black and white races."[33] Here Bonó appears to view Boyer's rule as a lost opportunity for both sides of the island to unify in the name of bringing about economic development and peace. He therefore blames the antagonism that existed between Haiti and the Dominican Repub-lic not on their supposed racial differences but on their leaders' "politics with white foreigners"—their relations with European countries and the United States. As Bonó asks, "Who doesn't understand that with its cosmopolitan tendencies the Dominican Republic is a constant threat to Haiti?"[34]

For Bonó, the difference between Dominicans and Haitians involved the divergent ways in which the two states approached their relations with Eu-ropeans. He appears to cringe before Haitians' racial consciousness, rooted (and rightly so) in a profound mistrust of Europeans. If Haitians' distrust of Europeans made Haitians too rigid, Dominicans' "cosmopolitanism" made Dominicans "too passive . . . which makes [us] accept without resistance or discussion the illegitimate schemes of voluntary or second-hand presidents."[35]

Thus far, Bonó appears to share with Galván a deeper interest in sustaining the privilege of white elites. He romanticized Spain, Spanish governance, and slavery; he elevated Hispanic cultural norms as an antidote to the racial chaos exhibited by St. Domingue and, later, Haiti, and rejected race-based political consciousness and mobilization. Revisionist scholarship about similar myths of racial democracy across Latin America argues that narratives such as these are fundamentally white supremacist in that they ultimately deny African-descended people full and equal citizenship, systematically position African-descended people as obstacles to economic development, and ignore racism as a structural problem with devastating consequences for people of African ancestry.[36]

According to Pedro San Miguel, however, Bonó's *dominicanidad*, while it "maintained a substratum of fundamental *hispanidad* . . . was far from defining itself merely as an extension of Spain."[37] Lacking this important characteristic, it would be hard to define Bonó as a white supremacist. Instead, San Miguel and Michiel Baud characterize Bonó's thinking as *mulatismo* (or *mulataje*) because he recognized blacks and mulattos as important in Dominican nation building and insisted on racial equality. The idea that Dominicans comprised a hybrid *raza* that played an important role for all mulattos and blacks throughout the hemisphere emerged in a letter Bonó wrote to General Gregorio Luperón in 1887. Excited by Luperón's return from Europe and his official announcement that he planned to campaign for the Dominican presidency, Bonó was overcome with emotion, writing, "This news [of your campaign] doubles my joy." He encouraged Luperón to "think seriously about the destinies Providence has reserved for blacks and mulattos in America. These futures are now manifest. . . . And I believe the island of Santo Domingo is called to be the nucleus, the model [for] the growth of this race in the hemisphere. And who better than you to begin to lay the first bricks, to build the foundation of this greatness?"[38]

In response, Luperón wrote, "Believe me, my friend . . . the prospects of this excite my [sense of] patriotism and since then, I have given much thought about the radical change that has to be introduced in the political [culture] of our country so that it can advantageously . . . fulfill the historical mission . . . assigned to it because of its geographic position . . . and the uncontestable perfectibility of the privileged race that occupies it."[39]

In an interesting piece published in 1895, Bonó develops this theme even further in an imagined congressional meeting that includes deputies from all over the country. In a general discussion about governance, Señor B from Santiago states,

We are a new race in the world, [a] product of the mixing of Caucasian, Indian, and African. . . . Our central and insular geographic position in

America, our affinities, our multiple ties to the rest of the Antilles, our relatively old independence place us in a position to pretend [we are] more fortunate than anyone else. . . . In effect, where and how could so many whites, blacks, mulattos, and *mestizos* who populate the Antilles be better situated if not in a powerful confederation that is a friend to European nations, as well as to North and South America? . . . We should show that we are a wise nation, although small, dignified to aspire to a higher calling, so that Haiti does not beat us out of our prize. . . . In effect, if [Haiti's] black exclusivity was, for her, for Europe, and for America, a guarantee in the past, today . . . this [is] an obstacle for the realization of [Antillean Confederation].[40]

In Bonó's formulations, Dominicans were not Indo-Hispanos but a new *raza* comprising blacks, whites, and mulattos who shared a bond through Hispanic cultural norms. Dominican *mulataje* made the country a model for racial inclusivity for the entire hemisphere. Nevertheless, in his letter to Luperón, Bonó added, "And who better than you knows how necessary the white race is for achieving [this future]?"

Why would Bonó insist on this? This last statement suggests his belief that European immigration and positive relations with European powers would help the Dominican nation develop economically and improve its racial stock. This belief gives some credence to reigning ideas about whitening as the mechanism for socioeconomic development, but Bonó's point was to contrast Dominican cosmopolitan moderation with racial exclusivity.

Bonó's critique of Haiti's racial exclusivity should not be read as solely anti-Haitian for another reason. According to David Nicholls, Haitian intellectuals such as the anthropologist Anténor Firmin (1850–1911) similarly advocated for Haitian governments to "liberalize the naturalization laws and . . . insisted that the prohibition of foreign ownership was a serious obstacle to the economic development of Haiti." Firmin wanted to bring Haiti onto the world stage through advancements in technology and education. As Michael Dash notes, Firmin's cosmopolitanism, like Bonó's, could easily be dismissed as antinationalist or, worse yet, anti-Haitian and antiblack. However, Firmin, like Bonó, was a nationalist who saw in Hispaniola's unique history a way to confront broader conversations about race, nation, and Pan-Caribbeanism. After meeting José Martí in 1893, he defended the concept of a raceless Caribbean federation based on the unification of Cuba, Puerto Rico, the Dominican Republic, and Haiti. As he wrote, "By joining together their national destinies and attracting all the other Antillean islands . . . they would ultimately form a substantial state capable of maintaining itself on its own." Confederation, thinking beyond national boundaries, in turn, required Haitians to eschew their own xenophobia. In this instance, pleas for racelessness and openness to others represent a political stance against tyrannical regimes that prohibited Caribbean peoples from seeing the benefits of Antillean solidarity.[41]

Anténor Firmin shared much with Gregorio Luperón and Eugenio María de Hostos, who represented a third current of Dominican nationalist thought, which spoke directly to Spanish and U.S. imperialism in the Caribbean. They advocated the creation of an Antillean federation based on the geographic and historical unity of Cuba, Puerto Rico, the Dominican Republic, and Jamaica. As the struggle for independence in Cuba and Puerto Rico unfolded and U.S. commercial imperialism expanded, they expressed a Pan-Antillean politics that, transcending race, would nurture freedom movements in Cuba and Puerto Rico, sustain democracy in the Dominican Republic, and secure Antillean political agency and sovereignty to counter U.S. influence.

Elaborated in the late 1880s and 1890s, Pan-Antilleanism combined support for the insurgent struggles in Cuba and Puerto Rico with advocacy for Caribbean unity. Luperón and Hostos insisted on the cultural, geographic, and racial cohesion of the people of the Greater Antilles: "In the Greater Antilles there is [a] nationality so natural . . . Cuba, Jamaica, Santo Domingo, Puerto Rico are not only members of the same body [but] parts of the same whole."

Hostos and Luperón's idea of a transnational collectivity was certainly derived from their own sense of shared exile. In 1895, for example, Hostos wrote from Chile to Luperón in St. Thomas, "I read [your letter] with great joy because it came from a beloved and esteemed friend, a hope of the Antilles. But at the same time, I read it with sadness, thinking that you, like me, are also uprooted."[42]

The last Cuban war for independence, which erupted in 1895, profoundly influenced Pan-Antilleanism in the Dominican Republic, which became a refuge for activists such as Hostos, Ramón Emeterio Betances (from Puerto Rico), and Antonio Maceo (from Cuba). Echoing Bonó, Luperón believed that the Dominican Republic served as an important model for Cuban and Puerto Rican insurgents as an independent nation: "[Our] liberty . . . will be like a very eloquent protest against [Spain's] tyranny and barbarities." As Antillean brothers, Dominicans had the responsibility of "bringing liberty to the archipelago . . . and breaking the chains that weigh them down."[43]

This fraternity was fully realized in the committees organized by Cubans, Puerto Ricans, and Dominicans from New York, Tampa, and Puerto Plata, and it allowed a few Dominican women entry into politics. Three women's clubs—the Cuban Star, the Daughters of Hatuey, and Homeland and Liberty—raised funds for the Cuban revolution.[44] Hostos believed, as did Bonó, that the Dominican Republic would play a key role in an Antillean (*antillano*) confederation, having produced men like Luperón and General Máximo Gómez, "son[s] of Santo Domingo by birth . . . [and sons] of the Antilles by choice."[45]

In addition to U.S. financial interference in the Dominican Republic, the U.S. invasion of Cuba in 1898 forced *antillano* activists to direct their anti-imperialist critique against the United States. For this reason, the political program of Antilleanism sought to "combat the influence of annexationism [and] to propagate the idea of an Antillean Confederation."[46]

Luperón, for his part, had a long history of venting his rage and frustration at U.S. interlocutors. He wrote in a letter to President U. S. Grant in 1869 proclaiming his resistance to any effort on the part of the United States to annex the Dominican Republic: "The oft-quoted Monroe Doctrine has its vices and its nonsense . . . we believe that America should belong to itself and [be] distanced from all European influence. . . . [We] do not think that [all of] America should be Yankee."[47]

Until 1898, Antilleanism provided an alternative to U.S.-sponsored Pan-Americanism. At the first Pan-American conference, held in Washington, DC, in 1889–1890, Secretary of State James Blaine introduced a plan to create a hemispheric economic system. Latin American countries—particularly those with the largest economies—rejected Blaine's ideas, however. Rather than an economic union directed by Washington, Hostos advocated for the creation of a Latin American confederation, the heart of which was Antillean unity. The point of building the Antillean Confederation was, he explained, "to help the continental countries of our Western Hemisphere to complete and extend civilization and set it on a sound footing, giving the Latin branch of America the legitimacy and weight [of] the Anglo-Saxon branch."[48] Luperón was even more direct and stark with his analysis. In a letter to Hostos, then residing in Chile, in 1895 he wrote,

We should look on [the North American republic] as an enemy and pirate against all other American nations. I believe that we should work for a political confederation of all Latin American republics, against North American filibusters. . . . They are both the greatest danger and the greatest threat [to] Latin American republics. . . . Yes, my dear Hostos, raise your strong voice in that noble Chile, so that all of America will hear it, for the league of the sovereign principle, for the solidarity of all Latin American republics, for brotherhood among all [Latin] republics and the people of its race and for its solid union against all filibusters and pirates, against all tyrannies and all injustices wherever they may be, to prepare for the grand future when all the American groups [become] one, vast political brotherhood.[49]

Given their belief in the unity of the Latin American republics, Luperón and Hostos grappled with the legacy of Spanish colonialism in the Americas. Like Bonó and Galván, Luperón also defined *dominicanidad* in terms of Hispanic cultural norms (Catholicism, the Spanish language, honor, and the defense of marriage).[50] His political radicalism led him to fight against Spain during the War of Restoration, lend support to anticolonial wars in Cuba and Puerto Rico, and advocate a Pan-Antillean project. Faced with U. S. hegemony, however, Luperón reconciled with Spain and its historical legacy in the Americas. For example, he once noted, "Today, Spain does not have enemies among those nations that were her American colonies, but rather, emancipated children who are, for Spaniards, true brothers." As a result, when Dominicans fought for their independence from Haiti, theirs was a struggle against a despotic regime and a defense of "their language, their familial honor, free trade, the morality of marriage, [their] hatred of polygamy, [for a] better future for their *raza*, better work, education for their children, respect for the religion of their ancestors, [and for the protection of] individual security and property."[51] Luperón, as Irmary Reyes-Santos argues, "ultimately [could not] imagine a stable independent nation that [did] not reproduce European/Hispanic cultural practices and religious mores" such as the ones he apparently defended—Spanish language, Catholicism, marriage, and nuclear families.[52]

By opposing an immoral Haiti where polygamy was practiced and where few embraced the "religion of their ancestors," it might appear that Luperón's *hispanicismo* was a consequence of antiblack, anti-Haitian thinking, but this seems unlikely, given his long history of political and military collaboration with Haitians. For example, in *Notas autobiográficas*, he points out that during his term as president (December 1879–September 1880) he "suspended the regime of strict orders along the Dominican border against commerce with Haiti . . . recognizing that it was neither legal nor wise to breed antagonism between the two sister republics. This harmony," he argued, was "the more necessary between the two peoples [given] the more tenacious, invading tendency of the North Americans."[53] Finally, he countered perceptions of Haitians' blackness as opposed to Dominicans' whiteness; for him Haiti and the Dominican Republic were sister nations not only of necessity but because they were the same people. Luperón insisted that "the island's population [was] formed by two races . . . the European and the African, which, mixing as they have, have produced another, mixed race."[54]

Luperón establishes here that Dominicans and Haitians comprise a new *raza*—a nation—produced by the mixture of races, itself a product of colonialism. To be Dominican or Haitian, in other words, was to be mixed-race (*mestizo* or mulatto) and both nations shared this history. In other words, in contrast to Galván, Luperón acknowledged (albeit in stereotypical ways) cultural differences between Haitians and Dominicans, but these did not become racial distinctions of the sort that produced xenophobia. Indeed, some regarded Luperón's thinking as so radical that they accused him of inciting race war. Writing in the 1920s, Sumner Welles, who served as head of Latin American affairs in the U.S. State Department, reported the unlikely story that while in exile from the island in 1871, Luperón proclaimed that "the African race shall dominate on [the] Island and that that race should unite in order to exterminate the other races."[55]

As in Bonó's case, we find in Luperón another example of Dominican nationalism that, while Hispanic-centric, was neither anti-Haitian nor Negrophobic. Luperón and Bonó, following Reyes-Santos, "produced a narrative of creolization that decentered whiteness while simultaneously affirming a Hispanic Dominican ethno-racial heritage."[56] They did so by regarding Dominicans' racial mixture in positive terms and by insisting that Dominicans and Haitians shared Hispaniola's unique historical legacies. Although Luperón represented Dominicans as culturally distinct from Haitians, his political activism, his generally high regard for Haitian heads of state, and his Pan-Antillean commitments suggest that neither whiteness nor blackness was central to his understanding of Dominican national character. Like Bonó, Luperón viewed Dominicans as a new *raza*, unified in racial harmony and as a nation with every right to proclaim and defend its sovereignty against foreign incursion.

Luperón's and Hostos's affirmations of racial mixedness as a positive force in Caribbean peoples' lives and for the future of their nation-states were quite radical, given the tenor of travel literature about the Caribbean produced for European and U.S. American audiences in the 1880s and 1890s. One North American tourist in Trinidad, Susan de Forest Day, frowned on the racial mixture she witnessed in the Caribbean, hypothesizing that the black children she saw with "flaxen hair" evidenced a "a mixture of races which cannot but result in demoralization." James Anthony Froude, for his part, also refused to believe that Jamaicans could govern themselves, given the "disproportion" of black blood, which increased the possibility of Jamaica's "reverting to cannibalism again."[57]

At the same time, Eugenio María de Hostos, who admired the Haitian government and the "inestimable benefit of democratizing and equalizing to the point of erasing [at the level of] ideas and customs the notion of privileged authority and caste difference" that Haitian rule brought to Santo Domingo,[58] did not include Haiti as part of the Antillean Confederation. Perhaps Hostos remained silent about that country's place in the federation because he feared that explicit support for Haiti could be used by Spain against independence movements in Cuba and Puerto Rico. Since the independence wars in the early nineteenth century and especially during the Ten Years' War in Cuba, the Spanish Crown and conservative forces had used the specter of "another Haiti" to scare moderate whites away from supporting independence; fears that revolution would produce racial warfare were also exploited to quash the political aspirations of African-descended men.[59]

Did such pandering to those fears evidence an antiblack undercurrent in Pan-Antillean thinking? Hostos did not ascribe Haiti's problems as being derived from Haitians' race; rather, the drastic break from slavery and colonialism produced profound fissures within Haitian society that were difficult to overcome. The Dominican Republic became central to Hostos's thinking because, as he wrote, "when it came time to expel Haitians, [Dominicans built] a government of equals, for whites, blacks, *mestizos*, without whites resisting the political elevation of *mestizos* and blacks and without those *mestizos* and blacks displeasing . . . white men as their bosses."[60] Having learned republicanism from Haitians, Dominicans had a commitment to equality that put them on a path toward racial transcendence. At the same time, Hostos recognized the colonial legacy: white men were still in power; black men were not.

As a result, it is important to understand Hostos's silencing of Haiti as an equal partner in the early configuration of an Antillean federation as evidence of the profound racism that confronted Caribbean societies engaged in liberation movements and, specifically, black men who aspired to political power. Gregorio Luperón embodied this embattled position. Before he became president for a brief period, Luperón refused overtures from his party to run for the presidency in 1876, because, as he wrote, "I do not want, do not want, do not want to become the occasion or pretext [for] disturbing the public's peace."[61] When asked to run again after his term as president, Luperón claimed that he "did not want to know anything about . . . politics . . . hated all things [associated with] the state . . . did not want its positions or its intrigues, only liberty and justice."[62] Luperón claimed to be antipolitical even as he led rebellions against administrations he deemed annexationist or authoritarian. Although an emblem of Dominican nationalism, Luperón twice refused to accept the political power he had earned.

Luperón's willingness to step away from power quite possibly stemmed from an ethical obligation to the idea that public service should not be monopolized for personal gain. Yet, when considered in light of the actions of his Cuban contemporary Antonio Maceo, who surrounded himself with white officers as he fought against Spain in 1898, one wonders if these "bronze titans" acted in conscious awareness of their difficult position as powerful black men. Antiblack racism, as Thomas C. Holt has argued in the context of nineteenth-century Jamaica, provided mechanisms for containing "the aspirations of a politically insurgent black citizenry [and structuring] a political system . . . nominally consistent with liberal democratic principles, while maintaining ultimate control over black expression."[63] In this broader context, therefore, Antilleanism's call for racial transcendence was not black denial: removing race from conceptualizations of the nation also undermined the possibility of its exploitation against African-descended men. Antilleanism, like racelessness in Cuba, could provide black men a way to broker their political power in a context that not only privileged whites, but that also viewed African-descended male leadership as dangerous and potentially seditious. Racelessness did not require that African-descended peoples forget or deny their heritage. Instead, it required antiblack racists to play the "race card"—to imagine reasons for denying people of color equality in these new regimes.

. . .

In this chapter I have argued that neither antiblackness nor anti-Haitianism was a central component of all expressions of *dominicanidad* as they emerged from the pens of theorists such as Pedro Francisco Bonó, Gregorio Luperón, and Eugenio María de Hostos. At the same time, it is also true that their imaginings of *dominicanidad* gave credence to a romantic and bucolic interpretation of Spanish colonialism that made race-based mobilization appear radical and extreme. A mythic Hispanicism appears to have been a lingua franca among intellectual elites in the nineteenth century. Their romantic narratives of a colonial past that produced racial and social harmony stemmed from the need to create a sense of national unity at a time when so many forces threatened Dominican sovereignty. Nevertheless, in the debate over the possibility of Dominican nationhood that vied for discursive hegemony at the end of the nineteenth century, only Bonó's, Luperón's, and Hostos's ideas were fundamentally democratic and conveyed optimism about a Dominican national project. For them, the legitimacy of the nation derived from the country's mixed-race population and its historically constituted common culture and identity rooted in Spanish language and Catholicism.

Nevertheless, Luperón's and Hostos's Antillean ideology allowed for a consideration of *lo dominicano* (Dominicanness) beyond the boundaries of the nation-state, transcending the limits of culture, language, and identity of their ethno-Hispanicism. Antilleanism bound activists together in a revolutionary

project oriented around sovereignty, solidarity, and resistance against imperialism in all of its forms, from Spanish rule to the commercial, political, and
military intervention of the United States.

This is poignantly reflected in the lives of Charles Fraser and Sarah Loguen
Fraser. As Frederick Douglass predicted, the Frasers built a comfortable life
in Puerto Plata. On December 23, 1883, they welcomed the birth of a little girl
whom they named Gregoria in honor of her godfather, Gregorio Luperón.
Then in 1884 President Meriño authorized a special license for Sarah to become the first woman permitted to practice medicine in the Dominican Republic. Gregoria recalled how Luperón and Ulises Heureaux often came to the
family's drugstore to spend time with her father. She described Heureaux as
"a Negro of splendid carriage, his body beautifully proportioned, his physique
untiring and untirable [sic], his nerves ever under the most perfect control due
to his lifelong abstinence from both alcohol and tobacco."

The Frasers also raised Gregoria to be aware of her multicultural heritage.
For example, when they celebrated her birthday, the Frasers would raise the
U.S. flag for Sarah, the Danish flag for Charles, and the Dominican flag for
Gregoria. Unfortunately, Gregoria's charmed life in Puerto Plata ended with
her father's tragic death in 1894. An astute businesswoman, though, Sarah Fra-
ser invested money from the pharmacy's projects and returned to the United
States after a stay in Paris in 1897.[64]

In some ways, Frederick Douglass had been correct: Sarah Fraser had experienced the fullness of her womanhood in Santo Domingo. Her daughter,
Gregoria, however, struggled to maintain the socioeconomic gains her parents had achieved. By the late 1890s, Jim Crow racism in the United States
put into stark relief the divergent life chances for people of African descent in
the Americas. Whereas Sarah was able to practice medicine in the Dominican
Republic, Gregoria confronted such intense racism in the United States that
she never achieved her dream of graduating from Syracuse University (her
mother's alma mater no less) with a degree in music. White students in the
department taunted her in the hallways with the words of a popular song from
that year, "Coon, Coon, Coon, I wish my color would change." At times, Gregoria's supporters used her Dominican birth as a response to this harassment,
as when a Dean M. commented, in earshot of white students, how Gregoria
missed her native Santo Domingo on snowy days. Nothing, however, seemed
to help. Assuming Gregoria worked as a maid, one professor remarked that
"dishwashing and scrubbing floors would [unfit] her hands for piano work."
Gregoria reported, "I told him, 'I had never done either for we had servants in
our home in Puerto Plata, Dominican Republic.'"[65]

Over time, in Upstate New York and in North Carolina, Gregoria became known as "Miss Fraser from Santo Domingo," but did this mean that she exchanged black pride for a racially transcendent Dominicanness? Not necessarily. Even as "Miss Fraser from Santo Domingo," Gregoria learned something about the fight against racial injustice from her personal experience with Jim Crow segregation and, I would argue, coming of age in Puerto Plata, the heart of the Pan-Antillean Confederation. Pan-Antillean ideology may have not addressed racism specifically, but it was an ideological force that demanded critical attention be paid to how racial ideas lubricated relations between states and social relations in general. In contrast, Galván's Indo-Hispanic, ethnic-racial nationalism erased African-descended people from the national narrative and adhered to a virulent, anti-Haitian Negrophobia. Antillean racelessness provided an alternative framework: Dominicans became a nation as they embraced an anticolonial, anti-imperialist stance and dealt critically with the implications of their shared unique history as racially mixed society. At the end of the nineteenth century, there were at least three arguments about the Dominican nation vying for discursive hegemony. As the Loguen-Fraser story suggests, only one opened a space for antiracist activism. The other laid the foundation for white nationalism.

We turn now to San Pedro de Macorís to examine how and why conceptualizations of Dominicans as a *raza* became arguments for Dominican whiteness.

2

THE CHANGING LANDSCAPE OF POWER IN
THE SUGAR-GROWING EAST

Debates over *dominicanidad* in the late 1880s coincided with significant economic, political, and demographic transformations in the Dominican Republic, and especially around San Pedro de Macorís. While Antillean activists organized in Puerto Plata, in 1876 refugees from Cuba's Ten Years' War injected money and new technology into San Pedro's hinterlands and initiated another kind of social, political, and economic revolution. Between 1876 and 1900, acres were cleared to make room for cane plantations; wrought-iron buildings that housed steam-driven mills towered over this cane-transformed landscape. By the 1880s San Pedro de Macorís, with its seven sugar estates, had become a major sugar-producing region. This dramatic transformation, Michiel Baud argues, provoked intellectuals and political elites to wonder about how "modernization and its failures to eradicate poverty and the destruction of traditional society" would shape the Dominican Republic's future.[1]

What occurred in San Pedro de Macorís is a familiar story throughout Latin America: wherever export-oriented economies took hold, governments and private enterprises forced the shift from communal to private property regimes; peasants were often displaced from their lands; and foreigners—whether as workers, managers, or owners of new agribusinesses—began to influence politics, shape cultural change, and contribute to economic development.[2] In oil-rich Venezuela, for example, as Miguel Tinker Salas argues, "the ascent of new political actors coincided with the restructuring of economic relations, the rise of foreign dominated . . . centers, the growth of labor, and rapid industrialization."[3] This chapter analyzes a similar process in San Pedro by discussing who became new political actors in the region after 1880 and how local governing structures changed as a result.

Scholars of enclave economies in the Dominican Republic and elsewhere in Latin America insist that agro-export production transformed local society as propertied natives often lost economic influence to foreign companies.

Yet, foreign-born owners and administrators were not always willing or able to exert political influence over the communities and regions in which they operated. The enclaves are unique, therefore, because even though they were quintessential spaces of foreign incursion, local governance often remained in the hands of regional elites.[4]

Among enclaves throughout the circum-Caribbean, San Pedro de Macorís was exceptional because it was not a "company town" in the traditional sense; no single U.S.-based corporation, like United Fruit Company in Central America, monopolized production.[5] Sugar estates such as Ingenios Consuelo, Angelina, and Porvenir were owned by investment firms and governed by corporate boards based in the United States, Cuba, Puerto Rico, and the Dominican Republic. Cuban and Puerto Rican participation in the Dominican sugar industry also uniquely influenced the region's economy because it brought wealthy, white, Spanish, Cuban, immigrant Italian, and Puerto Rican migrants to San Pedro. Some managed estates; others were *colonos* who grew sugar under contract to estates on land they owned or leased from the sugar companies; yet another group was urban-based merchants.

Immigrant Cubans, Puerto Ricans, and Spaniards shared with Dominicans the Spanish language, Catholicism, and a historical (in some cases, ancestral) connection to Spain, but San Pedro's native elite welcomed only those who were wealthy and considered white into their ranks. At the same time, while the city's elite consolidated its power, government officials dismissed armed, mobilized peasants as *gavilleros*, bandits. The emergence of the bandit as a social problem complemented the vertical shift of power and the incorporation of foreign white elites into local governing structures and as members of the dominant elites.

Large-scale sugar production and General Ulises "Lilís" Heureaux's dictatorship (1888–1899) provide the larger context in which this new, influential class took shape in San Pedro between 1870 and 1900. I begin with a summary of the growth of sugar production in San Pedro. I then assess General Heureaux's dictatorship and its impact on local and regional governance, particularly through financial patronage. While a political elite came into being in San Pedro de Macorís, a process that will be explored more fully in the next chapter, the city's hinterlands exploded in armed rebellion. Finally, I analyze the meaning of banditry in the early decades of the twentieth century and argue that the creation of the "bandit" reflected the changing dynamics of power in the eastern sugar zone. These transformations would only intensify during the U.S. occupation, as would war in the east.

. . .

Carol Rose reminds us that a "map, far from stifling the imagination, invites the viewer to reflect on the story behind the case."[6] The jagged outlines of San Pedro de Macorís Province tell a number of stories, in addition to forcing us to consider the rivers, creeks, and stretches of plains that serve as provincial boundaries. One sector embraces the plains (*llanos*) north of the city, while another draws its arm around the southern coastal plain until it reaches the Soco River farther east. The region's varied topography and fecundity caught the attention of Father Bartolomé de las Casas, the chronicler of the Spanish conquest and colonialism in the New World. In one description of Hispaniola he wrote about a settlement located a day's ride from the capital, Santo Domingo de Guzmán, along "a beautiful river called Macoríx [with] very fertile soil for [growing] cassava, raising swine and many other provisions and necessities."[7]

The plains of the Higuamo River experienced a brief period of prosperity in the sixteenth century, followed by precipitous economic decline and uneven development until the last quarter of the nineteenth century. Between 1600 and 1800, descendants of Spaniards, Indians, and enslaved or free persons of African ancestry took advantage of the east's varied topography and created a diverse economy based in ranching, lumbering, food crops, and, to a lesser degree, sugar. In the late eighteenth century, some *hacendados* (owners of large estates) established plantations and cultivated cane, but the golden era of the large estate, with hundreds of slaves cutting, harvesting, and grinding cane and shaping *melaza* (molasses) into blocks for sale in Spain ended almost without notice. Where the soil was rocky and poor, some landowners dedicated themselves to butchering cattle and preparing hides for sale in Santo Domingo.[8] The region's economic foundation in ranching was captured in the name given to the landscape. The region that was once simply denoted as "a day's ride from Santo Domingo" was known as two extensive tracts, the Yeguada del Este and the Yeguada del Sur, the eastern and the southern pastures. While the precise origins of the *yeguadas* remain unclear, the pastures may have been connected to and part of an even larger land grant (*merced*) that extended from the coast around what is today San Pedro and a town farther north and east, Hato Mayor (main herd). It is quite possible that over the centuries, this *merced* was entailed by its original recipients and leased, shared, or simply squatted on by poor whites or freed people of color.[9]

Sugar remained marginal to the local economy well into the mid-nineteenth century. In the 1850s, for instance, French observers commented that Dominicans were beginning to export sugar, but the sugar industry had failed to grow for lack of workers and because of "ancient machinery."[10] Until the 1870s, San Pedro's largest sugar producer may have been Manuel Asunción Richiez, whose *trapiche* (animal- or human-powered mill) was reported to be the largest in the area, producing 100 *quintales* (about 10,000 pounds) of sugar during the *zafra* (harvest).[11] Until the latter part of the nineteenth century, landowners, ranchers, and peasants were the eastern region's main social groups, and their products—low-quality sugar for local consumption, lumber, food staples, meat, and hides—formed the backbone of the region's economy.[12]

Then change came to the east. According to local lore, the most significant transformations began with the arrival of the Richiez family, which would become one of San Pedro's most influential. According to a descendant, Manuel Leopoldo Richiez, his forebears, "motivated by patriotic sentiments or . . . deeply horrified before the painful reality of the Haitian occupation,"[13] arrived in 1822, just after Dominican president José Núñez de Cáceres had accepted unification with Haiti.[14] Nearly thirty years later, around 1852, Juan Antonio Aybar became *alcalde pedáneo*, rural mayor. Shortly thereafter, in 1856, Father Carrasco organized the first Catholic congregation and unified the villages of Mosquito and Sol as a town he baptized San Pedro de Macorís. Two years later, San Pedro became a military outpost with an appointed commander-at-arms.[15] By the 1860s, a colony of Canary Islanders had joined about 180 farmers who lived in San Pedro's rural *secciones* (sections): Yeguada, Punta de Garza, and Soco.[16]

Most important, in 1876 Juan Amechazurra, a Spaniard who had fled Cuba during the Ten Years' War, built Ingenio Angelina and milled the first successful *zafra* (harvest) in 1879. As one writer put it, Amechazurra's Angelina transformed San Pedro from "an insignificant town of workers and fishermen [the moment] steam escaped from [its] whistle."[17] Other sugar estates quickly followed Angelina: Ingenio Porvenir (1879), Ingenio Consuelo (1881), Ingenio Santa Fe (1884), Ingenio Cristóbal Colón (1882), Ingenio Puerto Rico (1882), and Ingenio Quisqueya (1892)(map 2.1).

Foreign investment in sugar production in the Dominican Republic was facilitated by generous permits authorized by the president that allowed individuals or companies to import machinery, tools, and labor tax-free. The Dominican government also passed legislation to foment agricultural industry. In 1875 the Rural Police Law outlined the responsibilities of a local official in aiding large-scale agricultural production: "to prohibit gambling and diversions on nonfeast days, prosecute vagrancy, demarcate, fence in, enclose farms, procure the peace among habitants in his jurisdiction, to rein in [loose] animals from farms and the wilderness, to regulate lumbering both for export

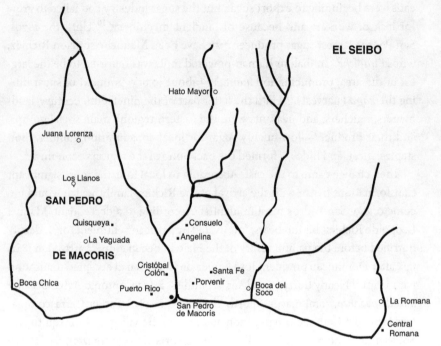

Map 2.1. Close-up of San Pedro Province, Dominican Republic. Bruce Calder, *The Impact of Intervention*, p. xxix.

and domestic consumption, to maintain and repair roads and boats and adopt whatever measures he deems necessary to fulfill the law."[18] Then, under the leadership of the Council of Secretaries of State and during the presidencies of Gregorio Luperón and Archbishop Fernando Arturo de Meriño, the Dominican government passed laws that allowed the sale of fallow state-owned property to land-hungry Dominicans and foreigners on the condition that they cultivate export crops such as coffee, tobacco, cacao, cotton, and sugar (promulgated July 8, 1876); declared all machinery, vehicles, instruments, and tools imported into the country and designated for agricultural use during the harvest duty-free (May 6, 1879); created municipal agricultural committees to oversee harvests, take censuses and surveys, and educate farmers (October 27, 1880); established committees in every town to educate citizens in the mechanical arts (October 10, 1880); and prohibited owners of sugar mills from cultivating cane on their property, forcing them to purchase their cane from *colonos*, contracted cane cultivators. (October 10, 1880).[19]

Although much of this legislation remained unenforceable until the U.S. occupation, the regulations outlined here reflected demands that flowed from regional landowners, not just from sugar estates. There were also clear disagreements among sugar producers, estate owners, and small cultivators over how the national government should respond to the very different needs of subsistence farming, large-scale agriculture, and ranching. For example, in 1870 El Seibo's city council sent a formal complaint to the minister of the interior, police, and agriculture about free-ranging animals that trampled fences and destroyed subsistence crops. Manuel Asunción Richiez, the owner of the largest rum distillery in the area, forwarded his own letter to officials in Santo Domingo, noting, "It has come to my attention that the *ayuntamiento* [city council] of this *común* (parish) has [written] to you [with] respect to the threat that a small number of cows that graze around here [pose]." Richiez concurred that oxen and cows roamed freely but insisted that this was a necessary feature of rural life and important to a population that depended on cows for milk and oxen for transportation. Richiez also explained that he and his neighbors "own a few oxen because we have cane haciendas and [the animals are] indispensable [for] grinding." In light of the claims made by the city, Richiez made this suggestion: "I think, Mr. Minister, that the best [solution] would be that those inhabitants whose fences [are in] a bad state [should] fix them, and if some animal [tears them down], [the owners] should pay for it and get rid of the animal."[20] Richiez's expressed disregard for the needs of peasant cultivators also reveals that the nascent sugar industry emerged within and also competed against traditional land-use and husbandry practices that had defined eastern life for generations.

The laws passed in the 1880s point to other unique features of the Dominican sugar industry that differentiated it from Cuban and Puerto Rican production during the same period. For instance, a noteworthy and confusing problem these new laws attempted to clarify was land titling and ownership. Sugar production required land, and the traditional property regime posed a significant problem for foreigners who did not understand customary landholding and land use practices and for investors who wanted to buy and secure private property to convert to cane. Members of the U.S. Senate Commission of Inquiry sent in 1871 to investigate the possible annexation of the Dominican Republic to the United States worried that potential settlers would find themselves caught up in land disputes if Dominicans refused to respect private property. At their request, William Gabb, a U.S. citizen resident in Santo Domingo, described the property regime as he understood it to function: "There are very few large landowners. . . . [Some] with one thousand acres, up to ten thousand acres in a few cases, the rest is divided among small landowners. Here there is a type of peculiar property right, called *comunero*, a species of community title in which all of the descendants of some large landowner possess land in common whose boundaries are well-defined and within which each inheritor has equal right as the others."[21]

The origins of this practice are murky. It appears that the practice of using lands in common (*terrenos comuneros*) arose from attempts by major landowners during the colonial period to avoid dividing their estates among numerous heirs: rather than apportioning land among the qualifying heirs, they determined the value of the estate and then divided that value, in the form of "land pesos," among them. Another theory states that the regime was consolidated in the eighteenth century when cash-poor landowners sold access or usufruct rights to unspecified areas of their estates. Richard Turits suggests that *terrenos comuneros* may have served the needs of Santo Domingo's cattle economy after the decline of the plantation economy in the late seventeenth century. Large herds required ample land, rivers, and meadows. One possible outcome of this economy was a system in which "jointly owned lands—comprising pasture, woods, streams, palm groves, and fertile terrain—[could be] collectively utilized rather than subdivided among heirs and other co-owners." In this context, "land pesos represent[ed] owners' relative rights or property share." Co-owners shared the expenses associated with cattle raising. In this regime, "sales of land pesos or divisions among heirs meant not diminished access to the estate, but rather only that growing numbers of co-owners enjoyed usufruct rights to the entire site."[22]

Over the years, this system of access to land and its exploitation appears to have degenerated into community property as squatters took over lands not used by titled owners or exploited such small areas that titleholders tolerated their presence. Land was cheap and official titles scarce. And as a result of peasants' intransigence, large landowners "were hardly encouraged . . . to attempt to evict the country's nearly ubiquitous, armed, and battle-ready peasant squatters."[23] This, combined with unclear boundaries and minimal face-to-face interaction among common owners, allowed some cultivators and herders to remain as nontitled exploiters of these vast territories.

Most significant, as Turits explains, the presence of squatters in *terrenos comuneros* transformed the institution to the point that peasants called the land *tierras comuneras*. In peasants' terms, there were titled shareholders, proprietors, and smallholders without formal titles. Property rights, it appears, "were not imagined as including the right to bar others from lands that owners were not using."[24] As a result, when Amechazurra's Angelina completed its first harvest at least three competing views of property relations and relationships to land had emerged by the late nineteenth century—those held by peasants, by titleholders, and by the Dominican state.

The laws highlight yet another important feature of the nascent sugar in-dustry: Dominican sugar did not build on slave labor nor did it emerge on the heels of emancipation. As a result, securing the labor necessary for large-scale sugar production required due diligence on the part of local authorities. Also, because the Dominican sugar industry took root long after emancipation in 1822, estate owners adopted both *ingenio* and *central* systems. In pre-emanci-pation Cuba, the *ingenio* referred to a plantation that cultivated and processed cane grown on land owned by the estate. Under this system, plantation own-ers increased their yield by purchasing more land and slaves. After abolition, both Cuba and Puerto Rico experienced a transition from *ingenio* production to the *central* system. The *ingenio-central*, or simply the *central*, referred to the sugar-milling operation. Unlike the *ingenio*, the *central* ground cane produced by *colonos*, or contracted cane farmers.

The centralization of the milling process in Cuba and Puerto Rico, as César Ayala argues, transformed the sugar industry: under the *central* system, cane farmers were no longer forced to invest in machinery, and mill owners could rely on contracts with cane-growing *colonos* to increase their yields. Mill own-ers were further advantaged in this system because *colonos* shared the financial risks of cane cultivation. San Pedro's sugar mills were all called *ingenios*, but they ground cane cultivated on properties owned by estates and/or *colonos*, just as *centrales* did (table 2.1).[25]

One exemplary model of the Dominican version of the *ingenio-central* sys-tem was Ingenio Consuelo, the sugar mill established in 1882 by the Cuban con-sortium Padró, Solaun y Co. Consuelo milled cane cultivated on land owned by the estate and by contracted *colonos*. In 1884 Ingenio Consuelo was already the tenth-largest sugar producer in the country. However, its bright future was

Table 2.1. Sugar estates in San Pedro de Macorís, 1870s–1880s

Ingenio	Owner	Nationality
Angelina	Juan Amechazurra	Spanish-Cuban
Porvenir	Santiago Mellor	Spanish-Cuban
Consuelo	Padró, Solaun y Co.	Spanish-Cuban
Santa Fe	Vásquez Rousset y Co.	Spanish-Cuban
Cristóbal Colón	Castro, Mola y Co.	Cuban
Puerto Rico	Juan Serrallés	Puerto Rican
Quisqueya	Juan Fernández Castro	Cuban

Source: Juan J. Sánchez, *La caña en Santo Domingo*, pp. 41–53.

Note: "Spanish-Cuban" refers to owners born in Spain who first migrated to Cuba and then to the Domini-can Republic.

hampered by an economic crisis brought about by a downturn in sugar prices, a process that began in 1882 and worsened in 1884–1885.

During the crisis of the 1880s, investment firms located in the United States stepped in to salvage debt-burdened *ingenios*, including Consuelo. The most notable change in the industry occurred in ownership. The Santo Domingo newspaper *Listín Diario* highlighted the alarming trend: three *ingenios* (Santa Fe, Quisqueya, and San Isidro in Santo Domingo) were in debt to Bartham Brothers in New York; Hugh Kelly and his shareholders owned two (Porvenir and Ansonia in Azua); another two (Consuelo and San Isidro) were financed by the Bass family business, Pioneer Iron Works; and four others, including Amechazurra's Angelina, belonged to a Cuban immigrant of Italian descent, Juan B. Vicini.[26]

When another crisis hit the sugar industry in the 1890s, Ingenio Consuelo's fortunes changed again once Alejandro Bass became the majority shareholder in the Compañía Azucarera de Macorís (Macorís Sugar Company). As owner of Pioneer Iron Works in New York, it is possible that Alejandro Bass was one of Consuelo's principal creditors, having provided the estate with machinery. On acquiring managing control of Consuelo around 1890, Alejandro turned it over to his son, William. If the economic crisis that hit the sugar industry in the 1880s resulted in the consolidation of sugar estate ownership, the slump in sugar prices in the 1890s, coupled with a worldwide economic depression, provoked a land grab in San Pedro by sugar estates through the *colono* system.[27]

For example, José del Castillo notes that by 1893 William Bass's Consuelo had 24,100 *tareas* under cultivation, distributed among twelve *colonos*.[28] Notary records show that between February and May of 1898, William Bass paid $40,144 for an additional 8,623 *tareas* (539 *hectares*).[29] Exiles from the Cuban War of Independence Santiago Mellor and Juan B. Vicini were also successful expansionists during this period of crisis. Veteran cane grower Manuel Asunción Richiez sold 1,287 *tareas* (about 80 *hectares*) of land that abutted Ingenio Porvenir, with an additional 42 "*varas* of virgin hillside [*monte*]," to Porvenir's owner, Santiago Mellor. Juan B. Vicini managed to put the 2,450-*tarea* (153-*hectare*) Colonia María Dolores under contract with his Ingenio Angelina estate by lending Don Evangelista Fuentes $2,000 for the purchase. When he bought the *colonia* (estate), Fuentes also assumed a cultivation contract with Vicini, agreeing to grow cane on 100 hectares and rent the property for ten cents per *tarea*.[30]

Hugh Kelly, of Ingenio Porvenir, increased the *hectares* under cane cultivation for his estate from 225 to 933, of which 820 were cultivated by *colonos*. In 1893

Ingenio Santa Fe had thirteen *colonos*; meanwhile, Ingenio Cristóbal Colón's *colonos* cultivated 563 of the estate's 688 hectares.[31]

As Arturo Martínez Moya concludes, the period between 1890 and 1900 witnessed a centralization of the sugar industry, which both increased production and strengthened the *colonato*—the *colono*-based cane-cultivation regime.[32] Roberto Marte has calculated that in 1890, 69.1 percent of proprietors in the region owned or worked fewer than 24 *tareas* of land, just about 4 acres. Fourteen individuals, accounting for 1.6 percent of proprietors, owned over 1,000 *tareas* (156 acres), consuming nearly 59 percent of property holdings in the region.[33] The impact of this centralization of land into the hands of fewer people continued into the early decades of the twentieth century (table 2.2.). Most important, as early as the 1890s, *colonos* had become an identifiable economic interest group, alongside estate administrators such as William Bass and Hugh Kelly, and those Cubans and Puerto Ricans who ran estates owned by their compatriots.

Available notarial records from the 1890s also provide some important details about *colonos*—their provenance, how they acquired their properties, and the nature of their contracts with sugar estates. Of the nineteen land sales recorded in Silvestre Aybar's notarial records from 1898, the majority of *colonos* noted in the book were foreigners—many of them Puerto Ricans—who had purchased the original titles from Dominicans: José Dolores de los Santos, a Dominican, sold his property to Señora Altagracia Guerrero de Ortiz, represented by her husband, Manuel, from Puerto Rico; when Eugenio Lugo from Puerto Rico sold his land to William Bass, he remained in charge of the property as a *colono* to "[grow] and [sell] good cane." Dominicans involved in the land grab included Antonio Aguayo, who sold his wife's properties to William Bass, and Judge Leovigildo Cuello, who sold land to Ingenio Colón.[34]

Table 2.2. Principal sugar enterprises in the Province of San Pedro de Macorís, 1925

Name	Nationality of owners	Area in acres	Value in dollars
Consuelo	U.S.	49.354	5,456,700
Quisqueya	U.S.	8.593	944,603
Las Pajas	U.S.	20.727	1,500,021
Santa Fe	U.S.	61.069	4,944,025
Porvenir	U.S.	10.877	1,644,867
Italia	Italian	8.269	Unknown
Angelina	Italian	13.317	1,930,640
Cristóbal Colón	Italian	22,175.0	1,454,660
J.J. Serrallés	Spanish–Puerto Rican–Dominican	12.275	Unknown

Source: Enciclopedia dominicana, vol. 5.

Little wonder, then, that Pedro Francisco Bonó and Eugenio María de Hostos harshly criticized the entire industry in their writings from the 1880s and 1890s. According to Pedro Francisco Bonó, easterners represented "the nation itself" in their willingness to introduce "a colossal agriculture on common lands." That industry had "dislocated, dispossessed, and forced with barbarity" an exploitive capitalist regime funded by foreigners. As a result, he says, easterners "will not exercise their citizenship responsibilities, nor will they live up to their responsibilities as fathers, and, falling into pauperism, they will ask of the nation impossible services or, of foreigners, protection and assistance." In his view, "monopoly destroyed the smallholders and their small ranches."[35] In another piece, Bonó asks, "Are we a colony or are we a nation?" The answer to that question lay in the state's capacity to protect workers, attack monopoly capitalism, and harmonize relations between city and country.[36]

For his part, Eugenio María de Hostos injected a Pan-Caribbean perspective, arguing in 1884 that mechanized sugar production created economic instability because the Antilles lacked the financial and economic infrastructure to support it. What few resources national governments had were devoted to sugar at the expense of other profitable crops like tobacco that provided peasants with a steady income while allowing them a degree of autonomy.[37] Even worse, "the sugar industry . . . from a historical point of view is abominable, it was forged in slavery." According to Hostos, the evil triad of low wages, cheap land, and monopoly capital revealed the colonial and imperialist roots of the so-called modern sugar industry. Resisting the impulse to invest everything in sugar should, he argued, be the first step in creating economic autonomy for the Antillean Confederation.[38]

As Bonó and Hostos feared, economic crisis forced San Pedro's *ingenios* to rely on *colonos* as a way to expand their productive capacity; most worrisome, foreigners made up a significant number of *colonos*, therefore reducing Dominicans' capacity to profit from the nascent industry. Although foreign-born *colonos* and estate administrators were economically dominant in the region, they were not politically powerful, at least not locally. The Ayuntamiento Law of 1856 prohibited foreigners from serving on city councils until they had resided in the country for one year and banned them from municipal positions until they had lived in their *comunes* for five years.[39] As a result, political power stayed in local hands. For example, Manuel Asunción Richiez served as city clerk (*síndico*) in 1867; his son, Manuel Leopoldo, assumed the same position in 1897. In April 1898 city council members elected Manuel Leopoldo vice president; in December 1898 he was elected city attorney (*síndico procurador*), only to return to the vice presidency on January 19, 1899.[40] Fernando Chalas was city council president in 1897 and then served as provincial governor in 1899, 1902, 1903, and 1912.[41] On September 10, 1882, the Dominican Congress installed General Ramón Castillo as the first governor of the Maritime District of San Pedro de Macorís.[42]

Despite the influx of estate administrators and *colonos* to the region, political power in San Pedro remained in Dominican hands thanks to the Ayuntamiento Law, but also because of General Ulises Heureaux, whose dictatorship greatly influenced local politics until his assassination in 1899. The number of *ingenios* operating in San Pedro doubled during his first term, 1882–1884, when he championed the region, noting San Pedro's "special gifts, . . . its port and . . . sugar haciendas."[43] When he assumed the presidency again in 1888, initiating what would be an eleven-year dictatorship, he gave a speech at the San Pedro Athenaeum.[44]

Heureaux's desire to secure social order and political unity, however, outweighed his commitment to democracy. Although the Constitution had granted suffrage to all Dominican men over eighteen (the age was lower if the man was married), the president insisted that city councils limit their list of eligible voters to literate men, merchants, property owners, ranchers, sugar estate owners, and professionals.[45]

Heureaux's approach to governance was rooted in his distrust of mass participation in the political process, a fact he noted in a letter, penned in English, to Charles Wells, explaining the problem with democracy in the Dominican Republic: "The special conditions of this country do not allow [the citizenry] to grasp its interests. . . . Almost always the people act by impulses derived from their first impressions, and it is only time and civilization that may teach them."[46] As this letter suggests, Heureaux, once the great defender of Dominican sovereignty as a general in the War of Restoration, believed that power belonged in the hands of a select few not driven by "impulses." The Dominican masses, according to him, required a dictatorship that would help them mature into civilization, which he defined as conscientiousness about the nation's economic interests.

Heureaux's dictatorship engendered stability, but the violence used to secure political loyalty planted sources of instability. For example, in March of 1895 General Ramón Castillo, Heureaux's handpicked governor of San Pedro Province and political ally, forwarded a petition to the president to remove the *jefe del orden* (district sheriff) from his post. Heureaux sent a reply in which he expressed concern about the subversive nature of the protest: "This document, even if the signatories are justified in submitting it, goes against public order and undermines the principle of authority." He ordered the arrest of the first five men who signed the petition and sentenced them to a fifteen-day prison term in Santo Domingo. He urged his "*compadre*" Castillo to warn other would-be protesters they would receive the same punishment for expressing disagreement with the regime.[47] By the end of March 1896, Heureaux had put Generals Castillo and José Estay, the interim governor of San Pedro Province, to death by firing squad on San Pedro's wharf.[48]

In addition to using violence, Heureaux managed his influence through financial patronage and borrowed-money-lubricated patron-client relations that tied local elites to regional officials and then to Heureaux himself. Throughout his regime, he received loans from foreign banks and wealthy men such as Juan Bautista Vicini, owner of several sugar estates, and Santiago Michelena, a banker from Puerto Rico. According to a story passed down in Dominican oral history, Heureaux is reported to have told Américo Lugo, a young writer who had a violent altercation with Vicini sometime in the 1890s, "Just so you know, I'm only the vice president. The president is Don Juan—he's in charge of the money."[49]

The same could have been said of Santiago Michelena, a Spanish immigrant who came to Santo Domingo in 1890 and established a branch of his family's commercial business. Michelena brought with him an extensive financial network that traversed the Hispanic Caribbean, Spain, and Germany and a sound reputation that helped him become a key player in Dominican political and economic life. Between 1893 and 1900, Michelena's loans helped General Heureaux feed his patronage system and also financed important *colonos* such as Juan Amechazurra and businesses in San Pedro. In October 1893, for example, twenty *petromacorisano* (San Pedro resident) firms and individuals owed Michelena $10,811.[50]

Heureaux secured even larger amounts from international firms. Roberto Marte calculates that, of the $12 million invested in the country's sugar industry in 1890, the bulk of it, just under $10 million, found its way to Santo Domingo and San Pedro Provinces.[51] The rest of it may have stayed with Heureaux. In 1888, for instance, he negotiated a loan from Westendorp & Company, a Holland-based financial organization, the terms of which placed the Dominican Republic at a critical disadvantage. The value of the first infusion of funds was $3,850,000, of which the government actually received just over $2,000,000 (57 percent of the loan's value after commissions and fees). Heureaux agreed to repay Westendorp over $8,000,000 and hand over control of the customshouse as a lien. By the 1890s loan payments for this and other advances took 40 percent of the government's revenue.[52]

Heureaux tried to renegotiate the loans using his personal connections with influential people in Washington, but to no avail.[53] Poor financial management coupled with an economic downturn secured his downfall. In 1899, a coalition of northern merchants disaffected with his regime had him gunned down as he traveled from Santo Domingo to the northern town of Moca.

After his death, regime changes and shifting political alliances significantly influenced San Pedro's provincial governance and its city council. Between 1882 and 1932, San Pedro had fifty-eight governors, of whom only three served their entire two-year term. The region's most politically volatile period was from 1903 until 1908, when twenty-one men occupied the governor's office. During the same period, San Pedro's city council had nine different administrations; in 1906–1907 and then again in 1914, three leadership changes occurred in the space of a year.[54]

By situating himself as the central node within a system of political graft financed by foreign and local loans, Heureaux fundamentally transformed regional power in San Pedro. Power became decidedly vertical and significantly enmeshed in patron-client relations organized around access to cash. Yet, in his analysis of the Dominican Republic's political geography, General Simon Campus derided only the proliferation of provinces as "the direct works of President Ulises Heureaux who formed them with the sole purpose of favoring some of his personal friends." Campus overstated the case: seven provinces came into being before Heureaux assumed power in 1888; he created only one.[55] Campus's analysis, nevertheless, was perceptive in another way: the provincial structure—and the vertical patronage system it reflected—appears to have protected local and regional political power for elite, native-born Dominicans.

My analysis of municipal records concludes that despite numerous personnel changes, there was enough stability among city council members to provide continuity between administrations. This stability was the product of nepotism, as in the case of the Richiezes (a Richiez remained on San Pedro's city council until at least 1899), the Berroas (notaries), and the Aybars (Juan Antonio served as *alcalde pedáneo* in the 1850s, and Silvestre Aybar became one of San Pedro's most important notaries). Only after Heureaux's death do we see the integration of foreign-born immigrants into San Pedro's governing structures: in 1905 James J. Brower, a British subject who worked as a bookkeeper for Ingenio Porvenir, was invited by the city council to serve as *suplente regidor* (assistant councilman), and in 1908 Spanish immigrant Dr. Emelio Tió y Betances became the city's medical officer.

Most important, professional men entered the ranks of local power at the turn of the century. Whereas Manuel Asunción Richiez and Elías Camarena, among the area's first settlers and *regidores* (city councilmen), derived their wealth from their estates, the men who headed San Pedro's city council by 1900 included lawyers, notaries, doctors, shopkeepers, pharmacists, and bookkeepers.[56]

In addition to estate administrators and *colonos*, therefore, the period between 1880 and 1900 also witnessed the emergence of a professional class in San Pedro that became politically influential in the city and across the region. This shift in political power began slowly at the level of provincial governor. Prior to the U.S. occupation in 1916, the majority of San Pedro's governors held the title of "General." As early as 1895, however, Don Antonio Brea held the post; in 1903 three *licenciados* (college graduates) served as governor. By the end of the U.S. occupation in 1924, and probably as a direct result of the intervention, civilians had replaced military men as provincial governors. Indeed, Heureaux's violent, anti-democratic regime buttressed by financial patronage made possible the transformation of local governance from military to civilian rule by economic and intellectuals elites. Heureaux's plan to keep the rural majority away from the ballot box worked. At the same time, Heureaux's financial relationships resulted in yet another important change.

Building on Alan Trachtenberg's insights regarding the Gilded Age in the United States, I argue that the shift toward professional and civilian men in local governance reflects a process Trachtenberg calls "incorporation," which he defines as "the emergence of a changed, more tightly structured society with new hierarchies of control and . . . changed conceptions of that society." The emergence of a corporate business culture complemented incorporation. According to Trachtenberg, corporate culture "wrenched American society from the moorings of familiar values" just as these new social hierarchies took root.[57] I want to suggest that incorporation was a transnational process that tied the United States with countries like the Dominican Republic through lending and debt servicing. Heureaux's steady appetite for cash assisted the Dominican Republic's vertical integration into the United States' commercial empire and facilitated the rule of civilian, professional elites in cities like San Pedro. This shift occurred as economies and financial systems in the Dominican Republic, Haiti, Panama, and Cuba fell under the direct supervision of U.S. diplomats, the period of Dollar Diplomacy. Particularly in San Pedro de Macorís and its immediate environs, the incorporation of the Dominican economy into the United States' commercial regime converted vast tracts of land into private property and cane fields, but this process also transformed governing structures and the meaning of political participation.

In contrast to the War of Restoration, which exaggerated the influence of the regional *caudillos*, one clear effect of Heureaux's dictatorship was the emergence of a closed power system in which the provincial structure served to further exclude peasants and the urban poor. It is in this context that we should understand the armed conflicts that exploded in the east as the sugar economy took hold and the debates over the role of the peasantry in the Dominican national project.

Armed opposition groups had long been active in the eastern countryside. Some of these groups had started as militias organized by military commanders in wars against Haiti in the 1840s and 1850s and then against Spain during the War of Restoration. In her comprehensive study of banditry in the early twentieth century, María Filomena González Canalda argues that some groups expressed a clear political agenda while others focused on the theft and sale of cattle. Following Henry Landsberger, González writes that armed peasants mobilized just as the power of the traditional landed elite diminished as sugar estates consumed more property. Banditry became visible after Heureaux's assassination in 1899, which resulted in the "breakdown of the chain of protection [and graft] created by Heureaux that generated and permitted the continued existence of autonomous groups [led by] powerful *caudillos*." These groups often "opposed state control and the modernization of traditional familial relations, clientelism, and politics represented by the state's modernizing project."[58]

In the wake of Heureaux's death, conflict swept the entire country. In early 1903 regional *caudillos* mobilized their forces and in effect divided the country into three regions. "Los del monte" (mountain men, or highwaymen), as they called themselves, appeared in official documents as *gavilleros* (bandits) in 1904. Among the first such groups were armed bands operating in the eastern region. As the governor of San Pedro de Macorís reported, for example, "There are people who should be attended to by the government; they are discontented, and [in them] resides a latent revolutionary germ."[59]

Julie Franks argues that many peasants in the east "engaged government officials and institutions in the contested construction of Dominican state power and authority in the early twentieth century" through armed revolt,[60] but during the Cáceres administration (1899–1911), peasant insurgency became a serious political problem. Dominican peasants ultimately collided with new forces of power and authority in the east; those who defended their interests in armed, mobilized groups became bandits.[61] According to González Canalda, it is unclear whether peasants embraced "*gavillero*" as a political identity, but it is clear that officials linked *gavilleros* with criminal activity and that local and national authorities viewed armed peasant men as criminals and not as legitimate political actors. As a result, González Canalda argues, it might be more useful to think of *gavillerismo* as an ideological construct that served the needs of a new political elite grappling with the profound contradictions of national state formation and agricultural export.[62] As the Dominican Republic became a sugar producer, peasants were pushed out of the political process. A civilian elite now ruled and these professionals justified their authority not by military achievements and titles, but, as we have seen, through nepotism and patronage.

Peasants' displacement from their lands and their formal dispossession accelerated during the U.S. occupation. In 1920, for example, the occupation government approved an executive order that provided a mechanism for the establishment of land titles. Executive Order 511 redefined the basis of property rights on the foundation of possession, which meant "cultivation . . . or other beneficial use"; the construction of "fences, walls, hedges, ditches, pathways or similar means of indicating boundaries"; and a cadastral survey. The order also made symbolic possession of land equal to the idea of improvements on property. As a result, although the law favored the sugar companies, it also represented an attempt, embraced by some within the military government, to assist peasants in their efforts to formalize their rights to lands they cultivated. Nevertheless, sugar companies were able to take advantage of the new law by demonstrating both tangible improvements and the symbolic possession of vast tracts of land. Richard Turits suggests that the participation of attorneys for the sugar estates "appear[s] to have successfully conditioned the equitable aspects of this legislation so as to meet the interests of their clients."[63]

Francisco Peynado would have been one of these lawyers, and an extant letter he wrote to Colonel Rufus Lane in 1918 evidences his contribution to the new land law. Peynado came of age at the height of Eugenio María de Hostos's distinguished career as an educator and philosopher in Santo Domingo.

After graduating from Hostos's Escuela Normal (Normal School) in 1884, Peynado studied surveying and then earned his degree in law and practiced in Puerto Plata in the 1890s and in Santo Domingo from 1893 onward. In 1918 Colonel Lane asked Peynado for his opinion about the constitutionality of a provision that required property owners to register their titles within a six-month period and sanctioned landowners who failed to comply by turning over their property to the state. Peynado argued that the plan was constitutional because legal precedent and even the Constitution itself limited the notion of property rights to mean the proper use and enjoyment of land. Interestingly, though, Peynado encouraged Lane to consider changing an element of the Executive Order such that those lands not duly registered would be exempt from takeover by the state and, instead, would be given over to the co-owners.[64]

Peynado's idea would have also benefited peasants, but it is more likely that as an attorney for William Bass, the owner of Ingenio Consuelo, Peynado knew that much of the land his client purchased in the 1890s officially made him a co-owner within the *terrenos comuneros* of various properties in the east. So his suggestion to require that delinquent titles be turned over to the co-owners would have worked to the advantage of well-financed people like Bass. Peynado's idea, then, perverted traditional collective notions of land use and ownership to favor the sugar economy.

Despite how changes like these affected rural communities across the Dominican Republic, U.S. officials refused to consider peasants who responded to dispossession by mobilizing armed groups as legitimate political actors and certainly not as anti-U.S. revolutionaries. Dismissing the political potential of peasant mobilization became part of the occupation government's overall strategy in its war against these groups, a conflict that intensified in 1918 and ended in 1921. Marines on the battlefield claimed that on asking ordinary Dominicans, they learned that *gavilleros* were, for the most part, "fugitives from justice" or men "who found banditry an easy way to make a living."[65] In 1919 the occupation governor, Thomas Snowden, reported to his superiors in Washington that the "so-called bandits" were "bands composed of a few real outlaws [and] refugees from justice . . . [who] have no political aims whatever and [whose] activities consist solely in robbery and other outrages upon their own countrymen." Snowden proudly reported, "There is no political unrest [among] the people of the Dominican Republic. They are now absolutely happy and content in an assured peace," a peace that was threatened by criminality.[66]

Documents about *gavilleros* produced during the U.S. military occupation present peasant mobilization as a result of criminality. Military authorities noted that many raids of estate stores occurred on payday. For example, the assistant manager of Ingenio Consuelo, H. W. Turner, reported that between August 4 and September 8, 1918, three different bandit groups had continually raided the mill, stealing from the store and attacking workers. Martín Peguerro's band of about fifty men attacked the *ingenio* on August 4, "inflicting wounds on one English negro" and taking $1,250 in merchandise, clothes, and cash. The same group also robbed an estate store, the overseer's house, and workers' houses, taking another $235. Later that month, Peguerro's men robbed Bodega Consuelito, taking $1,000. In the process, they "killed Mono de la Cruz, who resisted their entrance into [the] store, went into the houses, forced the women . . . and beat up many laborers, taking away about six prisoners."[67]

According to both U.S. military officials and some Dominican commentators, bandits also kept rural people "in a state of abject terror" and hid themselves in a wild countryside where "concealment [was] extremely easy and the successful pursuit of a man or a body of men [was difficult]."[68] One of the most powerful *gavilleros* in the region, General Salustiano de Goicoechea (Chachá), evaded capture by marines even though he was reportedly entrenched near Ingenio Consuelo with some 100 to 200 men under his command.[69]

U.S. military authorities claimed that rural violence was simple lawlessness and developed policies aimed at identifying and imprisoning suspected bandits such as disarming the population and removing entire peasant communities from areas under revolt.[70] A marine stationed in Seibo Province dismissed the idea that bandits were political actors with popular support, claiming that they were unlike the majority of Dominicans, "who are friendly to the Americans and ... desire to lead the lives of law-abiding citizens."[71]

For example, despite their many problems with armed peasants, military officials wondered if "a large part of the disturbances ... [were] not from without the estates but from within." Indeed, some evidence suggests that estate administrators exploited the problem of banditry in order to use government funds to build private armies; a few, it appears, negotiated their own agreements with bandit groups. Colonel Thorpe made this point in a memorandum to Admiral Knapp, the military governor, when he claimed, "Consuelo management with its system of employees and jefes (crew chiefs) undoubtedly obtain much information of the whereabouts of criminals and fugitives and if they would give me that information it would be of great use. But instead of giving the local military authorities such information they send the false criticisms to Washington with the hope of obtaining, under false pretences (*sic*), troops for their private interests instead of the best public use."[72]

And it seemed as though internal disputes among *colonos* might have prompted some of the activity because, as the same report indicates, five men out of twenty who reportedly raided the estate were identified as working for Herr Leevey, a German *colono* for Consuelo. Military authorities noted that "bandits have never done a dollar's damage to Herr Leevey's property," even though they destroyed property and burned cane on other *colonias*.[73]

Some bandits, meanwhile, drew a radically different picture of their activities and motivations. As one marine commented, there were peasants who claimed to have "patriotic motives," boasting "that they had driven the Spanish and the Haitians from the Republic and [would] soon drive the Americans out." They considered themselves "heroes ... and the food and clothing that they steal as prerogatives of their position."[74] At one insightful moment in 1918, marines were fighting against an entrenched group of insurgents in Las Pajas when an *alcalde* taunted the insurgents by calling them bandits. Some rebels responded, "We are not bandits; we are revolutionaries!" A group led by Eustacio "Bullito" Reyes in San Pedro between 1913 and 1920 called itself La Revolución, and in 1920 insurgents in Higüey released a prisoner after giving him a letter to deliver to the military government in which they explained that they were revolutionaries and not killers.[75] Another influential leader, Vicentico Evangelista, called his struggle a "revolution" against the United States and its occupation forces.[76]

During the occupation, U.S. officials believed that guerrilla leaders such as Nateras, Evangelista, and Reyes merely cloaked themselves in the language of revolution to secure symbolic and material support from a broad spectrum of Dominicans who resisted the occupation. Francisco J. Peynado, for his part, provided some insight into the forces that pushed some peasants into armed groups—criminal or otherwise. Peynado, who helped craft land reform legislation with U.S. authorities, once noted that the Dominican peasant, "not being able to derive usefulness from his land or from laboring on it, is forced to sell his actions for a low price . . . and becomes a peon, a bum, and later, a bandit."[77]

Ventura Rincón was a Dominican whose economic plight, lack of political power, and interactions with U.S. authorities exemplified the series of events that, as Peynado noted, could transform an autonomous, peasant producer into a "peon" and, later, into a bandit. U.S. military officials labeled Ventura Rincón as a "Dominican negro," a "dangerous character," and a "bandit leader" after he led a rebellion against U.S. Marines in 1918. Released from prison on a suspended sentence in January of 1919, Rincón returned home and, according to police, continued to enrich himself and his family "by means and methods of irregular nature." Publicly known as "a bad man with a big heart," because he donated a large part of his personal wealth to Dominican officials, Rincón, according to U.S. authorities, led "at least 500 men." He had also spent ten years working variously as a machinist or as a contractor for a number of Ingenio Colón's *colonias* (colonies). According to U.S. authorities, over the course of his time at Colón, Rincón cultivated a close relationship with William A. Gowrie and his son, William Scott Gowrie, both British subjects, former employees of Colón, and, in 1922, colonists who grew cane for the company. Together, the Gowries and Rincón unofficially "ran things" on the estate, accumulating wealth and expanding their property holdings through, officials argued, graft and larceny.[78]

During a police interrogation, Rincón poignantly discussed the events that, in the end, undermined his ability to cultivate for his own benefit and how the sugar economy might have pushed him toward banditry:

Before, I possessed two thousand *tareas* of land on *colonia* Tolerancia, which I bought from Antonio Draiby and his brother Abraham Draiby[.] [When I was] clearing the ground in order to build up a *colonia* for the sugarcane, I was told by Santo Domingo Agriculture Company that this land did not belong to Antonio Draiby and he did not have a right to sell it to me[.] [In] the meantime, William A. Gowrie came to some understanding with Mr. Frita of the Santo Domingo Agriculture Company in order that he might buy 3,000 *tareas* of land for $30,000. . . . Mr. Despaigne [manager of Ingenio Colón] had bought up all the land that belonged to the Santo Domingo Agriculture Company and leased it to us . . . for eight years to work without paying him anything[.] . . . This contract was made between Mr. Despaigne and Mr. [William A.] Gowrie. I did not make any contract with Mr. Despaigne or Mr. Gowrie. I was only in charge of the land.[79]

Military authorities accused William Scott Gowrie and Rincón of conspiring to kill Jerôme Dufrense, Ingenio Colón's traffic manager, because Dufrense changed the *ingenio*'s cart allocation system in a way that put the Gowries and Rincón at a disadvantage. An angry Gowrie was left with too few carts to haul his cane to the mill, so he "left the entire matter to Rincon." At first, Rincón tried persuasion, but "after learning that he was unable to control [Dufrense] as he [did] with others of the [Colón] Estate," he decided to murder Dufrense. One of Rincón's friends, Augustino Díaz, a "light" Dominican who worked as an overseer and porter on William A. Gowrie's estate in Hato Mayor, carried out Rincón's plan.[80]

Historians have since tried to determine whether men like Rincón, as a result of their dispossession and displacement from their lands and traditional cultivation practices, became anti-imperialist revolutionaries or had the potential to become such as a result of the occupation. Writing in the 1970s, Félix Servio Ducoudray applauded the bandits as leaders of a nationalist, anti-imperialist movement that waged a justified war against U.S. occupation and the sugar estates.[81] Bruce Calder's study of guerrilla warfare in the east points out that while peasant warriors sometimes expressed anti-U.S., even revolutionary, sentiments, their overall political consciousness remained "inchoate."[82]

Orlando Inoa challenges Servio Ducoudray's analysis by arguing that, for the most part, destroying the sugar industry was not the primary goal of peasant insurgents; extorting money from sugar estate managers by providing "protection" services was a lucrative source of income for cash-poor communities, and the occupation government represented a threat to their money-generating scheme. To prove his point that the bandits were hardly "revolutionary," Inoa notes an agreement signed in 1915 between Enrique Jimenes, minister of interior, policing, and agriculture, and prominent bandits, including Evangelista and Goicoechea. In that document the bandits made demands that appear to represent the needs of ignored communities. They asked that the national government build highways into the eastern region, end a judicial dispute that involved other bandits and the state, and authorize them to organize rural guards (presumably made up of their own men) on Ingenios Angelina, Consuelo, and Santa Fe.[83]

Following María Filomena González Canalda, it appears that distinctions made between "revolutionary" and "bandit" peasants by governing elites tell us less about the collective consciousness of armed peasants than about the limits of the politically possible at the turn of the century in a region now fully incorporated as an enclave of sugar production.[84] Armed peasants claimed to be "revolutionaries" because they might have accepted authorities' framing of political identities for rural men. While the bandit was little more than an insolent peasant who robbed the rich to feed the poor, the revolutionary was a man with legitimate claims. Therefore, as an insurgent figure the bandit symbolized the central tension of Dominican state formation from Heureaux's dictatorship through United States occupation: rural people's pursuit of political power and elites' efforts to consolidate state power in their hands. As Juan Pablo Dabove argues, being a bandit in early twentieth-century Latin America was not a matter of what one did but "an identity effect embedded in a political [and economic] conflict."[85]

This conflict, as this chapter has shown, began in the last quarter of the nineteenth century, when the sugar industry took root in San Pedro de Macorís Province. As the Dominican Republic became incorporated into the U.S. economic sphere and its financial institutions began to be supervised by U.S. authorities, vast landscapes were transformed to make way for sugar, and this process was complemented by a significant political shift. Three features characterized this political transformation: relative stability, mainly through nepotism within municipal governance; the eventual removal of military men from the governorship in favor of civilians; and the narrowing of the franchise to the exclusion of the peasant majority.

In the first instance, the *gavillero* embodied the problem of peasant disenfranchisement from the political process. Between 1876 and 1916, political institutions were fostered "to reproduce the role of dominant classes."[86] That being the case, the political struggle between the Dominican countryside and the emerging power of the province and the city involved replacing horizontal networks of power, usually nurtured by patron-client networks that tied local strongmen with regional authorities, with vertical bureaucratic structures built upon a patronage system financed by cash and credit and with Heureaux as the central figure disbursing favors. This shift upward did not necessarily undermine the myriad ways that armed groups, their leaders, merchants, and landed elites were connected; indeed, these ties could not easily be erased, and peasants responded precisely to this widening gap between customary forms of power brokering and emerging institutions designed to structure influence in a particular direction.

An incident in 1912 is particularly illustrative of this. In December of that year, a group of rebels from the east was waging war against the national government and President Nouel, who had assumed control over the country as the result of pressure from the U.S. government. The governor of San Pedro Province attended a special session of the city council to inform them "that he was there to turn his authority over to the municipality" because the president had appointed another governor in the hopes of securing the peace. In a move that speaks to the multiple loyalties that characterized political culture in San Pedro, the city council, after a "lengthy discussion," voted to reject the governor's resignation. And rather than assist the national state in its efforts to end the revolt, the *ayuntamiento* decided that it "was not obligated to assume command of the province under these conditions" nor could it "diverge its funds" to cover the costs that would incur. Instead, assuming the role of mediator, the *ayuntamiento* offered to help promote "harmony between authorities and revolutionaries."[87]

While it is more likely that San Pedro's poor financial situation influenced city council members' decision, it seems to be the case that the councilmen simply refused to support Nouel's administration out of a sense of loyalty to the beleaguered governor. The idea, moreover, that the council could negotiate with the "revolutionaries" suggests that members of the *ayuntamiento* may have supported the armed insurgency and that urban elites were connected to rural unrest aimed against the national state. This is also implied by the secretary's use of "revolutionaries" as opposed to *gavilleros* in the minutes. Revolutionaries had legitimate grievances and political claims; *gavilleros* did not. This point underscores González Canalda's argument that those who emerged as *gavilleros* in the documentation were denoted as such after they had been fully excluded from (or refused to accept) political agreements that brought peace between regional *caudillos* and the national state. Since peace agreements usually included "cash or naming to public office [and] immunity from military or civil prosecution,"[88] one can imagine the city council considering itself to be in the better position to secure the peace than the national government. In this instance, San Pedro's city council decided to treat these rebellious peasants as legitimate political actors. Most important, this decision did not occur as a function of what the peasants did, but how the city council perceived their activities and wrote them into the historical record.

· · ·

In 1863, during the War of Restoration against Spain, Pedro Francisco Bonó inspected troops along the eastern front. As the minister of war for the revolutionary government, Bonó noted the poor condition of the cannons used by insurgents. The men were rustic *monteros* (mountain or highway men) who slept on and beneath *yaguas* (royal palms) woven together to make mattresses or roofs. They were often "half naked"—one man he described as wearing "a black cotton tailcoat but underneath which . . . there wasn't event a shirt or another piece [of clothing] that impeded contact with his body; he only had underwear." And because they "lived marauding," they provisioned themselves with plantains and pumpkins. Most important, though, many of them knew precisely why and for what they fought. Bonó asked a young colonel, Santiago Mota, if he was prepared for an upcoming battle against Spanish troops. Mota responded, "As always and every day more desirous to fight and to finish throwing out these whites."[89]

During the War of Restoration, armed peasants were neither bandits nor revolutionaries. Some appear to have been politically conscious actors fully aware of the significance of the struggle against Spain. This ragtag army would ultimately defend the sovereign rights of the republic and secure independence from Spain. Its revolt, in turn, prompted some Cubans to take up arms against Spain when a full-blown insurgency exploded in Cuba in 1868. As a result, as James Sanders has argued for Afro-Colombians in the nineteenth century, armed Dominican peasants were "part of a pan-Atlantic movement . . . [that contested] the meanings of liberalism and republicanism."[90] Ironically, Italian and North American refugees from Cuba's conflict built a new sugar empire in the Dominican Republic that led to conflicts over land and political power in the same nation whose peasant armies had so inspired the move toward Cuban independence.

This chapter has shown that much had changed between 1863 and 1924, when U.S. Marines left the Dominican Republic. As a result of foreign investment and Dollar Diplomacy, the Dominican Republic was incorporated into the United States' sphere of influence. With this incorporation came profound changes in landownership, cultivation practices, and political organization.

The growth of the sugar industry in the eastern region is central to this story. Complementing the birth of an enclave economy were local processes and decisions by dominant elites that also redefined the nature of governance and excluded peasants from these new political structures.

Whether mobilized peasants understood themselves as bandits or as revolutionaries is difficult to prove with the available evidence. That armed peasants could be represented only as bandits or revolutionaries suggests their removal from San Pedro's new political landscape. Instead, urban-based elites would refashion a new ideal of sociability and governability anchored in an associational culture organized around promoting progress, civilization, and modernity.

3

THE CULTURE OF PROGRESS
IN SAN PEDRO DE MACORÍS

Addressing the question of whiteness and national identity in the Dominican Republic, Michiel Baud argues that Dominican nationalism of the late nineteenth and early twentieth centuries reflected disillusionment with modernization, its failure to eradicate poverty, and its threat to tradition. According to Baud, to resolve their dismay, some Dominican elites opted to look (again) toward Spain as a model of civilization; others oriented themselves toward Europe and the greater Caribbean.[1]

In this chapter I focus on the making of an elite in San Pedro between 1890 and 1916. I argue that *hispanicismo*—the elevation of Hispanic cultural norms and the privileging of European heritage—became a lingua franca that helped a new elite, comprising native-born Dominicans and wealthy white immigrants, cohere as a dominant class in San Pedro de Macorís. In San Pedro, as wealthy white immigrants became members of the city's governing elites, local leaders turned to Hispanic values and norms to define culture, progress, and modernity for the city's residents.

Hispanicismo was important to a process Barbara Berglund has termed "cultural ordering." In her study of nineteenth-century San Francisco, Berglund argues that ruling elites imposed a hierarchical social order through the language of civilization. She argues that San Francisco became "American" once it became "civilized": "Civilization emerged as a powerful conceptualization of social order that, in a word, signaled the sort of technical progress and class relations associated with industrial capitalism, white—especially Anglo-Saxon—superiority, and a gendered order."[2]

A similar process of cultural ordering took place in San Pedro, where it achieved its fullest expression in municipal governance, the elaboration of urban development projects, and the organization of associational life. These activities allowed San Pedro's governing elites to identify themselves as a class with a particular set of interests and a cohesive ideology; to consolidate their political power by expanding their ranks to include wealthy, foreign-born, immigrant white elites; and to narrow membership among the dominant elite to those who embraced new norms such as cultural refinement and education. Most important, cultural ordering through *hispanicismo* linked whiteness with civilization, progress, and modernity.

. . .

San Pedro's new political and cultural class—"new" in the sense that it included educated professionals, novelists, poets, essayists, merchants, and small business owners—cohered around an optimistic, forward-looking ideal of national progress. Members etched their hopefulness onto San Pedro's urban landscape (map 3.1). By the 1890s San Pedro's main streets included Caridad (Charity), El Sol (Sun), Progreso (Progress), Perseverancia (Perseverance), Porvenir (Future), Comercio (Commerce), Libertad (Freedom), La Fe (Faith), La Esperanza (Hope), Adelanto (Advancement), Industria (Industry), La Aurora (Dawn), and La Estrella (Star).[3] The early press also reflected the outlook of this group: *El Civilizador* (The Civilizer, 1882), *El Progreso* (Progress, 1889), *La Razón* (Reason, 1894), *La Idea* (The Idea, 1895), and *La Soberanía* (Sovereignty, 1899).[4]

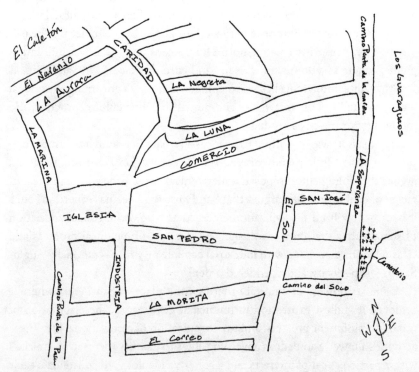

Map 3.1. Map of San Pedro, c. 1890s. América Bermúdez, *Manual de historia de San Pedro de Macorís.*

Journalists, among others, helped create a cultural identity oriented around civilization and progress. As one headline from San Pedro's *El Cable* proclaimed, "Todo es Progreso," everything is progress. Progress was the visible sign of change, reflected in *ingenios*, rail lines, telegraph poles, lighting fixtures, and other features of urban life in San Pedro. Specifically, Luis Bermúdez and Antonio Soler, the editors, applauded as progress estate owners laying the necessary rails to transport cane to the mill. In another article about the Chicago World's Fair, they touted the United States as an exemplary model of progress because its people felt empowered; in yet another article, education and the recognition of one's "*deberes*" (duties), as opposed to one's rights, was noted as a key development on the road to progress.[5] Progress, then, also involved economic development, especially of the kind for which San Pedro was famous: large-scale agricultural production. As one editorialist wrote, "What a great pity that the entire republic does not imitate this nascent district!"[6]

San Pedro's residents were well within their rights to celebrate their quick march toward progress. After a devastating fire in 1891, the city council made enormous efforts to rebuild the city and transform its principal buildings into showcases. Toward this end, the *ayuntamiento* embraced a trinity of interdependent responsibilities: designing and improving storm drains, roads, sidewalks, railroad tracks, and lighting fixtures; creating a body of legislation and methods of enforcement to supervise the city's spatial growth and to monitor materials used on residential and commercial buildings; and constructing parks and public buildings such as schools, hospitals and clinics, marketplaces, and municipal offices. In 1891 the city council made plans to build a *casa constitucional*, a project supported by the national government. The hardwood building was to have a spacious meeting room, a kitchen, and a zinc roof.[7] By 1902 numerous buildings that housed provincial affairs—a governor's mansion, hacienda administration, post office, courthouse, and police headquarters—dotted San Pedro's cityscape.[8] The city council also facilitated important infrastructural changes. In 1887, for instance, Santiago Mellor, the owner of Ingenios Porvenir and Santa Fe, received the first telephone line concession in the Dominican Republic. Mellor's historic line ran from his sugar depository to the Lenos warehouse across town. In April 1891 and October 1892, the city council allowed Mellor to build rail lines from Ingenio Santa Fe to his warehouse near the port area. In exchange, Mellor agreed to pay for periodic repairs of Adelanto Street, over which the tracks ran. By February 22, 1893, the route was finally completed, and the city council celebrated its inauguration with the estate owner and his administrators.[9]

As early as 1888, the council developed plans for street lighting and received donations from business owners around the plaza and the administrators of

Ingenios Santa Fe and Colón to finance the project. By January of 1889, twelve streetlights were ready for installation in San Pedro's downtown areas.[10] In 1895 a drainage system was built in the center of town to prevent flooding during the rainy season because, as José Hernández pointed out in a letter to the city, when it rained, "the water rises and enters [our] houses, even the bedrooms."[11]

"Civilization," in turn, referred to governability, how ordinary people understood their relationship to the government. For example, an *El Cable* editorial encouraged Dominicans to work hard, build a country that valued progress, and dismiss the "fatal belief that governments are obligated to distribute bread to the people, to a nation with its arms folded."[12] Resonant with the call for people to educate themselves about their responsibilities, the paper's editor equated civilization with hard work but also defined being civilized as the willingness to be governed. In this instance, the author's idea of governance was reciprocal: only when good citizens worked hard should governments be generous.

If economic criteria alone were used to define San Pedro's elites in the late nineteenth and early twentieth centuries, one would find that immigrants enjoyed more economic success than native-born Dominicans. In San Pedro, progress was in the hands of the sugar industry and the wealthiest, and members of these groups tended to be foreign-born.[13] As we have already seen, notary records from the late 1890s suggest the predominance of Puerto Ricans as sugar estate *colonos*. The term "wealthy" would have also applied to a Cuban immigrant such as Lorenzo Zayas Bazán, who had made $55,583 in private loans. José Tedeschi, an Italian immigrant, was similarly well off, judging from his ability to provide $25,000 in loans to Antonio Casanovas, a Spaniard resident in San Pedro.[14] To be sure, the sugar economy put Dominicans at an economic disadvantage with regard to white immigrants who arrived wealthy or had accumulated wealth as a result of access to credit. In other words, as Juan Bosch has argued, sugar production failed to produce a Dominican bourgeoisie.

However, in San Pedro, as in Santo Domingo, visible wealth was only one of many criteria that determined who acquired "elite" status. As Teresita Martínez-Vergne points out, many of the men who served on Santo Domingo's city council regarded themselves and others like them as elite because they were educated, highly respected, and upwardly mobile. In San Pedro, the dominant class constituted an elite because, quite simply, it regarded itself as such. Since command over progress belonged to others, Dominican *gente de primera* (educated, cultured elites) took charge of bringing civilization to San Pedro by welcoming wealthy white immigrants as equal members of the dominant class through Hispanic cultural norms. This process of integration turned out to be so successful that Manuel Leopoldo Richiez would insist in 1914 that San Pedro's greatness was the product of its having been settled by "good, well-mannered people and white islanders: [a] valiant, pristine gem of *blue blood* who [kept] themselves pure and unpolluted."[15]

Richiez's "good, well-mannered people" were undoubtedly those educated *petromacorisanos* (San Pedro residents) who began, in the late 1880s, to build an associational life for themselves in the city. San Pedro's associational culture was both an expression of Dominican elites' political and ideological power and the primary means by which white immigrants celebrated their ethnic identities and were assimilated into Dominican governing structures.[16] Associational life nurtured modernity—the marriage of progress with civilization. As José Ramón López wrote in a short, biting article in which he poked fun at Dominicans for "not associating except to conspire [against the government] and to dance," associational life was important "if we want to prosper." He advocated the organization of clubs to help the country pursue its economic goals and chided Santo Domingo's elites for not doing so.[17] Associations helped make civilization and progress a lifestyle. As Lopéz wrote in another article, "civilization and progress are nothing more than the transformation of wealth"; they are "little more than wealth invested in all the necessities of an existence eminently active and intellectual." Associations made possible an investment in an active, engaged life.[18]

Among the most important clubs was the Athenaeum of San Pedro, founded in 1890 by the sons of San Pedro's leading families, including Félix and Manuel L. Richiez; Quiterio Berroa, a poet; and José Ramón Monzón, who served as president of San Pedro's city council in 1899. First organized as Amantes de Estudio (Lovers of Knowledge), these young men established San Pedro's first library in 1894 with books donated by *El Cable*'s editors. Celebrating the group's first anniversary, poet and intellectual Rafael Deligne praised the Amantes for their "fighting spirit" as men who guided society toward its "highest aspirations" through "a dynamic force of action."[19] Presumably, this meant creating the necessary social, cultural, and economic conditions to nurture Dominican progress. They also organized San Pedro's commemoration of the four hundredth anniversary of Columbus's arrival in the Americas and, when Salomé Ureña de Henríquez (1850–1897), the Dominican poet laureate, died in 1897, paid homage to her life and work in *El Cable*. In celebration of San Pedro's fifteenth anniversary as a district, the Amantes held a *velada* (literary soirée) in which the daughters of San Pedro's elites—women such as Lucrecia de Zayas Bazán, the wife of the Cuban immigrant and landowner Lorenzo de Zayas Bazán—played the piano and young men such as Federico Bermúdez, a poet, spoke on current events.[20]

Meanwhile, members of the Club Dos de Julio (Second of July Club) sponsored dances and other activities considered respectable by the *gente de primera*. The club became famous for the Saint Andrew Dance and the Cane Festival, the latter held on the club's anniversary and celebrated with literary readings and beauty contests.[21] Perhaps Dos de Julio patterned its Cane Festival after Ingenio Consuelo's annual harvest. On the sugar estate, as in town, administrators elected a festival queen and hosted a number of public parties.[22]

Women were also involved in the city's associational culture through feminine branches of male societies or in independent clubs. One of the earliest clubs for women was El Abanico (The Fan), founded in 1880 by women from powerful Dominican families (Richiez, Camarena, de Soto, Ysambert, Aybar, Acevedo, Bermúdez, and Castillo) and foreigners (Read and Santoni). According to América Bermúdez, a reorganization took place such that Abanico ceased to exist; on July 2, 1890, the male-only Sociedad de Recreo y Ornato "Dos de Julio," (Second of July Society of Recreation and Adornment), later the Club Dos de Julio, was established; in 1894 men from this new club organized its female counterpart, the Sociedad de Señoras y Señoritas "Dos de Julio."[23]

Another important element that tied Dominicans in these groups together appears to have been Eugenio María de Hostos. In a speech honoring the Amantes de Estudio, Señor Lowenski Monzón noted that the Amantes "revolutionized the ideas and the most [important] discourses of Hostos, the predestined, [who] saturated the air with his *moral social* [social morality]."[24] Lowenski Monzón's declaration may not have accurately reflected the Amantes's motivations for founding their organization in 1890, but it does suggest that Dominicans active in San Pedro's clubs were familiar with Hostosian social thought.

Hostosian social thought as described here complemented the Antillean ideology Hostos crafted in collaboration with Gregorio Luperón. Whereas *antillanismo* outlined a plan for Caribbean self-determination and cooperation, the *moral social* was a philosophy of nation building. Hostos defined the *moral social* in contrast to religious-based conceptualizations of morality. Rather than deriving its legitimacy from religious doctrine, social morality emerged through conscientious learning and application of the principles of natural law to society. Hostos defined "*moral*" (moral/morality) as "a consequence of [our] understanding of our relationship with nature, with our own being, and with the social being" and "*inmoralidad*" (immorality) as the corruption of the natural order.[25]

Cultivating the *moral social* was critical in the work of bringing economic progress, sound governance (civilization), and modernity to the Dominican Republic, and Hostos believed that Dominicans educated in secular schools founded on the principles of scientific inquiry were the best equipped for "bettering, completing, harmonizing, and moralizing" the community as a whole, especially given the disruptions occasioned by economic development.[26] In addition to education, the family was the pillar of a civilized society. The family completed "the biological tie with the sociological, [strengthened] the moral bond with the juridical tie, [and] [perfected] ... the natural and legal dependency of inferiors on superiors."[27] The family, in other words, was the cradle of social order and secular education, the key to developing a civilized citizenry.

For Hostos, immigrants also played a role in cultivating the *moral social*. Participation in city governance and in the process of cultural ordering assisted the assimilation of foreigners into the power structure and facilitated the process by which white immigrants became elite Dominicans. By equating the work of civilizing the nation with citizenship and political power, Hostos made immigrants yet another vanguard group in the cultivation of progress and culture. Ever a sharp critic of half-baked plans, Hostos insisted that to "populate for population's sake doesn't get you anywhere." In a typical essay on the topic he wrote, "The republic cannot be considered civilized, not even on the road to civilization, until it begins to populate, on the largest scale, its depopulated territory; until it has put into production all of its natural resources; until it has established a rational system of rents ... and free trade ... until, educated by this free trade in products, it adopts the free exchange of ideas and ... [until] ... it truly opens its ports to men from all places, religions, and all opinions."[28] Hostos recommended organizing agricultural colonies for immigrants so that the civilizing forces that they brought to the country would have a lasting impact: "Colonization doesn't [simply] mean gathering around a capitalist, the proprietor and owner of a mechanized mill, a number of sharecroppers ... who produce cane for the mill ... who earn some thousands of pesos in a few years and, in the end, lose all right to the land."[29] He hoped that immigrant colonies would form the basis of a new society in which capitalist modernity was moderated by the conscious cultivation of civilization.

The significance of Hostosian thought among San Pedro's lettered elites is suggested by the city council's commitment to secular public education and the absence of the Catholic Church's influence on curriculum and local politics. According to América Bermúdez, public instruction in San Pedro began as early as 1848, when Elías Camarena, one of the first settlers in the area and a trained teacher, voluntarily taught local children.[30] By 1895 Rafael Deligne, then serving as San Pedro's superintendent of schools, reported that nearly 200 children attended the city's six public elementary schools: four for boys, two for girls.[31]

Hostos's influence on pedagogy in San Pedro was especially pronounced in the city's early investment in female education. Educated women were critical to cultivating progress and civilization within the family because they instructed children. Eusebia Rodríguez y Rodríguez, the principal of Perseverancia, one of San Pedro's primary schools for girls, once insisted to the city council, "Educated women are important for society . . . [as you well know] a morally and intellectually prepared woman has a highly civilizing role to play in her family, the foundation of society." Toward this end, her school offered courses in mathematics, grammar, history, ethics, calligraphy, and various forms of embroidery.[32] In 1887 the city opened its first high school for girls, the Salomé Ureña Institute, named after the country's beloved poet and founder of the Young Women's Normal Institute, the first school for advanced education for young women in Santo Domingo. Anacaona Moscoso, a graduate of the Normal Institute, served as the first principal and trained the daughters of San Pedro's *gente de primera*, including the Richiez sisters and Ulises Heureaux's daughter Casimira, for careers in teaching. These women, in turn, became the first licensed high school teachers in San Pedro and, as we will see in chapter 5, many of them, such as Dr. Evangelina Rodríguez and Petronila Gómez, became leaders in the feminist movement.[33]

Secular and female education proved too provocative for some Dominicans, but apparently not for San Pedro's city council. In 1887 Juan Tomás Mejía, the minister of justice, development, and public instruction, openly criticized teachers who were trained in Hostos's methodology for lacking religious training and urged the government to deny them teaching licenses. Mejía must later have realized his outburst had been a serious misstep; when he spoke to the crowd gathered at the inauguration of San Pedro's renovated church in July of that year, his outrage was considerably muted. He rescinded his rigorous defense of Christian education since, as he claimed, his stand "was the cause of rifts among the people."[34]

Mejía's changed posture gives credence to Lowenski Monzón's claim that Hostos's *moral social* influenced elite *petromacorisanos* intellectually and in terms of their governance. The centrality of the municipality in Dominican political theory had long united people on opposite ends of the political continuum. In an article he published in 1862, Manuel de Jesús Galván proclaimed that the city council "brings together all of the residents of a city into a common bond; it makes of them one big family." He went on to note, "City councils are the principal axle and spring of this simple machine; its tasks are as those of a head of household: to govern prudently and inspired by a good understanding of the economy."[35] Later, in his address as president of the provisional government in 1880, Gregorio Luperón also attached both symbolic and political significance to the municipality: "The municipality [is] respected by the republic just as the family respects society; [the city] contains in itself the generating principle of democracy, because [it is] a depository of a portion of sovereignty and is appropriately the government of the people by the people and for the people; [it is] called to consecrate the majesty of citizenship." The *municipio*, in other words, was the kernel of social order, progress, and economic vitality to the entire nation.[36]

San Pedro's governing elites understood this and applied Hostosian ideals to how they managed local problems. As noted above, they encouraged progress in terms of infrastructural development. This also meant legislative intervention to regulate how people lived and moved within the city. These efforts, at times, clashed with Hostos's desire that local governments help bring harmony to social relationships negatively affected by the economy. Throughout the 1890s and early decades of the 1900s, the city council desperately tried to make living in town as comfortable as possible. In 1891 the *ayuntamiento* banned oxen-pulled carts from the city limits, but after some "lighthearted" discussion, as the secretary noted, the council rescinded the initial proposal but still limited cart traffic to Industria Street and charged drivers a twelve-peso tax.[37] In 1901 the city council passed a resolution banning thatched roofing and the use of woven *yaguas* (royal palms) to build houses.[38] A year later, the city council passed another ordinance banning the use of plant material on houses constructed along Industria between Diez de Septiembre, La Aurora, Santana, and La Marina Streets—essentially, in the center of town.[39] Provincial Governor Fernando Chalas, a former city council member, sent a letter admonishing the city—in Hostosian terms—for its decision, claiming that the poor "need to be protected by those who are supposed to ensure [the] tranquillity of [the entire] community." Chalas indicated that while "it is undoubtedly true that [the law] favors the development of public embellishment . . . there are so many poor families who edify their homes with great sacrifice . . . whose savings would not allow them to use better materials." The law was, in his mind, "unjust to the poor [who live] far from the life of luxury and comfortably with what they honorably acquire."[40] Chalas's warnings went unheeded by the city council. Several residents simply refused to obey the growing number of rules, as evidenced by yet another ordinance passed in 1906 reminding *petromacorisanos* that "all houses built in the city [must] be wood."[41]

Governor Chalas's arguments in favor of relieving the poor from the growing list of demands made on them by the city council highlights the singularity

of political will and vision when it came to making San Pedro a capital complex. Yet this process produced tensions and disadvantages that highlighted
the contradictions inherent in Hostos's social morality ideology. To be sure,
elites drove urban development and San Pedro became the perfect and primary vehicle for native-born Dominicans to exercise their power and influence. At the same time, when the city council followed the precepts of the
moral social, they were challenged to place limits on their vision of progress.

Secular schools and social/literary clubs provided important spaces that
gave expression to Hostosian ideals through debate, intellectual development,
respectable social interaction, and the elevation of Hispanic cultural norms.
Print media also proved important in the dissemination of Hostosian thought.
San Pedro's elites most likely read the Santo Domingo–based magazine *Revista
Ilustrada*, which regularly featured articles by or about Federico Henríquez y
Carvajal, one of Hostos's early collaborators and among his most loyal supporters. In the March 1899 issue, Henríquez y Carvajal published an article
in which he addressed the emergent cultural space that literary magazines
provided the Dominican intellectual vanguard. Applauding the publication of
both the *Revista* and *Letras y Ciencias* (Letters and Sciences), Henríquez y Carvajal underscored how they "inspired patriotism and [satisfied] the wishes of
enlightened opinion" and completed the project begun by those "founders of
the Antillean Confederation," who strove for "civility in action."[42] San Pedro's
literary societies and social clubs were also spaces where the city's dominant
groups cultivated social networks and reaffirmed their sense of identity as *gente
de primera*, a status they conferred on themselves based on ancestry, occupation, education, and prestige.

The absence of detailed censuses, however, makes it difficult to count the
numbers of Cuban, Puerto Rican, and Spanish immigrants in San Pedro. According to Harry Hoetink, for example, San Pedro's population grew from a
few hundred in the 1870s to nearly 8,000 in the 1890s, thanks to internal and
international migration. A contemporary source claimed that in 1895, almost
9,000 people lived in San Pedro; by 1902 that number had increased to ap-
proximately 11,000.[43] A municipal census taken at the end of the sugar harvest
in 1917 reported the city's population at 9,298,[44] and by the first national census
in 1920, the city's population was just over 13,000.[45]

Census takers reported that Cuban, Spanish, and Puerto Rican immigrants
tended to reside in urban areas, where many were shopkeepers. For instance,
by 1920 about 250 Spaniards lived in San Pedro; the first among them had
founded the Centro Recreativo Español (Spanish Recreation Center) in 1911.[46]
Wealthy Puerto Ricans established the Club Unión Puertorriqueño (Puerto

Rican Union Club) in 1914. Interestingly, wealthy Cuban immigrants did not establish a club of their own. Since many of them were Spaniards, they may have participated in the Spanish Recreation Center. Others joined Dominican social clubs and literary associations from the start, helping establish El Abanico and Amantes de Estudio, among others.

Although the presence of these ethnic clubs suggests that wealthy white immigrants remained at a distance from their Dominican counterparts, Francisco Richiez Acevedo argued that interclub rivalries and joint activities nurtured a shared identity as *petromacorisanos* and as elite, Hispanic Dominicans.[47] Seasonal games were a particularly powerful way in which immigrants elaborated a Dominican nationalism rooted in a Hispanic ethnic identity. The Juegos Florales (Floral Games), held in May, and the Juegos Invernales (Winter Games), held in December, were spectacular events organized by San Pedro's cultural and literary clubs. According to Ernesto Armenteros, the son of Spanish immigrant and wealthy merchant Juan Armenteros and an active participant in these activities in his youth, participants in games did not have to be members of the organizing clubs but were required to be "people with a correct moral education."[48] In April 1916 the Union Club in Santo Domingo held the Juegos Florales Antillanos (Antillean Floral Games), elected a queen and her court, and awarded prizes for the best poems about Dominican independence and essays about free trade and the intellectual exchange between Cuba, Puerto Rico, and the Dominican Republic.[49]

Magazines, newspapers, and a literary culture also helped a Hispanic-oriented elite identity take shape in San Pedro and beyond. Magazines such as *Revista Ilustrada* published pieces by San Pedro's Luis Bermúdez and Rafael Deligne and Nicaragua's Rubén Darío.[50] A young feminist and journalist from Puerto Plata, Mercedes Mota, gave voice to this "new generation arising in America" in an article she wrote and published in *Revista Ilustrada* in 1899. "Our generation," she declared, "deserves to be considered worthy and noble; [we] deserve to be called advanced and progressive." The America that Mota embraced included the "young republics of Hispano-America," defined by the young generation of poets, essayists, and writers, including José Enrique Rodó of Uruguay, among others.[51] Education and the creation of a Hispano-American tradition composed the basis of a new identity for women and men who came of age at the turn of the century.

Pictures and stories published in another Santo Domingo–based magazine, *Blanco y Negro*, reveal that elites' privileging of whiteness was implicit yet visible. For example, nearly all of the young women whose pictures grace the pages of surviving issues of *Blanco y Negro* are clearly of European descent, and

poems tie these women to the nation. In his ode to floral queen Herminia Rodríguez Gautier, Apolinar Perdomo proclaims, "The homeland . . . [celebrates]
your triumphs in the victory of art and love."[52] The queen and her court often
wore white dresses. In the case of this "lovely group," mythology and whiteness
blended easily (figure 3.1).[53]

The whiteness of the queens, such as Josefa Báez (figure 3.2), is in stark
contrast to the minuscule number of images that feature darker-skinned Dominicans. In issues of *Blanco y Negro* before 1916, darker-skinned Dominicans
appear as criminals, as in the case of Ramón Fernández and Luís María Espinal, who stood accused of robbing a warehouse owned by the Vicini family.[54]
Or they are documented as laborers, in one instance working in J. Parra Alba's
new, modern bakery (figures 3.3–3.5).[55]

The difference between the associational cultures of cities such as San Pedro, Santo Domingo, Santiago, and San Francisco de Macorís and daily life
for the majority of Dominicans is captured in photos taken of children from
Santa Cruz Orphanage and the Colegio Eugenio María de Hostos. The majority of girls in the orphanage were darker-skinned, in contrast to the children at
Hostos school, who were mostly light-skinned.[56] The public that watched the
horse races and participated in the *juegos olímpicos* (Olympic games) held during carnival was a world apart from the poor children who attended "Charity"
School, run by Franciscan friars (photos 3.6 and 3.7).[57]

Most important, these magazines and clubs provided venues for intellectual
elites to display their educational achievements. Club Unión's games, for instance, gave a prize for the best medical science article that "[advised] mothers
about hygienic measures and [other] prophylactic measures they should take
to avoid gastrointestinal diseases." The magazine *Renacimiento* held contests
to select "the best civic-minded/educated child who understands his civic
responsibilities," "the farmer who used the most advanced scientific technology," "the rancher who, within a one-year period, [could] introduce the best
breeds," "the poor housewife who, despite all odds, manages to raise healthy
and robust children," and, perhaps in recognition of the changing times, "the
career woman who distinguishes herself in the workplace and in the home."[58]

Through games, lectures, and literary contests, San Pedro's wealthy white
immigrants and Dominican elites identified themselves as models of progress and civilization who brought modernity to the city and to the nation as a
whole. This occurred thanks to an apparent consensus among elites about the
city's commitment to secular public education. Prior to the U.S. occupation,
interactions among Dominicans, Cubans, and Puerto Ricans also fostered a
rapprochement with Spain as the homeland and emphasized the centrality of

Figure 3.1. "Bellísimo Grupo." *Renacimiento* (April 22, 1915), p. 125.

Figure 3.2. "Srta. Josefa Báez, Reina de la Mi-Caréme." *Blanco y Negro* 1, no. 31 (April 18, 1909).

Figure 3.3. "Ramón Fernández." *Blanco y Negro* (May 9, 1909).

Figure 3.4. "Luís María Espinal." *Blanco y Negro* (May 9, 1909).

Figure 3.5. "Nueva panadería del Sr. J. Parra Alba." *Blanco y Negro* (August 1, 1909).

Hispanic identity.[59] For example, in 1915 Enrique Deschamps and other "citizens" sent a letter to the council requesting that the city pay "homage . . . to the mother country [and] resolve to designate with the name 'Avenida España' the street currently called 'Marina,'" and the city council did so. The *ayuntamiento* followed up this request with a renaming campaign in which a number of streets in San Pedro featured an important figure from Dominican or San Pedro's history (table 3.1). In one instance, the city council changed the name of the West Indian neighborhood Yocotón (Jacob Town), to Juan Amechazurra.[60] By paying homage to a sugar estate owner, educators, and poets in this way, San Pedro's dominant elites elevated these key figures as models of progress and civilization. Naming the city's main thoroughfare after Spain expressed a sense of cultural unity among dominant elites. Finally, honoring Juan Amechazurra, the founder of Ingenio Angelina, suggests the council's commitment to supporting the sugar industry as the primary vehicle for economic growth.

Between 1890 and 1916, San Pedro's dominant elites established norms that guided urban development based on the principles of Hostosian social

Figure 3.6. "Colegio E. María de Hostos—Sus Directores [las] Srtas. Aybar con un grupo de niñas y niños." *Blanco y Negro* (March 20, 1910).

Figure 3.7. Escuela "La Caridad." *Blanco y Negro* (January 16, 1910).

Table 3.1. San Pedro de Macorís street names, 1932

Former name	New name
Industria	Duarte [Juan Pablo]
El Sol	Sánchez [Francisco del Rosario]
La Marina	Avenida España
Comercio	Independencia
La Aurora	Duverge
Caridad	José Reyes
La Luna	Núñez de Cáceres [José]
San Pedro	Anacaona Moscoso
Estrella	Mella [Ramón]
San José	Gastón Deligne
Santana	General Cabral [José María]
El Naranjo	Hostos [Eugenio María de]
La Esperanza	Rafael Deligne
Libertad	Luis Arturo Bermúdez
Retiro	Federico Bermúdez

Source: Richiez, "Historia de la provincia."

thought, created an associational culture oriented around ideals that united progress with civilization, and defined Dominican modernity through values associated with high culture and Hispanic ideals. "Civilization" meant the purposeful, conscientious embrace of one's responsibilities within a social order. Becoming civilized signaled an internal transformation of individual *petromacorisanos*, assisted by reading newspapers, attending schools, and participating in interclub competition. The city's dominant elites were the most identified with these ideals, and their social world, grounded in a sense of cultural unity through Hispanic norms, remained far removed from the city's working classes and from poor immigrants of color.

In San Pedro, *hispanicismo* initially operated to expand the ranks of the city's dominant groups by incorporating wealthy foreign-born whites. It provided a sense of cultural unity and a common identity among whites otherwise differentiated by wealth. Through Hispanic cultural norms, San Pedro's dominant groups substantially narrowed the ranks of those who embodied progress and culture to those who expressed cultural refinement in their social practice, were wealthy, and who were of European ancestry. Finally, *hispanicismo* guided the process of cultural ordering. Associational life in San Pedro and elsewhere throughout the republic gave expression to the links between progress, civilization, and whiteness. As we will see in the next chapter, the enforcement of rules designed to bring about progress and civilization provoked another kind of racialization, this time, for San Pedro's working-class majority.

4

POLICING THE URBAN POOR

During the harvest of 1901, Francisco Méndez, a Dominican who worked at Ingenio Porvenir, demanded the return of property held by James Alexander, a contracted employee from St. Vincent who worked in Porvenir's engine house. Méndez refused to offer Alexander proof of ownership and called on the estate's security chief, another Dominican, to referee the dispute. According to witnesses, Alexander had been on his way home to retrieve the items but, rather than permit him to retreat peaceably, the guard called him a "vagabond." Alexander responded, "I am no more a vagabond than you are. You have no right to say that to me." The guard arrested him and ordered Méndez to escort him to San Pedro's jail (figure 4.1).[1]

The North American administrator of Porvenir, who considered Alexander a man of "excellent character," reported the following: "I told Alexander, as he was being led away, 'I will meet you in town within a few minutes and will see that justice is done to you' . . . [and] . . . , just as I was about to leave for town, I saw [Méndez] returning. Inquiring what was the matter, I was told that . . . Méndez had returned saying that he had shot Alexander in the leg because the latter had tried to escape from him. I went immediately to look for Alexander and, not far from the estate, found his dead body lying beside the road shot through the heart. I went to town and reported the affair to the Governor."[2] British vice-consul Gosling found Alexander's attempted escape "extremely unlikely" and concluded that Méndez had murdered him, "based on the testimony and on the numerous complaints which have been made to me from time to time by British subjects."[3] In the end, and under much pressure from the British government, the Dominican Congress agreed to pay Alexander's family a $5,000 indemnity for his murder.[4] Meanwhile, San Pedro's provincial court acquitted Méndez of homicide, but, bowing to the demands of the British officials, the Dominican Supreme Court overturned the acquittal and eventually sentenced Méndez to an eighteen-month prison term.[5]

The murder described here presents a sharp contrast to the world of literary readings, *juegos*, and floral queens described in the previous chapter. Yet San Pedro was also home to thousands of English-, Dutch-, French- and Kreyòl-

Figure 4.1. Ingenio Porvenir, 1940s. Colección Hugh Kelly IV. Centro de Investigación Histórica, Universidad de Puerto Rico at Río Piedras.

speaking workers, many of whom had labored for banana companies in Limón, Costa Rica, or worked in Panama's Canal Zone or for sugar companies in Santiago de Cuba before they arrived in San Pedro. These Afro-Antillean migrants made up the city's working class and the sugar estates' seasonal workforce. They also lived in a remarkably transnational space comprising affective, economic, political, and cultural networks that linked Afro-Antilleans throughout the circum-Caribbean region.

As I argue in chapter 3, governing elites in San Pedro incorporated wealthy, white elite immigrants into their fold through a process of cultural ordering given expression through Hispanic cultural norms. This chapter focuses on another aspect of this cultural ordering process, one that occurred through policing foreign workers and the immigrant poor. It argues that through policing Afro-Antilleans remained largely excluded from an emerging national community taking shape in San Pedro.[6]

Even though Hostos-inspired city councilmen were especially invested in making San Pedro a beacon of modernity and progress, they were less convinced that San Pedro's racially and ethnically diverse working poor could be drawn out of barbarism into civilization. Through Hostos-inspired social policy and policing, city council members hoped to manage the chaos of this multiethnic, multiracial city. Although policing was not explicitly conceived in racist terms, I argue that San Pedro's city council and police forces assigned the region's Afro-Antillean workers a lower status through the creation of a "moral geography" and by policing immigrant women's sexuality.[7] Antiblack racism, I propose, evolved in San Pedro as a reaction against Afro-Antillean migrants. San Pedro's unique ties to the greater (Afro) Caribbean world, then, add richly to our understanding of nation making as a process that marked some as "raced" through the violent monitoring of their labor and sexual practices.

. . .

As sugar production became more important to the Dominican economy in the 1880s, the national government in Santo Domingo debated the best means to attract foreigners to the country and which ones were preferable. For example, in a report written while he was minister of the interior, Ulises Heureaux noted that the "importation of *braceros* [contracted workers] from the neighboring small [islands] . . . had caused harm as they were people unfamiliar with work and unused to the countryside."[8] In response to this concern, the national government explored the possibility of bringing in Asian workers but rejected it as too expensive. The Dominican government, like governments throughout Latin America, then set its sights on white families from Europe or, given the Dominican Republic's location, white peasants from Puerto Rico (*jíbaros*) and Cuba (*guajiros*) as investors in colonization schemes aimed at helping sustain the sugar industry.[9]

Officials in Santo Domingo who rejected Afro-Antillean labor migration converted their disfavor into the Law of Agricultural Enterprise of 1911. Article 9 prohibited any agricultural enterprise from bringing "immigrants who were not of the white race . . . [except] when it is demonstrated that the crops or harvest of any year may suffer by the lack of help, then the Executive Power may authorize immigrants of any other race from the neighboring islands" to harvest that year's crops only.[10]

Estate owners and managers such as William Bass and Hugh Kelly ignored these rules and contracted black workers as early as the 1880s. In fact, Bass, the owner of Ingenio Consuelo and a founding member of San Pedro's Immigration Society, hired so many West Indians to work at Ingenio Consuelo that elite *petromacorisanos* questioned his allegiance to their determination to populate San Pedro's hinterlands with white colonists. In response to this criticism Bass rejoined, "Who wants to stand by while machinery, boilers, locomotives, or towing grinders are in the care of someone who lacks competent knowledge of how to operate them?"[11] Black West Indians also spoke English, a feature that probably appealed to North American managers. Similar considerations may have influenced Hugh Kelly's decision to hire West Indian workers at Porvenir. By the time his grandson Hugh Kelly IV began to manage the mill in the 1940s, English- and Dutch-speaking Antilleans had worked and lived at Porvenir for nearly fifty years. Some of the West Indians, Hugh Kelly IV said, were accountants, and the mill manager was a Dominican-born Dutch islander. These men "were the ones running the place. They were the ones who showed me the ball."[12]

In the 1890s, however, San Pedro de Macorís suffered from an image problem as a result of its placement along the migration routes of an increasing number of Afro-Antillean people: the region, it was said, was awash in criminality, violence, and social disorder. These claims inspired an investigation of crime in the sugar zone by the editors of El Cable. The newspaper's contributors rejected the argument that San Pedro was crime-ridden but admitted that the sugar economy's reliance on foreign labor produced social tensions that were often expressed violently. They blamed Dominican and Afro-Antillean workers equally, claiming that rural violence and disorder were caused by peasants' "lack of respect for the institution of the family" and the "abundance of liquor [consumed] at cockfighting rings, dances, and wakes." A trio of dangers—"gambling, women, and wine"—was held responsible for the increased criminality in and around San Pedro.[13]

One writer wondered how one might expect to retain control over an area where 4,000 "different kinds of people" lived during the harvest.[14] An El Cable reporter made the interesting suggestion that San Pedro's crime rate might be higher because Dominican peasants influenced black Antilleans to behave violently.[15] Citing crime statistics for the week of December 21, during the tiempo muerto (end of harvest) of 1897, he reported that in a regional population of perhaps 14,000, there had been fifteen homicides in the city and in San Pedro's immediate rural areas (tables 4.1 and 4.2).[16]

The available evidence fails to show whether crime actually increased in San Pedro and its environs in the 1890s, but the governing elites and outside observers believed that violence and criminality infected the sugar zone. The disconnect between the perception of criminality and its actual occurrence may have been the result of elite anxieties about the region's increasing orientation toward the Afro-Caribbean region. This was not quite the demographic outcome envisioned by the national government or by local elites, who sought to attract white immigrants.[17]

In the 1880s and 1890s, the desperate living conditions that afflicted Afro-Antilleans living on islands in the British, French, Danish, and Dutch Carib-

Table 4.1. Crimes for the week of December 21, 1897

Crime	Total
Homicide	15
Assault	9
Robbery	9
Slander	1
Defamation	3
Attempted murder	1
Total	38

Source: "Comparad i juzgad," *El Cable*, December 21, 1897.

Table 4.2. Offenses committed by prisoners in the San Pedro de Macorís jail, December 1897

Offense	Number of prisoners
Robbery	9
Homicide	11
Total	20

Source: "Juzgado de instrucción de Macorís," *El Cable*, December 21, 1897.

bean created a mobile and cheap labor force for plantations across the Spanish-speaking Caribbean rimlands. Annual reports submitted by colonial governors during the last quarter of the nineteenth century detail the famines, droughts, epidemics, floods, and economic depressions that forced people to migrate as a survival strategy. Emigration relieved population pressures on smaller islands while remittances sustained local economies and eased social tensions produced by the pressures of unemployment and economic desperation. Banana production, railroad building, and transoceanic canal projects provided Afro-Antilleans who moved to Nicaragua, Panama, and Costa Rica opportunities to work and, in some cases, to become small landowners.[18]

It appears that in the 1890s the number of Afro-Antillean workers in San Pedro increased—as did perceptions that a crime wave was sweeping through the region. Recruitment in the British islands for one-year contracts in the Dominican Republic began in November or December. Workers made their way to the San Pedro port by January and returned to their home islands once the harvest ended in April or May.[19] In 1895, 400 West Indians living in San Pedro de Macorís signed a petition seeking consular representation from the British government.[20] Two years later an *El Cable* article reported that 14,000 foreign workers had come to work during the harvest. José del Castillo estimates that in the 1890s, an average of 3,000 West Indians cut cane on Dominican sugar estates every year. For the harvest of 1902–1903, sugar-estate owners contracted over 4,000 workers, including many Haitians and British West Indians. In 1915, according to del Castillo, nearly 11,000 British subjects passed through the port of San Pedro.[21]

During the U.S. occupation, the military government rescinded the 1911 law that had made recruiting black workers difficult. Military authorities also enhanced the national government's role in labor procurement. The government now required estate managers to send formal requests to the secretariat of agriculture and immigration in which they specified how many workers were needed and from where they expected to recruit them. At the end of the harvest, estate managers filed another set of permits with the government indicating the number of workers they repatriated or to request permission to retain a few during the *tiempo muerto*. Between June 1919 and June 1920, the occupation government counted over 4,000 contracted laborers, accompanied by 1,278 family members. Haitians, whose country was also under U.S. occupation (1915–1934), outnumbered both Dominicans and West Indians as workers in provincial cane fields, making up the majority of the 22,121 black immigrants who requested permits to remain in the Dominican Republic after their contracts expired. Nearly 13,000 of these workers resided in San Pedro. The rest, presumably, lived in housing (*bateyes*) provided by either *colonos* or the sugar estate.[22]

In the 1890s *El Cable*'s editors, while they denied that violence was rife in San Pedro, drew a connection between Afro-Antillean migration and changes in social relationships that heightened and exacerbated social tensions, a perception lived out, a decade later, in James Alexander's tragic death. In the first decade of the twentieth century, the city council resolved to manage San Pedro's working classes more aggressively so as to exercise some control over space and labor. For example, in 1906 the city council prohibited non-Dominicans from joining the police force.[23] That same year, the city council also passed one of its most aggressive pieces of municipal legislation, aimed at coachmen who drove in the city. The new law required them to obey strict guidelines governing dress, behavior, and licensing. They had to be of "good moral character," at least eighteen years of age, and they had to pass a police interview. Immigrants could not legally drive a coach until they had resided in the city for a year, and all coachmen were subject to fines if they failed to appear for the regular inspections held on the first Sunday of every month.[24]

The regulations governing coachmen were not aimed specifically at Afro-Antilleans but appear to have affected them disproportionately. For example, of the twenty-three plaintiffs who faced coach- and cart-related violations in

1915 and 1916, twenty-two were foreign-born, hailing from Barbados, St. Kitts, St. Thomas, St. Martin, Nevis, Haiti, Puerto Rico, Guadeloupe, and Antigua (table 4.3).

Afro-Antilleans were also prominent among those accused of "scandalous behavior" and "mistreating others." These misdemeanors usually involved fighting in public or hurling insults. Twice as many men as women and nearly twice as many Antilleans as Dominicans were charged with these misdemeanors (table 4.4). According to the national census taken in 1920, West Indians constituted 17 percent of the total foreign population residing in the country, and in 1915 and 1916, they made up 99 percent of those accused of coach- and cart-related infractions and more than half of those charged with misdemeanors.[25]

As a result, the intense monitoring of urban workers took on a racial cast. This became particularly acute (and tragic) when private and public security forces used violent force to subdue Afro-Antilleans. As in James Alexander's case, abuse by a police officer or his agent sometimes resulted from an exchange of fighting words. For instance, W. H. Rawleigh from Tortola filed a $50,000 claim against the Dominican government for the "ill treatment" he had received from a police officer, Víctor Vargas. Vargas had pushed Rawleigh, who, to defend himself, had "used an expression [to refer to] Vargas which exacerbated the matter and the assault took place" in which Vargas beat Rawleigh with a stick and broke his arms. In their report on the case, British and Dominican officials admitted that "there [was] a good deal of ill feeling between the Spanish speaking population of Macorís and the British Subjects."[26]

One day a porter named James Jeffers arrived at the consular office with "black and blue marks all over his body," complaining that a police officer had mistreated him "without justification."[27] A *petromacorisano* night watchman assaulted J. G. Somersall, a British subject, who was standing on the corner of Libertad and Porvenir Streets watching a dance. Luckily, the officer's superior arrived in time to stop the abuse.[28] Charles Greenwich, a British West Indian subject employed at Ingenio Angelina, had a particularly grim confrontation with the police chief from Ingenio Santa Fe: "It seems that Ingenio Santa Fe's Police Chief was searching for the police chief of Ingenio Angelina. Finding Charles Greenwich in the batey of the latter Ingenio, he asked if [Greenwich] knew [the police chief's] address. Charles's negative response was motive enough so that the police officer made use of his knife and cut his face (you can see the scar) and hit him various times."[29] Finally, John Roberts, a native of Antigua who worked at Ingenio Santa Fe, was arrested in 1920 and accused of stealing tools from his workstation. Roberts reported that after searching the estate, Santa Fe's security guard placed "a rope . . . around [his]

Table 4.3. Nationality and occupation of those accused of coach/cart-related violations, 1915–1916

Crime as recorded	Defendant's nationality	Defendant's occupation	No. of incidences
Obstructing the road	Barbados	Cart man	1
	St. Kitts	Cart man	2
	Puerto Rico	Factory owner	1
	Nevis	Cart man	1
	St. Kitts	Cart man	1
	Haiti	Cart man	1
	St. Kitts	Cart man	1
	St. Thomas	Cart man	1
Leaving coach on the road	St. Martin	Coach driver	1
Having more than 4 people in the cart and parking outside designated areas	St. Kitts	Coach driver	1
	Antigua	Coach driver	1
Carrying more than 4 people in the cab	Puerto Rico	Coach driver	1
	Dominican Republic	Coach driver	1
Running cart into the street and endangering others	St. Kitts	Cart driver	1
Failure to drive coach with lamps	St. Martin	Coach driver	1
Having a damaged cart and forcing municipal animals to pull it	Barbados	Cart driver	1
Wearing a dirty uniform while working	St. Martin	Coach driver	1
Leaving carts in a prohibited zone at a prohibited time	St. Kitts	Cart man	1
	St. Martin	Cart man	1
Going out with carts before six in the morning	Nevis	Cart man	1
	Guadeloupe	Cart man	1
	Antigua	Cart man	1

Source: Alcaldía de San Pedro de Macorís, Libro 31 (February 1, 1915–March 26, 1916), AGN.

neck and . . . [he] was pulled off [his] feet and . . . suspended in mid-air." As they threatened him with lynching, Roberts reported, "the Judge stood near me with a machete in his hand and threatened to strike me if I did not say who had the tools."[30]

These stories from San Pedro resonate with the experiences of many Afro-Antillean workers throughout the circum-Caribbean area. Scholars of the region have long noted the tensions between Hispanics and Afro-Antilleans as deriving from competition for jobs and wages or from antiblack prejudice reinforced, at times, by differential pay structures (as on the Panama Canal).[31]

Table 4.4. Origin and sex of those charged with scandalous behavior and mistreatment, 1915–1916

Origin as stated in *alcaldía* records	Number of incidents	
	Male	Female
Dominican Republic	17	12
St. Kitts	12	6
St. Martin	6	2
Antigua	5	1
St. Thomas	4	2
Nevis	1	3
Guadeloupe	1	2
St. Croix	1	1
Barbados	1	
Montserrat	1	
Curaçao	1	
Haiti	1	
Jamaica	1	
Dominica	1	
Puerto Rico	3	2
Cuba	2	
Spain	2	
Switzerland	2	
China	1	
Total	63	31

Source: Alcaldía de San Pedro de Macorís, Libro 31 (February 1, 1915–March 26, 1916), AGN.

Police violence against migrant West Indians in agro-export regions appears to have been the product of class conflicts articulated as racism.

The evidence from San Pedro suggests, however, that a reversal of the equation may be necessary. First, it appears that the black workers who experienced police brutality in San Pedro were not always among the lowest paid. Many of them were among the most privileged laborers on sugar estates—mechanics, administrators, or engineers—and perceived themselves as equal to or even better than the local Dominican police. The assertiveness with which some Afro-Antilleans defended themselves against verbal or physical abuse suggests a degree of self-assurance (or arrogance) that is inconsistent with the image of the browbeaten worker (see figures 4.2 and 4.3). Finally, that many black workers sought assistance from their consular representatives underscores the point that, quite apart from being migrant laborers, Afro-Antilleans were also subjects of powerful empires. For example, in the wake of James Alexander's death, Vice Consul Gosling reported, "[Dominican] authorities are most careful how they arrest British subjects and once or twice in their desire to avoid

Figure 4.2. Samuel Isaac with friends, 1940s. Colección Hugh Kelly IV. Centro de Investigación Histórica, Universidad de Puerto Rico at Río Piedras.

Figure 4.3. West Indians with railcar, 1940s. Colección Hugh Kelly IV. Centro de Investigación Histórica, Universidad de Puerto Rico at Río Piedras.

complications have communicated with me before arresting them." Police caution sometimes went too far: Gosling noted the case of a Crown subject who "was arrested by a policeman and taken to the Policía (Police Headquarters)[then] was immediately released on the discovery that he was a British subject."[32]

Rather than the product of racial prejudice or class conflict, it appears that the liberal use of violence against Afro-Antilleans by public and private police forces in San Pedro was crucial in the ideological work of constructing Afro-Antilleans as degraded, low-status workers and associating blackness with foreignness. Policing was one of those key processes that made "racial and cultural identities take priority."[33] The growing significance of racial identity became even more apparent in the monitoring of sexual behavior, specifically, the policing of sexual labor in San Pedro before and during the U.S. occupation.

As we saw in the previous chapter, San Pedro's elites participated in an associational culture rooted in activities they regarded as respectable. They created spaces in homes and constructed buildings owned by the clubs that gave physical expression to the world they inhabited, one characterized by lectures, theatrical productions, and rhetorical competitions. In these spaces, progress and civilization became associated with elite Dominicans and wealthy white immigrants. In other words, within their social world, San Pedro's elites forged a relationship between race, progress, and civilization in which European ancestry was privileged.

In sharp contrast, the policing of migrant workers and female sex workers resulted in the creation of other kinds of spaces far removed physically and ideologically from the Athenaeum (Ateneo), the Columbus Theater (Teatro Colón), and the Spanish Club (Club Español). Opposite the geography of club life, an "urban geography of vice" took shape in San Pedro between 1890 and 1924, thanks to the heavy-handed monitoring of prostitution.[34] Policies designed to protect public or collective morality, as Michelle Mitchell argues for African Americans in the United States, helped make the control of women's sexuality, especially that of immigrant women of color, important in governing San Pedro.[35]

Between 1890 and 1920, San Pedro became embroiled in a series of efforts to control prostitution. Throughout the nineteenth century, brothels, bars, and cantinas were legal and taxable businesses in the Dominican Republic, but for reasons missing from the documentation, San Pedro's residents increasingly petitioned the city council to monitor prostitution and remove brothels from the center of town. In the 1890s a near-consensus emerged among the governing elites that citizens had the right to shop in the market, stroll in landscaped municipal parks, and conduct their affairs without being confronted by prostitutes and their clients. For example, a group of neighbors living on Colón Street demanded that the city council remove a house of prostitution from the neighborhood. Manuel Richiez bemoaned "the scandals that these women [cause] day and night with their bad conduct, which [undermines] morality." That same year, in another effort to quell public dissent, the city council resolved to fine and arrest those who organized and sponsored *bailes de rameras* (prostitute dances), at which prostitutes solicited clients.[36]

Despite calls for eliminating prostitution from the city, the council simply passed an ordinance in 1893 prohibiting prostitutes from riding in coaches during the day. The editors of *El Cable* published a scathing article lampooning the law: the writer deemed the legislation both counterproductive and ridiculous, arguing that the cover of darkness would only make prostitutes more dangerous to social morality. In dramatic language, he explained that the light of day "infused respect" among prostitutes and their clients, whereas beneath the shadow of night, "the imprudent whistles, burlesque peals of laughter, and drunken voices" would echo unrestrained throughout the city. He argued that prostitutes should be banned from riding in coaches at any hour of the day or night because they were "degenerates" and their acts were "immoral." Interestingly, he did not think it necessary to outlaw prostitution completely.[37]

The 1893 codes apparently failed, because in 1908–1909 yet another controversy over prostitution erupted. This time it was led by a coalition of healthcare professionals and community leaders mobilized by the chief medical officer and a Spanish immigrant, Dr. Emilio Tió y Betances. Problems had begun to surface in 1906. In August of that year, Councilman Aybar presented a motion to remove the Hotel Venecia from its location near the port, because the brothel's employees flaunted their "immoral acts" and undermined public decency. Anticipating Aybar's protests, the city council president explained that he, the police commissioner, public-health officials, and Venecia's madam were already searching for a more appropriate place for the brothel's residents to live.[38]

The council's actions in the Venecia case mark the beginning of a trend that would later define public policy regarding prostitution in general: removing brothels to newly created tolerance zones, usually located on the southern edge of town, near Miramar, the predominantly West Indian neighborhood, and within walking distance of the port.[39] Records from 1908 indicate that the city council considered renting a house for the sole purpose of identifying and examining prostitutes and removing them from "the center of the population."[40] This action may have been taken in response to Councilman

James Brower's proposal that the city submit "women of the bad life" to weekly exams in order to prevent the spread of syphilis. Then in March of 1909, the city council passed San Pedro's first Prostitution Regulation.[41] A key element of this legislation required prostitutes to register with the city and submit to regular physical examinations. The city transferred syphilitic women to Santo Domingo for treatment.[42]

In 1909 through 1911, tolerance zones fell under even more serious vigilance. A public-health bureaucrat, Dr. Héctor Marchena, who, persuaded by an international scientific consensus about the dangers of syphilis and the mysteries of its transmission from women to men (and not the other way around),[43] believed that prostitutes were "finishing off San Pedro's humanity" and urged the city council to take quick and decisive action to treat "hundreds of infected women."[44] Citywide inspections began on February 1, but within two weeks, a council member complained that few women were coming forward. The representative had a point: the two extant reports (from March and April of 1911) indicate that about fifty women had appeared for their required checkups.

In San Pedro as elsewhere throughout the Americas, the problem of syphilis was gendered female. The syphilitic woman became a symbol of the social ills associated with urban growth and economic expansion.[45] A similarly negative image of female sexuality was captured in San Pedro, where one of the city's tolerance zones was known as "La Draga." "*Draga*" refers to the sludge, trash, and sewage that dredges removed from the seabed to clear the River Higuamo for shipping. Women who sold sex were no longer human, just receptacles that collected the "discharge [of] humors, secretions, and excretions."[46] Such an indictment may explain why, in San Pedro, many prostitutes failed (or refused) to appear for their obligatory inspections. According to city officials, many women were Puerto Ricans or British West Indians who may have wanted to avoid being deported. Also, women may not have wanted to appear on the city's tax rolls as prostitutes if selling sex was just one of their many income-generating activities. Dr. Marchena argued this point: "There are certain women who, during the day, present themselves as respectable women, but become prostitutes at night when they cannot be monitored by our staff or by the police. For this reason, it is difficult to classify them as prostitutes without sufficient proof."[47]

If these same women feared public exposure, the location of the examinations—the municipal cockfighting arena—posed an additional problem, especially if, after being diagnosed with syphilis, they were hauled away to Santo Domingo in a health department vehicle. Equally unattractive was the standard treatment for venereal disease: doctors recommended an extensive cleaning of the genital areas with soap, water, and a mercury-based douche injected into the urethra.[48]

Finally, it appears that many women refused the humiliation simply because they were not infected with syphilis. The small sample I obtained from three medical reports suggests that women examined by Dr. Marchena's team suffered from a variety of venereal diseases and infections, but not syphilis. During the three weeks for which there are data, doctors diagnosed twelve women with gonorrhea and sent two to Santo Domingo for syphilis treatment. The rest suffered from chronic metritis (inflammation of the uterus), vaginitis, scabies, and other diseases of the vulva. Forty-one women had some type of communicable disease while eleven received clean bills of health. Dr. Tió was forced to admit that policing prostitution had failed to prevent diseased women from engaging in commercial sex and that the city lacked the necessary resources—among them a specialized hospital for women—to cure those who suffered from venereal disease.[49]

As Laura Engelstein argues, the mystery of syphilis's transmission and course through the human body made it "the perfect vehicle for the doctor's assertion of professional authority."[50] This appears to have been the case in San Pedro, where very few women received actual treatment for their vaginal infections, but where many were policed into so-called clandestine prostitution because officials claimed they spread syphilis. This fear justified the elaboration of policies and direct intervention, which, in turn, served as ideal instruments through which doctors, police, and municipal officials consolidated their power within San Pedro's burgeoning public-health regime. Indeed, the spectacle of inspections, registration, and the transport of prostitutes to Santo Domingo for treatment made local government appear effective and powerful. At the same time, however, the antisyphilis campaign revealed the limits of health officials' power in regulating illicit sex and female sexuality. By focusing on foreign women and women of color as the transmitters of syphilis, health officials in San Pedro legislated gender inequality and sexual racism into the public-health bureaucracy.[51]

The preoccupation with prostitution in San Pedro occasioned an opportunity for social groups outside the geography of club life to participate in the creation of additional respectable spaces for leisure and entertainment. The fight against prostitution broadened the coalition of men who defined themselves as authorities over San Pedro's residents.[52] These included Dr. Emelio Tió y Betances, a Spanish immigrant; John Brower, a council member; and members of the British West Indian Industrial Lodge, who, in collaboration with residents of Amechazurra Street, complained to the city council about the "presence of whorehouses" in a neighborhood "populated, for the most part, by honest families." These citizens asked the council to relocate the house "farther away," into a tolerance zone.[53]

After 1916, the protests of local residents found a more receptive audience among U.S. military officials, who, for quite different reasons, considered the creation of tolerance zones unsatisfactory and encouraged city councils to take more drastic action against prostitution. The occupation government drastically reorganized the existing public-health administration and abolished provincial health and sanitation boards when it issued a Sanitation Law in 1919, Executive Order 388. Under this legislation, new sanitary districts were created and placed under the jurisdiction of the Public Health Secretariat, located in Santo Domingo. U.S. officials also argued that the Dominican government had failed to secure a workable national health policy, because many municipalities continued to rely on police officers rather than trained health officials to conduct hygiene inspections. The occupation government also ordered city councils across the island to elect health officials and directed them to spend between 10 and 15 percent of their municipal budgets on sanitation projects. This law also gave the Public Health Secretariat jurisdiction over medical training and provided a regulatory apparatus for the certification of doctors.[54]

San Pedro de Macorís, with its well-established public-health infrastructure directed by Dr. Tió y Betances, was ahead of other Dominican cities except in the area of prostitution. In 1918 Major James McLean wrote the city council complaining about a number of women at the "Santa Fe Port [bordello]" who worked "with absolute disregard for municipal regulations" and recommended that the business be shut down. To make matters worse, as Councilman Antonio Marmolezo testified, the brothel often "held dances on workdays, and, as a result of poor police vigilance, large mêlées frequently broke out."[55]

In response to these complaints, the occupation government passed the Tolerance Zone Law, which required prostitutes to carry an identification booklet when they left tolerance zones for other parts of the city and to have their books signed by military officials after their weekly physicals.[56]

Then the debate over prostitution and tolerance zones exploded in the fall of 1919. In October the provincial governor accused the city council of allowing the expansion of tolerance zones in San Pedro. A month later, he recommended that the council shut them down; on both occasions, the city council rejected his request.[57] Then in November, just before the implementation of the Sanitation Law, the city council met in a special session with Provost Marshal Stack, Major Knoche of the Dominican National Guard, and the provincial governor to discuss a disturbance that had occurred in the tolerance zone. Apparently, the mixture of "gambling, women, and wine" had caused a nasty confrontation between U.S. Marines and members of the Dominican National Guard. Obviously embarrassed by what took place, the military authorities argued that closing down the zone was the "only remedy" to prevent future clashes between Dominicans and North Americans. For his part, the governor suggested that the council deport prostitutes from San Pedro. Despite the tide of opinion against them, however, city council members decided to keep the tolerance zones intact and, in a surprising move, simply outlawed the sale of liquor to all U.S. Marines stationed in San Pedro and prohibited the consumption and sale of alcohol within and around the red light district.[58]

The passage of the Sanitation Law in December of 1919 converted the city council's defiance into a moot, symbolic gesture as the occupation government launched a frontal attack on "clandestine" prostitution. Documents produced during the campaign against prostitution from 1920 to 1923 suggest that U.S. and Dominican officials fundamentally disagreed over the meaning of the tolerance zone with regard to governing San Pedro's multiethnic and multiracial population. For example, U.S. officials in the Dominican Republic aggressively policed and incarcerated women suspected of clandestine prostitution rather than trying to reform them, as Dominican officials had attempted. In San Pedro between May 26 and August 25, 1920, police arrested fifty women, and the courts levied hefty fines against them, ranging from U.S.$15 to U.S.$50. Some were even sentenced to jail: Margot Cortera was brought to trial in June of 1920 for selling sex and fined $25 with jail time; five prostitutes, all with Spanish names and perhaps working out of the same house, were arrested a few weeks later and fined $40 each with an additional forty days behind bars.[59] As in many cities in the United States, under the Sanitary Law any young woman who contracted a venereal disease was defined as a prostitute, regardless of how she became infected, and was penalized for having a sexually transmitted disease.[60]

A combination of laws, policing, public-health policy, and morality discourse positioned prostitutes on the same level as the West Indian washerwomen, domestics, and street vendors who filled San Pedro's police ledgers with their scandalous behavior. Violent enforcement of the law became a weapon wielded against immigrant working women. Eileen Findlay's reminder that sexuality "becomes explicitly politicized at certain historical moments" and is used to identify new sets of actors and political projects prompts us to consider these persistent interventions and attempts to make prostitution less visible as sexual racism. Policing migrant women for their sexual activity complemented the violence meted against Afro-Antillean men by Dominican security forces.[61]

Kevin Mumford's concept of the "interzone" helps us understand the policing of prostitution as sexual racism. In his analysis of Chicago and New York during the Progressive Era, Mumford defines interzones as marginal and marginalized neighborhoods that "should be understood foremost as [an area] of cultural, sexual, and social interchange." Interzones were mostly confined to African American neighborhoods, and their creation signaled "white reformers' abandonment of African-Americans settling in the urban North." According to Mumford, interzones in the United States "served to create a new complex of racial and gendered politics" in which the use of sexual stereotyping to define racial attributes was "constructed into the infrastructure of [the city] and everyday lives, not only in bureaucracies and schools but also saloons, brothels, even sidewalks and alleyways."[62] In and around the estates, physical violence helped establish racial hierarchies; in the city, forcing women who may have sold sex to live in tolerance zones or to submit to physical exams highlighted their foreignness and their lower status.

. . .

Regulating the tolerance zone complemented the cultural ordering process defined by associational life and *hispanicismo*. In that world, *hispanicismo* defined the norms and values of a dominant elite that identified with its European heritage. At the same time, racial bias in the enforcement of laws, the violent policing of Afro-Antillean men, and efforts to control or eliminate sexual labor helped identify racial others and sexual migrants as populations that required intervention and monitoring. As a result of both cultural ordering and policing, attributes associated with modernity and deviance became ethnoracial signifiers. Whiteness was linked to civilization; blackness adhered to those identified with criminality, disorder, and sexual immorality.

Most important, antiblackness in San Pedro was not simply anti-Haitianism. The region's racialization emerged from its particular relationship to foreign capital, symbolized and actualized through the presence of Afro-Antillean workers who became "black" in "a matrix formed by labor, politics, and an evolving racial ideology" that linked morality with inclusion in the body politic.[63]

San Pedro's elites left a spatial legacy of power and privilege, an urban order characterized by race and class hierarchies, and social differentiation rooted in gendered notions of morality and respectability. British West Indians understood these dynamics much better than either the U.S. military officials or the Dominican governing elites. As an established West Indian community took shape in San Pedro, some of its members began to organize and challenge racist ideologies. The actions and voices of these new political actors, mobilized around specific race and gender identities, set the stage for a racial politics of a different order.

5

DEBATING DOMINICANS' RACE
DURING THE U.S. OCCUPATION

On September 7, 1921, members of the San Pedro de Macorís branch of the
Universal Negro Improvement Association (UNIA) paraded down Sánchez
Street to protest the arrests of their leaders, which had taken place on September 3. Men, women, and children from St. Kitts, Nevis, Antigua, and Trinidad
marched under two flags: the British Union Jack and the red, black, and green
UNIA banner. As they passed the home of the Reverend Archibald Beer, the
white rector of San Esteban Episcopal Church and the British vice-consul in
San Pedro, some Garveyites (as members of the UNIA were called in honor
of the organization's founder, Marcus Garvey) flipped the British flag upside
down. Outraged, Beer demanded that they carry the flag properly, raising
such a protest that the Garveyites relented and marched away. Later, however,
when they reached their regular meeting place at the Independent Episcopal
Church's Emancipation Hall, they trampled and spat on the flag.[1]

The Reverend Beer's complaints about the protest and an apparently radical celebration of British Slave Emancipation Day the week before, on August
31, reached the sympathetic ears of U.S. military officials and the Dominican
authorities, weary from years of rural and labor unrest. Starting in 1919, U.S.
Marines were engaged in a protracted battle against *gavilleros*, groups of armed
men from the countryside who raided sugar estate stores (*bodegas*), attacked
workers, and fought U.S. Marines encamped in San Pedro's hinterlands.

Labor protests had also become a regular feature on San Pedro's sugar estates, and the fear that the UNIA might have some connection to labor mobilization prompted authorities to move quickly to end UNIA activity in San
Pedro. According to documents produced by Dominican officials, including
Judge José Pedemonte and his secretary, Manuel Jimenez, the organization's
primary purpose was "to promote the dominance of the black race over the
white race." District Attorney Fernando Brea advised his superiors that the
UNIA's leaders promoted a sense of racial difference that was foreign to the
Dominican Republic: "We believe organizations like these pose a particular

threat in a country that has never known racial differences—at least not as they are manifest in other countries and especially in the way that groups like these envision them."[2]

U.S. military officials echoed Brea's concerns. Provost Marshal Kincade believed that a UNIA-led race war would threaten the white Dominican minority's political, social, and economic power: "While [dominance over the white race] would be impossible in the United States, it is not at all impossible here after the occupation ceases."[3] Accordingly, three UNIA leaders were deported to their home islands.

Similar arguments animated state actions against UNIA chapters throughout the Caribbean. In 1929, for example, Cuban president Gerardo Machado launched an investigation into UNIA activities and labeled the UNIA a "racist" organization because members considered themselves "enemies of the white race."[4] Across the circum-Caribbean, Afro-Antillean activism provoked vigorous responses among Spanish-speaking officials, who worried that black workers might ignite labor unrest or, as in Cuba, inspire race-based mobilization among people of African descent.

In San Pedro, the U.S. occupation of Haiti and the Dominican Republic influenced official response to the UNIA. Building on Luis Martínez-Fernández's insight that race "was a key determinant of U.S. policy toward the Dominican Republic and, for that matter, toward the entire Caribbean region,"[5] I argue that the U.S. occupation of the island occasioned another debate about Dominicans' race. During this period, the idea of "race war" espoused by Dominican and U.S. military officials was not mere hysterics. U.S. intervention was predicated on the idea of white racial superiority and the racial inferiority of African- and Asian-descended peoples. While this racist thinking was used to justify invasion, the U.S. occupation tested the hypothesis that those deemed racially inferior could overcome their deficiencies and build stable political regimes and improve their economies under U.S. tutelage. U.S. officials' insistence that intervention was a logical response to race warfare, then, prompted authorities to quash antiracist, problack theories of race and nation, particularly those presented by Afro-Antillean Garveyites.

This chapter argues that Dominican antioccuaption activists crafted a new idea about Dominicans' race not only in reaction against U.S. occupation, but in the face of black mobilization from below. I begin this chapter by examining the British West Indian community in San Pedro and the cultural, religious, and economic forces that made the UNIA possible. Then, building on the conclusions regarding policing and race in chapter 4, I analyze the role U.S. military authorities played in institutionalizing race and racism. The chapter ends with a critical study of nationalist writings produced during the occupation. I will demonstrate that in sharp contrast to the nineteenth century when a similar debate erupted over Dominicans' race, the U.S. occupation made appeals to Antillean unity and celebrations of racial mixture less tenable as ideological positions.

. . .

Historians agree that between the 1890s and the end of U.S. military occupation in 1924, the number of black workers in the Dominican Republic and in San Pedro increased dramatically. During World War I and the interwar period, many of these migrants remained stranded in San Pedro; others chose to try their luck in the Dominican Republic after having already worked elsewhere.

Although Afro-Antillean migration to the Dominican Republic was predominantly male, women and children were significantly represented among migrants. Immigration lists from the 1920s indicate that West Indian women and children migrated to San Pedro without male companions. Of the sixty-three names on a list of workers who arrived between May and December 1921, only ten were men with labor contracts; the rest were twenty-nine children under thirteen years old and twenty-four women, most of them from St. Martin and St. Kitts. Forty-year-old Florence Webb and twenty-two-year-old Susana Webb from Nevis arrived in San Pedro along with Susan James, a single mother of four, from St. Martin, and Olive Jarvis, a thirty-four-year-old mother of five from St. Kitts. These women probably immigrated to San Pedro for the same reasons that had motivated their lovers, fathers, or brothers.[6]

Some West Indians amassed considerable fortunes in San Pedro. For example, Edwin Autuen from St. Thomas arrived in San Pedro at the turn of the century and worked at Ingenio Puerto Rico as an electrician. In 1920 he was employed as a telephone operator (*telefonista*) and owned two homes. Rafael Mitchell, a native of St. Thomas, went to Juan Antonio Hernández's office in March of 1921 to notarize the value of his properties in anticipation of his marriage to Manuela Pickering from Tortola. His estate, including twenty wooden houses, two concrete houses, thirteen plots of land, seven coaches with fourteen horses, and 8,000 pesos in cash, was valued at 108,000 pesos. Mitchell was there to ensure that "this amount not become part of the community property" so that his "natural" daughter, Erotida, would retain her inheritance rights.[7]

The presence of women and property owners in addition to religious institutions and residential intimacy were decisive in transforming this migratory population into a permanent one. Beginning in the 1880s and 1890s, West Indians settled in Locomotora (a neighborhood bisected by railway lines from Ingenio Santa Fe), Jacob's Town (Yocotón), New Town, and Miramar and in smaller neighborhoods such as Farmyard, Market Street, and King Street. A West Indian missionary, the Reverend Charles Williams, organized the African Methodist Episcopal Church in Miramar in 1886; black ministers from St. Kitts founded the Moravian Church around 1895; the Reverend Benjamin Isaac Wilson, from St. Croix, established Holy Trinity Episcopal Church near Ingenio Santa Fe in Locomotora in about 1897; and San Esteban Episcopal Church, in Miramar, was founded in 1922. On their heels, and drawing from the same congregations, West Indian men of means founded fraternal lodges. By 1910 there were three such lodges; the oldest, Logia Independencia (Independence Lodge), was founded in 1883. Another, Logia Industria (Industry Lodge), was affiliated with the Grand United Order of Oddfellows, and Logia Experiencia (Experience Lodge) catered exclusively to English speakers. All these lodges organized women's auxiliaries.[8]

For the most part, British subjects appear to have preferred endogamy, and in some cases they chose to raise their children speaking English and as Protestants. Emille Washington recalled that his very proud British West Indian father, who had married a British West Indian woman born in San Pedro, insisted that his children were British subjects, not Dominicans. He often said, "You cannot put duck eggs under a hen and, when they hatch, call them chickens."[9]

Marriage and baptismal records from San Esteban Episcopal Church suggest similar sentiments. In 1921 and 1922, thirty-eight West Indian couples celebrated their nuptials; only five couples involved an Afro-Antillean and a Dominican, and all of those paired a British West Indian male with a Dominican woman or a woman of West Indian and Dominican descent.[10] Out of 140 children baptized in San Esteban Episcopal Church and its satellite missions in Ingenios Consuelo, Angelina, and Quisqueya, only one appeared to have had a godparent who might have been Dominican or Spanish speaking. Only sixteen of those children received Spanish first names. Children born to parents who selected Spanish first names were most often male, and a slight majority, ten, were born in the city. George Atilano Sprouse and Elena Romano Matos formulated an amusing compromise for their twin boys: they named one Charles Lewis and the other Marcos Vinicio.[11]

The liturgical calendar brought together Anglicans, Moravians, and Methodists, and public rituals—funeral processions, Christmas Eve serenades, Easter pageants, and May Day festivals—undermined strict denominationalism. As did endogamy, these events nurtured cultural cohesion among West Indians from various islands. Doña Martha Williamson sighed when she remembered the church services and religious activities she attended with other West Indians from various churches: on "fore day [Christmas Eve], people would leave at midnight and go from house to house, playing guitar, serenading, and singing hymns until four in the morning." On Christmas Day, "a set of people [would] go around and sing. When you go and sing, the person living there, they get up and open the door, they listen to what you're singing, they have the guaravberry [wine], and they'd give you guavaberry to drink." Neighbors exchanging Christmas cakes and meats with visiting carolers made the season "a happy time."[12]

These events hint at the class and gendered politics of Protestant piety and respectability that also shaped an emerging Afro-Antillean identity. Elderly women who grew up in the late 1920s and early 1930s recall the dress codes that governed participation in public ceremonies. Doña Martha Williamson remembered that during Holy Week "you had on your white dress and your black skirt, and white bodice. You [didn't] wear color on Good Friday. And you'd always wear your hat." Male and female lodge members were also expected to exhibit sobriety and religiosity at all times. Indeed, the lodges provided West Indians with respectable social interactions within an exclusive space.[13]

San Pedro's UNIA emerged from an associational culture that differed significantly from the one described in chapter 3: West Indian community life centered around Afro-Anglo cultural traditions, Protestant churches, lodges, and public memorial practices steeped in sacred symbolism, with separate spheres for men and women. The dense religious, familial, social, and economic networks that characterized San Pedro's West Indian neighborhoods provided Afro-Antilleans venues for cultural and religious expression free from the racial hostility of Dominican police or estate security. Memorial processions in San Pedro, as Helen Regis has argued in the case of African Americans in New Orleans, provided "a space for the expression of individual and communal grief, while joining local histories with contemporary experiences."[14] Complementing lodges, the Moravian, African Methodist Episcopal, and Episcopal churches provided Afro-Antillean men (and, to a lesser degree, women) with powerful venues for leadership and community building. This may have been particularly true for poorer West Indian workers, who could not afford to pay dues for lodge membership. Taken together, the black West Indian church in San Pedro, like the African American church in the United States, served "as a base for building a sense of ethnic identity and . . . community interest among its members."[15]

Churches, lodges, marriage, godparenthood, and religious processions brought together West Indians who, as a group, were economically diverse. As we have seen, West Indians occupied nearly every aspect of San Pedro's urban and regional economy: some owned and rented houses; others worked on sugar estates as mechanics, engineers, or clerks; yet others comprised the urban workforce as coachmen, laundresses, domestics, and sex workers.

World War I also proved to be a defining moment in creating a sense of commonality among British West Indians from different islands. First, the demands of war meant that fewer ships were available to return British West Indians to their home islands at the end of the sugar season.[16] British officials reported that a great number of British subjects living in Spanish-speaking countries "[were] indigent and unable to earn a living owing to old age, sickness, etc," but officials remained disinclined to offer assistance because "there were no funds available for the relief or repatriation of such persons."[17] As a result, many British West Indians who would otherwise have returned home remained in San Pedro.

World War I was pivotal in uniting British West Indians for another reason. As a result of the significant racial discrimination they experienced in the British Army, West Indian veterans began to question their status as British subjects. Many among the thousands who served in the West Indies Regiment began to demand greater political autonomy and expanded juridical rights. Legislation passed immediately after the war made such expectations tenable. In 1918, for example, the Representation of the People Act granted suffrage to all those who had been part of the war effort, including women and colonial subjects.[18] Despite this gesture, however, the government's segregation policies enraged West Indian troops. Soldiers stationed in Taranto, Italy, for instance, mutinied against white officers to protest a racially tiered system of labor, command, and wages.[19]

After the war, the Crown backed away from its promises to make all British subjects, regardless of race, equal under the law and dashed hopes of reforms in colonial administration and island governance. As a result, British West Indian men, emboldened by their war experiences, returned from the battlefields of Europe to organize protests against the Crown on their home islands. Former soldiers in Belize and Trinidad became the leaders of unions and nationalist movements.[20] For others, World War I prompted conversations about a West Indian federation and black self-governance.[21] This new boldness, centered on the pursuit of racial justice, provided the basis of a new nationalism, one that unified black populations under black leadership.

One measure of the attractiveness of these new ideas was the popularity of the UNIA. Branches sprang up throughout the Americas in the 1910s and 1920s. Marcus Garvey's message of black racial pride and economic uplift inspired millions of people of African descent to become race-oriented. In Spanish-speaking countries, moreover, the UNIA was a vital social and po-litical organization for West Indians, who were often the targets of antiblack nationalism. The Dominican Republic's sugar-producing regions proved es-pecially fertile soil for Garveyism: by the 1920s, the provinces of Barahona, La Romana, Sánchez, Santo Domingo, and San Pedro de Macorís all had UNIA branches.[22] By 1921 the UNIA had roughly six million members around the globe.[23] Interviews with elderly men and women whose British West Indian parents migrated to San Pedro indicate that well into the 1940s, and despite Marcus Garvey's personal and political decline, the UNIA remained an attrac-tive organization among Afro-Antilleans.[24]

Many people of African descent found Garvey's charisma and his power-ful message inspiring, but the reasons British West Indians embraced Garvey-ism varied according to the context in which they lived and worked. During the early years of its existence in Limón, Costa Rica, for example, the UNIA forwarded a damning critique of West Indians' economic and social circum-stances rooted in the common history of African-descended peoples. Al-though it "reflected the class and social interests of different factions" in West Indian communities in Costa Rica, the organization rose above such rivalries in its struggle against racism.[25] As a result, the UNIA was important for com-munity cohesion in the face of labor exploitation and Hispanic racism.

In Cuba the UNIA's black nationalist discourse challenged the pervasive ideology of a raceless Cuban national identity. There, Cuban and British West Indian Garveyites accused white Cubans of perpetuating antiblack racism and advanced a political agenda that represented the specific economic and political interests of black Cubans. In contrast to Costa Rica, where even the white managers of United Fruit viewed the UNIA as relatively harmless and preferable to trade unions, some white and black Cubans responded to the UNIA with great hostility because of its potential to turn the social and eco-nomic demands of Afro-Cubans into a foundation for race-based political power.[26]

Unfortunately, it is difficult to gauge Garveyism's impact in San Pedro. There were no English-language newspapers that recorded West Indian activities there, nor did the UNIA receive much attention from the Dominican media or state authorities until the September 1921 march. UNIA documents collected by the U.S. military authorities suggest that reading *Negro World*, the UNIA's official paper, prompted the establishment of a branch in San Pedro. On December 17,

1919, the San Pedro branch of the UNIA–African Communities League held its first meeting at the African Methodist Episcopal Church in Yocotón. Three hundred people attended the first meeting; by 1920 the organization claimed two thousand members, according to the documents.[27]

The UNIA's initial membership was drawn largely from San Pedro's urban West Indian population, which included independent artisans, businessmen, and housewives; of the sixteen arrested in 1921, for instance, only one listed his occupation as "cane worker." It also appears that, despite its claims to the contrary, San Pedro's UNIA was a relatively small group.

Dominican and U.S. officials believed, however, that members of the UNIA were somehow involved in the labor disputes that provoked unrest in San Pedro Province in the 1920s, since its founding coincided with an increase in labor disputes on local sugar estates. Between 1916 and 1920, when World War I temporarily ended European beet production, the price of sugar increased, and sugar exports jumped 79 percent. Between 1905 and 1916, the average price per kilo of sugar was $0.05; in 1920 it was $0.285.[28] The new wealth did not trickle down to laborers, however. The heady days of La Danza de los Millones (Dance of the Millions), when San Pedro's economy boomed thanks to higher sugar prices, ended abruptly in 1920: Dominican sugar plummeted to its prewar low of $0.05 per kilo. As sugar prices fell, food prices increased, sugar estate managers reduced wages to stay afloat, and the Public Works Department ceased operations, forcing the military government to fire hundreds of Haitian and West Indian workers.[29]

Sugar workers organized strikes as early as 1919, demanding higher wages to offset inflation. The longest work stoppage, in March and April of 1920, occurred at Ingenio Consuelo and resulted in a few wage concessions. In that instance, Afro-Antillean workers provided the leadership and were the majority of participants.[30] At the same time, the collapse of the sugar market shook the foundations of provincial power in San Pedro.[31] Once sugar prices returned to their pre-1918 lows, many colonos sold their heavily mortgaged properties to foreign banks or to sugar companies. In turn, devastated ingenios were sold to foreign investors. By 1924 investors in the United States owned thirteen of the twenty-one sugar mills in the country. The Cuban Dominican Sugar Company was one such group, operating five sugar mills worth over $16 million.[32]

U.S. and Dominican officials suspected UNIA involvement in these labor strikes, but the evidence suggests otherwise. Since most of those arrested lived in San Pedro, it appears that the UNIA found a home among some West Indians precisely because it seamlessly wove together the key elements of urban West Indian life in San Pedro: expressive Protestant piety; black religious lead-

ership; and moral reform. Nevertheless, that UNIA members deemed it necessary to march in front of the British consul's home and display their anger by
disrespecting the Union Jack suggests that they, like other blacks living in the
empire, "found themselves asking deeper structural questions of capital and
the political world around them."[33]

In San Pedro, the Reverend Beer of San Esteban Episcopal Church became
the focal point of a powerful critique that British West Indians developed toward the empire and its representatives. Simply put, the Reverend Beer was
a racist whose paternalist attitudes an increasing number of outspoken West
Indian ministers refused to tolerate. Beer was born in England and became a
priest in the United States, where he spent most of his life. In 1921 the U.S. Episcopal Church sent him to minister to U.S. Marines and organize new congregations. The British government then selected him to serve as its vice-consul in
San Pedro. Beer's congregation grew quickly because he had financial support
from the U.S. Episcopal Church and, it was said, because he offered potential
congregants money "borrowed" from his consular funds.[34]

As a vicar and a consular representative, Beer approached his work with
British West Indians through the lens of racist paternalism. His views become
evident in letters he wrote to Dr. Gray, his ministerial supervisor and secretary
for Latin America of the Episcopal Church in the United States. In August of
1921 he informed Dr. Gray that black people had "infantile minds" and "learned
better by seeing," arguing that "their actions and thoughts [were] no better
than those of [his] son Kenneth." As he explained, "If they were children, one
could give them a 'pow-pow,' but as they are adults, one always has to scold
them and the more one does this, the more they seem to enjoy it."[35] Beer
admitted that he disliked having physical contact with black people because
he feared contamination. He once wrote, "I refuse to take the bus that takes
people of color to the various centrales. After having been face to face with diseases such as 'constitutional syphilis' [referring to the physical manifestation
of syphilis, such as ulcerations of the nose and mouth] and every other illness
you can imagine, I am obligated, out of respect for my family, to always ride
my horse." Despite the tropical heat, Beer rode and walked from San Pedro to
outlying *ingenios* to celebrate mass, dressed in his black priestly attire.[36]

Long before the confrontation on September 7, other Episcopal ministers, such as the Reverend Beer, were already in a pitched battle against
the UNIA and, perhaps even more so, black church leadership in general.
As Beer wrote to Dr. Gray, "I always tell people that they are not African,
but Black West Indians. This, I do in order to dilute whatever racial preju-
dices Garveyism promotes."[37] Beer even refused the sacraments to anyone

affiliated with the UNIA and to those who attended the Reverend Phillip Van Putten's Independent Episcopal Church and the Reverend D. E. Phillips's African Orthodox Church, both associated with the UNIA. The Reverend William Wyllie, archdeacon of the Dominican Episcopal Church, warned Beer that Garveyites in San Pedro could undermine his evangelical work, since they "had successfully destroyed the Moravian mission in San Pedro de Macorís."[38]

As they had done in their religious lives, Garveyites used a public procession to express their frustration with Beer, their commitment to racial justice, and their support of black ministers. When the military arrested the Garveyites who had participated in the march, supporters quickly rallied around the organization. Members of the Experience Lodge, for example, sent a letter to the military governor asking him not to deport their brothers—the Reverend D. E. Phillips, James Halley, Charles Henry, William Butler, and David Hicks—describing them as upstanding, altruistic citizens who promised to quit the UNIA if allowed to stay in the country. James Cooks, a fellow Garveyite, traveled to Santo Domingo to protest the "injurious arrests" of his friends.[39] Cooks was a Dutch subject who had lived in the Dominican Republic for many years and had substantial real estate holdings; unfortunately, his bravado encouraged the U.S. military government to initiate deportation proceedings against him.

Concerns that the UNIA could provoke labor unrest or, worse yet, a "race war" were especially pronounced when Garvey embarked on his Caribbean and Central American tour in September 1921 to encourage Garveyites to buy shares in the Black Star Line.[40] Garvey's tour may have prompted U.S. officials to take steps to deport San Pedro's Garveyites. They requested deportation for the Reverend Phillip Van Putten, the president and founder of the UNIA, but Van Putten voluntarily left San Pedro. One report sent to Rear Admiral Samuel S. Robison, acting military governor, described Van Putten's successor, the Reverend Phillips, as an "arrogant [man] with little respect for the law" and pointed out that other officers harbored similar feelings. The commanding general called the UNIA leaders "habitual offenders." Charles Henry, William Butler, and J. Grayon-Carey, three men deported to St. Kitts in January 1922, claimed the military authorities had labeled the UNIA a "menace to the Dominican government" to justify banning it from Dominican soil.[41]

Just as economic policies in the British Caribbean had created a labor force primed for exploitation in enclave areas from Cuba to Venezuela, Garveyism and black church denominations facilitated the creation of transnational activist networks and religious leaders capable of mobilizing their compatriots. Men like Sydney DeBourg and the Reverends Phillips and Van Putten were not migrants in the usual sense: they taught other West Indians to challenge the racist paternalism of U.S. hegemony in the Caribbean and the racial injustice of the British Crown. When they confronted Beer, San Pedro Garveyites transformed a local conflict into a broader critique of their status as British subjects. Holding high the UNIA banner, they challenged racial paternalism and racial injustice with a boldness that resonated with the nascent labor and anticolonial sentiments emerging in the British Caribbean in the postwar era.

The deportation of UNIA leadership proved devastating, and the remaining UNIA members, who had been released in November, returned to their homes. Although many of them continued as members of the churches founded by the Reverends Van Putten and Phillips, the UNIA ceased to exist in San Pedro except in the minds and hearts of its proponents.[42] Lodges and churches remained strong forces in the West Indian community, but as an image from the 1940s suggests, team sports such as baseball began to fill the void left with the end of the UNIA (figure 5.1).

The U.S. military authorities, who embarked on a "race war" of their own by suppressing San Pedro's UNIA, were clearly motivated by anti-UNIA investigations in the United States. Yet, the racist and violent underpinnings of U.S. intervention in the circum-Caribbean region had always been clear, especially to Haitians who suffered abuse at the hands of white marines. Mary Renda notes that marines fighting against Cacos in Haiti often referred to the war as "hunting Cacos." Commenting on one particular battle against Cacos

Figure 5.1. Porvenir baseball team, 1940s. Colección Hugh Kelly IV. Centro de Investigación Histórica, Universidad de Puerto Rico at Río Piedras.

who had entrenched themselves behind a boulder, Faustin Wirkus noted that the "black heads . . . appeared very much as those behind the 'hit the nigger and get a cigar' games at American amusement parks." Renda cites one white Baptist minister who witnessed "members of his own congregation 'roped tightly and cruelly together, and driven like slaves toward the Gendarmerie headquarters."[43]

Dominicans also complained about abusive, racist treatment by U.S. Marines. Bruce Calder notes that some U.S. residents reported that marines often called Dominicans "spics" and "niggers." One officer, assigned to investigate the killing of several men by a marine, eventually dropped the charges, claiming that "because of the basic 'difference in psychology' . . . the Dominican 'race has a totally different conception of right and wrong from that held by the white race.'"[44] In an interview in 1999, ninety-four-year-old Juan Valdés Sánchez recalled that "the Americans killed many workers from our farm," because, in some cases, "few Americans spoke Spanish, and this occasioned many misunderstandings and tragedies."[45] Philip Douglass, a correspondent for the U.S.-based *Nation* magazine, commented on the marines' rough treatment of Dominicans. While Douglass was walking around in Santo Domingo, a marine approached him and yelled a question: "Where the hell the wharf was" in "five per cent pidgin Spanish." Douglass concluded, "I probably avoided a two-to-one street-brawl by answering him in English." While returning to his hotel, Douglass witnessed a marine grab one of the "colored boys" nearby: "The marine was about to give him a good beating with the stick the boy was carrying when I intervened." The marine accused the young man of throwing a stone at another officer but admitted that he had not seen him before. The marine let the boy go, but not without a "shove in the neck and an aspersion on his parentage."[46] One especially sadistic marine, Captain Frederick Merkel, committed suicide after his arrest for the deaths and torture of Dominican civilians under his command. "To this gentle soul [Merkel]," one commentator noted, "the water cure [water boarding] was but the merest reprimand."[47] U.S. authorities arrested Merkel after discovering he had tortured a Dominican prisoner by pouring salt and orange juice into the prisoner's wounds and then cutting off his ears.[48]

The violence and racism that buttressed U.S. occupation was placed into full relief as more critical evaluations of the occupation saturated debates in the U.S. and Dominican press about ending military governance. In 1920 the U.S. Senate organized a committee of inquiry to investigate accusations that U.S. Marines were abusing their authority and mistreating Dominicans and Haitians. That same year, the U.S. Senate, the military authorities, and Dominican officials began discussing the withdrawal of the marines from Dominican soil. Two plans were announced for ending the occupation. The Wilson Plan, formulated in 1920, outlined a gradual withdrawal of U.S. troops under the guidance of a Dominican consulting council selected by the military governor. The Harding Plan, offered in 1921, stipulated an immediate withdrawal on the condition that Dominicans commission a U.S.-officered national guard, broaden the terms of the U.S. receivership established in 1907 to include collecting internal revenues, and validate a $2.5 million loan for public-works construction. The collapse of the sugar market in 1921 added a sense of urgency to the question of ending the occupation when it became clear that the military government would not be able to finance much-needed infrastructure projects and public-health programs or expand the national police force without financial support from Washington.[49]

The idea of race war and the need for racial improvement framed how military officials understood the goals of the occupation. By the 1920s, these same ideas framed debates about Dominicans' readiness to govern their country. The first element of U.S. military officials' understanding of "race war" in Hispaniola concerned the training of the Dominican National Guard, established by Executive Order 47, signed in 1917 by the military governor, Admiral Henry Knapp. The Dominican National Guard absorbed within its ranks the Dominican Navy and the Republican Guard. As in other countries under U.S. occupation, the goal of creating a national police force was to "support the government established when the new Constitutional President [was] elected."[50]

Lieutenant Edward A. Fellowes, a captain in the Dominican National Guard, opened a training school for officers in Haina. Writing about the school's first day, he remarked, tongue-in-cheek, that "the prospects looked black." He described Dominicans' responding to his "halting and inaccurate Spanish . . . with a smile showing the wide expanse of white teeth against an ebony background." After quelling the initial "tantrums" that made his first day at work particularly difficult, he and his staff worked on transforming "green (dark green) rookies" and "wild bushwhackers" into officers. Most important to my argument, Fellowes admitted using skin color as a way to assess the readiness of troops under his command, since phenotype allowed him to guess their biological race and their capacity for leadership: "As a general rule, the degree of intelligence increased with the decrease of the ebony tinge. . . . Those who were of clearer complexion usually were more intelligent, and could be trusted with responsible jobs. . . . Practically all of our best non-commissioned officers were either of Porto Rican descent, or had a larger proportion of Spanish than Negro blood in their veins."[51]

In this instance, Fellowes may just have been following orders from his superiors. When the marines established the guard, the governor claimed to have received complaints from the "better class" of Dominicans because they allowed too many Dominicans of a "lower class" to join it. An anonymous letter from someone high up instructed marines to recruit white or lighter-skinned Dominicans in an effort to cultivate good feelings between Dominicans and the military government: "I have given unofficial instructions to 'lighten' the Guardia a little. My observation indicates that it was a little too black, since the people do not pride themselves on their percentage of black, but on their percentage of white."[52]

Rafael Trujillo's rapid rise through the ranks of the national guard may best demonstrate how those perceived as lighter in color and therefore with more European blood in their veins, benefited from institutionalized racism. As a child growing up in San Cristóbal, Trujillo often played "the general," using bottle caps as medals. As a young trainee at Haina, Trujillo quickly earned the respect of his marine trainers. Once an officer, his personal wealth grew and his social status improved.[53] Given the U.S. military's preference for officers of less visible African ancestry, Trujillo appears to have reaped the benefits of an emerging racist system to whiten himself. Once he was president, Santo Domingo–based elites disregarded him as "a ruthless mulatto arriviste with Haitian [black] lineage,"[54] but Trujillo nurtured his strong ties to U.S. military authorities, who evaluated his commitment to order, cleanliness, and professional appearance as hallmarks of his officer's training during the occupation. Eric Roorda cites a British official who once commented, "[In] appearance [Trujillo] is slightly mulatto, but this is off-set by good military bearing."[55]

Racist violence characterized many interactions between marines and ordinary Dominicans, but at the level of official policy and institution building, U.S. military officials appear to have accepted that those Dominicans who were lighter skinned were European enough and therefore equipped with the capacity to learn how to govern correctly under U.S. tutelage. As mulattos, therefore, Dominicans fared better than Haitians, whom U.S. military officials often regarded as pure "black." The racial difference between Haitians and Dominicans, in which some Dominicans were perceived as racially mixed and thus closer to Europeans, justified, for many U.S. authorities, continued military governance of Haiti and the end of occupation for the Dominican Republic. For example, George C. Thorpe, former chief of staff of the brigade of marines in the Dominican Republic, opined that Haiti had been populated by "savages" and thus constituted a "Black Republic [that was] far less civilized than Santo Domingo, known as the *Mulatto Republic*":

While there is a high percentage of ignorance in both countries, the Dominican is far more amenable to educating processes than is the Haitian
caco [peasant insurgent]. During my two years' stay in Santo Domingo,
the doors and windows of my house were always open and my personal
effects often unguarded, but the only time I was robbed, the thief was a
Haitian. In fact, a large part of the so-called bandits in Santo Domingo
are Haitians.[56]

As a mixed-race people, Dominicans fared better in the struggle for racial
improvement because, according to the theories of the time, their European
blood bequeathed them the capacity for intellectual growth through apprenticeship to U.S. military officials and foreign policy elites. Dominicans' racial
mixture was demonstrated in the 1920 census, which found that the country
was more *"mestizo"*—the preferred term to indicate mixed race—than white
or black. The census, the first national one in the modern era, engaged directly
with the idea of "racial" warfare and deepened the process of creating Dominicans as a mixed-race people on the basis of their proximity to European ancestry. In other words, U.S. military officials and census takers played a key role
in conflating Dominican *raza* with U.S.-centric meanings of racial identity. By
this, I refer specifically to "race" as "a theory of the organization of human difference that, even with the best of intentions, hides (or reveals) within itself a
structure of hierarchy."[57]

As Bruce Calder notes, military officials regarded the census as an important experiment in the government's efforts to make the Dominican civil service less partisan, more efficient, and more accountable to its citizens. Previous
Dominican governments had made provisions for national censuses to take
place, but these efforts had ultimately proved futile as regional warfare, bureaucratic inefficiency, and the lack of a workable transportation infrastructure undermined the government's well-intentioned efforts to count the population.
In contrast, the military government was aided by a centralized bureaucracy,
paid staff, the help of the marines, and the blueprints for a national census
designed by previous Dominican administrations. Although the extensive network of roads that the military government planned to build remained woe-
fully incomplete by the time census work began in 1919, the existing roads, the
military automobiles available, and the cooperation of district marine commanders enabled enumerators to travel with greater ease and complete their
important work.[58]

Teaching sound governance through data collection was not a neutral en-
deavor—much was at stake in organizing the social landscape of occupied

territories. In the Philippines under U.S. military rule, Governor-General William Taft noted that "the taking of the census will . . . form a test of the capacity of the Filipinos to discharge a most important function of government."[59] Census taking in areas colonized by the United States, Vicente Rafael argues, was meant as a test of self-governance and self-mastery, qualities that the U.S. authorities believed were forged through "a long apprenticeship of obedience" that resulted in political and cultural maturity.[60] Data collection and the provision of civil services, in other words, were part of the civilizing mission of a global empire meant to prepare Dominicans, Filipinos, Nicaraguans, and Haitians for home rule.

The 1920 Dominican census was completed under the direction of the provisional president, Juan Bautista Vicini Burgos, and the ministers of the interior and police, José del Carmen Ariza and Manuel de Jesús Troncoso de la Concha, and it was administered by educators. Like the U.S. census, it was designed to quantify what U.S. officials regarded as a "social and political order [that] was largely defined by race,"[61] in other words, a social system in which skin color, a signifier of ancestry, overdetermined one's access to goods, services, and political power. U.S. military authorities were not simply interested in managing a racially mixed population. Quantifying, ordering, classifying, and imagining a social landscape in terms of how North Americans understood race meant transforming color—*blanco, mestizo,* and *negro*—into fixed racial categories based on blood quantum. In U.S.-occupied Hispaniola, racist paternalism operated at two levels: as racial betterment to prepare Haitians and Dominicans for self-governance; and through racist practices within institutions that redefined variations in color as racial differences.

The 1920 census used the same color categories as those employed in Santo Domingo's 1908 census—white, *mestizo,* black—and in U.S. censuses, including the one taken in 1919–1920.[62] U.S. military officials would have been very familiar with a three-tiered racial classification system because, since 1850, the Census Bureau, at Congress's insistence, had recognized mulattos as a segment of the U.S. population distinct from blacks. In 1890 federal officials added "quadroons" and "octoroons" to the count in order to determine whether the racially mixed portion of the black population was disappearing or becoming more "Negro." By 1920, however, the Census Bureau had dropped "quadroon" and "octoroon" from the schedules, but "mulatto" remained. A person was deemed "mulatto" if he had "from three-eighths to five-eighths black blood." "White," however, was also a contested category in U.S. censuses produced between 1850 and 1920. In addition to debating whether all Europeans should be counted as "white" or grouped in terms of their nationality, politicians and statisticians differed over whether classification by "race" should be limited to the foreign-born immigrants, include the world's major races (whites, blacks, yellows), or be abandoned altogether.[63]

The U.S. military authorities in occupied territories achieved what the U.S. Congress and the Census Bureau in Washington could not: they came to a consensus about who counted as white. In the Dominican Republic, U.S. military officials limited "*blanco*" to native-born persons regarded by the census taker as "white"; "*mestizo*" included "*amarillo*" (Asian) and "*negro*" was applied to Haitians and others deemed black.[64] The Dominican census of 1920 brought into sharp relief the small size of the white minority on which U.S. authorities could depend to take political power once occupation ended. Moreover, "*blanco*" was the most narrowly defined category and included European and Middle Eastern immigrants. Census takers counted a total of 894,655 inhabitants of the Dominican Republic, of whom 25 percent (223,144) were white. The whitest provinces were those in the north, Santiago and Pacificador, but even there, where whites accounted for 35 percent of the population, the "colored" population was twice its size. "*Mestizo*" was the broadest category, accounting for nearly half of the Dominican population, 49.7 percent (444,587). According to Félix Evaristo Mejía, writing at the time, "*mestizo*" "ranged from genuine mulatto to almost white."[65] "*Negro*" included 25 percent of the population, although this category apparently caused some confusion among enumerators. In contrast to the 1908 census, census takers in 1920 incorporated Haitians as part of the "*negro*" category. They also distinguished Dominican and Haitian *negros* by counting Haitians as foreigners, noting that Haitians made up 57 percent of the foreign population (49,520).[66]

By this reckoning, *mestizos* and *negros* outnumbered whites three to one. The *negro* population, however, did not include Afro-Antillean West Indians, whom census enumerators counted among the foreign-born and who made up 16.8 percent of the immigrant population. West Indians and Haitians combined made the foreign resident population mostly black, accounting for nearly 75 percent of the 49,520 foreign-born residents.

Closer to the ground, the numbers are even more significant. By 1920 San Pedro had become the third-largest city in the country, after Santo Domingo and Santiago, with a population that reached almost 13,802 within the city's limits. San Pedro *común* brought the population to 25,300. The province of San Pedro, with a total population of nearly 28,500, had the highest percentage of foreign residents in the country, about 26 percent (some 10,145 people).[67]

By 1920 the Dominican Republic was clearly a multiethnic and multicultural nation, but it had also become one in which race organized the social order. As District Attorney Fernando Brea had feared, "racial differences [of a sort] the country [had] never known" had indeed become part of official government policy. Among the lessons Trujillo and many others probably learned during the U.S. occupation, perceptions of Dominicans' race mattered greatly in foreign affairs, and the closer Dominicans were to whiteness, the more positively they would be received in the international arena. This was the case because, according to Lloyd E. Ambrosius, antiblack racism motivated Woodrow Wilson's liberal internationalism explicitly; the United States' mission in the world was ostensibly to bring liberal democracy to all, but what it actually meant was protecting white supremacy at home and abroad.[68]

Whether Dominican elites became more or less anti-Haitian or antiblack as a result of U.S. occupation is difficult to gauge. Vocal antioccupation activists did demonstrate, though, an awareness that a new politics of race had emerged thanks to U.S. occupation and hegemony in the western hemisphere. In its version, the United States had engaged in a race war against sovereign nations whose peoples it deemed racially inferior. For example, in a broadside encouraging Dominicans to abstain from participating in the vote to end the occupation according to the terms outlined in the Harding Plan, radical nationalists (so called because they advocated immediate withdrawal without a treaty) exposed the racist nature of the occupation: "Just think about the contempt they have for us because we are not white like them!"[69] Moderate nationalists, who supported the idea of voting for an appropriate plan to end the occupation, also dismissed race-based justifications for the occupation. Former presidential candidate and member of the Supreme Court Federico Henríquez y Carvajal published a letter in the New York–based newspaper *Las Novedades* in which he argued that the racial and ethnic composition of a nation-state did not nullify its membership in the family of sovereign nations. Nor did race determine a nation's economic, social, and political trajectory or make one nation superior to another:

> It is incorrect to find within the ethnic composition of a people the only, exclusive, and original cause of the precarious political state of those nations. As in those countries where the population includes a strong proportion of the black race, in the rest of [the] Americas where that race does not exist or has been extinguished through the diffusion between other races, revolutions have existed or continue to this day, alternating between authoritarian governments . . . one can be assured that if, all of a sudden, the entire institutional system of the United States transformed

itself unfavorably . . . the most terrible revolutions would break out in this country, perpetuated by the blue-eyed race.[70]

Occupation in the name of modernization was a grievous injustice, even more so because it was perpetuated on the basis of racist assumptions. These nationalists appear to have understood, as Matthew Guterl argues in the case of occupied Haiti, that "the multifaceted superiority of 'white America' was inscribed upon the life of [the Dominican Republic] by the legions of bankers, technophiles, artists, anthropologists, politicians, soldiers, and scientists who approached the island as an experiment in social engineering."[71] Jacinto López, for example, denounced the occupation because foreigners had inflicted a number of cruelties on a nation he described as a "civilized, Christian people" living in the "cradle of Christian civilization in America."[72]

Despite overwhelming evidence that U.S. foreign policy elites and military officials regarded and treated Dominicans as racially inferior, nonwhite people, Dominican nationalists did not embrace the progressive theories of race and nation from their late nineteenth-century intellectual traditions—*mulatismo* and *antillanismo*. Nor did they flock to the UNIA or to the National Association for the Advancement of Colored People (NAACP) for support in their anti-imperialist efforts. At the same moment when activists such as Garvey, W.E.B. Dubois, Hubert Henry Harrison, and James Weldon Johnson began to imagine the possibility of a worldwide revolt of the colored masses against white colonizers, Dominican nationalists elaborated an ideology of *dominicanidad* centered on Dominicans' biological and cultural connections to the "Latin" race, *latinidad*. *Latinidad* comprised a reactionary, conservative response to the U.S. occupation that, like *hispanicismo*, elevated Spanish cultural norms but also emphasized social order, patriarchy, and racial identity. *Latinidad* proponents also drew on Galván's reconciliation with Spain and the idea that Hispanics were fundamentally a white race, but in contrast to his idea that Dominicans could not be a sovereign nation, occupation-era activists insisted that "Latin" people were morally superior to Anglo-Saxons, as they described their U.S. and British counterparts. Nationhood for Dominicans became possible once they embraced their racial difference as members of the "Latin" race through which they could claim parity with Anglo-Saxons.

The intellectual José Ramón López evidenced this shift toward *latinidad* in articles he published between 1913 and 1917. Born in Montecristi in 1866, López grew up and attended a school in Puerto Plata directed by an exiled Cuban, Antonio Benítez y Correoso. The school was housed in a building owned by Gregorio Luperón and shared space with the Sociedad Liga de las Antillas (Antillean League Society). During his studies, López could have easily crossed paths with Eugenio María de Hostos, Ramón Emeterio Betances, and Luperón himself.[73] Although López was not trained by Hostos, Hostosian ideals were interwoven in his thinking about governance, the work of civilizing Dominicans, and the role of the intellectual. In 1913 he published a piece in which he outlined a future for Dominicans as "domínico-antillanos." As he explained then, "I am not for *latinidad* . . . because the speedy approximation [of all things] Latin in our times undermines the Antillean Confederation or, at the very least, retards it indefinitely."[74] However, in 1916 López, in a piece that outlined the six stages of U.S. imperialism in the Americas, declared, "The Dominican nation is mentally and morally Latino," and that this reaction against U.S. occupation had turned friends of the United States into its enemies.[75]

In addition to their anti-imperialism, Latin men rebuked violence as a legitimate form of protest, primarily because Dominicans could not militarily defeat North American troops. One editorialist made the distinction between a "bandit" of the like who had recently kidnapped Thomas Steele, a sugar-estate manager, and a "patriot." The patriot was "the citizen who loves his country, who desires and procures its well-being as he is able to do so"; the "bandit" was "a thief, [a] highway robber, who ordinarily runs with an armed band." The true citizen defended liberty "within the realm of civility"; a Dominican bandit was, he insisted, like "Apaches, the Ku Klux Klan, and all those who, in one form or another, disturb social tranquillity with their savage acts."[76] The interesting reference to the Ku Klux Klan notwithstanding, Dominican nationalists clearly felt it was within their interests to present themselves and the Dominican nation in the most civilizing way possible. Unable to claim whiteness and unwilling to claim Pan-Africanism, they opted for *latinidad*.

For Dominican nationalists and the U.S. military authorities, the return of Dominican sovereignty in 1924 was part of a racialized and, as we will examine in the next chapter, a gendered debate over the successes and failures of the U.S. occupation. Military officials understood U.S. hegemony in the Caribbean as part of a larger civilizing mission to bring the "lesser" races into modernity through racist paternalism. Dominican nationalists offered powerful critiques of the racist assumptions that motivated the occupation; they opened the possibility of reimagining Dominican national and racial identity in different ways. Clearly, however, the limits of the politically possible had changed drastically since the late 1890s, when the Dominican, Cuban, and Puerto Rican anticolonial struggle inspired creative, even radical, ideas about race and nation.

As in the 1890s, Dominican nationalists in the early twentieth century reflected on their condition in hemispheric terms. In contrast to that earlier period, antioccupation activists did not respond to the racist politics of the occupation with an idealized notion of racial mixedness (as in José Vasconcelos's *raza cósmica*) or even the racial transcendence of Pan-Antilleanism. They embraced *latinidad*, rooted in the idea of their biologically derived difference from Anglo-Saxons, based on Latinos' distinct moral compass, sentimentality, and spirituality. Through *latinidad*, Dominican nationalists were able to claim whiteness.

This was an important strategic move; in occupied Hispaniola black domination was a real threat. For both Dominican nationalists and the U.S. military authorities, the return of Dominican sovereignty depended on the monopoly of political power held by white or light-skinned Dominican men. Garveyism challenged and threatened white supremacy and the future of Dominican independence. Essays and editorials produced by leaders of the nationalist movement evidence the choice made by Dominican elites. Rather than regard the black male as representative of the body politic, they opted for a discourse of "civilized" patriarchal authority that laid the foundation for the acceptance of a virulently antiblack nationalist ideology, *hispanidad*. What remained to be accomplished was the diffusion of *hispanidad* across the country.

GENDER AND *HISPANIDAD* IN THE NEW ERA

Many years after her mother, Sarah Loguen Fraser, made a similar journey from the United States to Puerto Plata, Gregoria Fraser Goins returned to the Dominican Republic in 1939. Disembarking in San Pedro de Macorís, Goins traveled by car to Puerto Plata and arrived there on July 29: "Down we came in spirals . . . and finally the Atlantic Ocean . . . what breathtaking beauty . . . and Puerto Plata came into view. Into the town and the first thing I recognized was the Wesleyan Church." People recognized her too: ninety-five-year-old Mary Ann hugged her and spoke kindly about her parents; the children of domestics who had once worked in their home, a son of the intellectual Eugenio Deschamps, and members of the Brugal family personalized the return home. As she wrote, "How I love this spot on earth. The ice wall formed by so many years of repression is gradually beginning to melt, will I actually once more live and feel?"[1]

Returning to a Dominican Republic under General Rafael Trujillo's rule certainly helped Gregoria "feel" her Dominicanness again. She had apparently continued to speak the Spanish she grew up with but also converted to Catholicism, leaving behind the Protestant heritage of her parents and late husband. Shortly after her return to Puerto Plata, Gregoria's particular longing to feel connected to a place and to a people found its answer in Trujillo-era pageantry when the "Padre de la Patria" (Founding Father) also arrived for a visit. Gregoria cried during the mass in honor of the Virgin of Las Mercedes and noted that taking communion in Puerto Plata differed from approaching the rail in the United States: "there seems to be more awesomeness and reverence in my attitude . . . the partaking seems to bring me more spiritual strength." After General Rafael Trujillo's yacht appeared in the port, Gregoria and friends from the Women's Club went down to get a view. "The crowd was so great and congested that I was properly squeezed," she wrote. Being nearly trampled, however, did not deter Gregoria from rising at five the next morning to join the children and "truckloads of men" to have "one grand time . . . for our own."[2]

"For our own." This phrase echoed Frederick Douglass's claims made nearly a half century earlier that U.S. African Americans could feel the full measure of their manhood in the Dominican Republic. Like her forebears, Gregoria went to the Dominican Republic for opportunity; she swapped racist repression in the Jim Crow United States for active engagement with Trujillo-era nation building. Trujillo's national project (1930–1961), draped in the religious piety of devotion to Mary and lived vividly through large, public marches and rallies, attracted numerous educated, reform-minded women. Mass demonstrations, fairs, and pageants helped Dominicans believe in Trujillo and see in him the nation's future. As an educated and religious woman, claiming ownership of a national project, "for our own," hints at the gendered dimensions of Trujillo-era nationalism.

This chapter bridges the gap between the historiography on women's activism and studies of the Trujillo era. I begin with the premise that modernizing state regimes and changing gender norms are mutually constitutive processes.[3] For example, just one year into his thirty-one-year dictatorship, Trujillo carefully nurtured the loyalties of feminists when he championed suffrage in a speech he gave during the first-anniversary celebration of Dominican Feminist Action (Acción Feminista Dominicana, AFD), held at Santo Domingo's Athenaeum on May 14, 1932.[4] By then, AFD was the country's largest feminist organization, and the Athenaeum was the nation's most prestigious intellectual venue. General Trujillo used the occasion to win the AFD's support when he proclaimed his support for women's suffrage: "It would benefit Dominican society if our women brought their delicate sentiments to the public arena."[5] The Dominican Congress finally granted women the vote in 1942; that same year the AFD became the Women's Branch of the Partido Dominicano (Rama Femenina del Partido Trujillista adscrita al Partido Dominicano).[6]

However, in one of the first major studies about the Trujillo dictatorship, published in Chile in 1956, political exile Jesús de Galíndez dismissed the feminist movement as Trujillo's creation. Prior to 1940, Galíndez argued, "there was no spontaneous movement." Even worse, he reported, when Trujillo made clear his intentions to change Dominican women's legal status, this "triggered a hotbed of jealousies between those women who aspired to lead the movement and take advantage of its benefits." The struggle, according to Galíndez, pitted feminist leader Abigaíl Mejía and Delia Weber de Coiscou, an artist, against another contingent of reformers headed by Carmen G. de Peynado, wife of former president Francisco J. Peynado.[7] Roberto Crassweller was equally dismissive in his assessment of Trujillo feminism, labeling it a strategic marketing campaign aimed at deflecting criticism of his regime. Embracing feminism, according to Crassweller, allowed Trujillo to construct an image of his government as progressive, modern, and democratic.[8]

One possible result of this dismissive attitude toward the women's movement during the Trujillo era has been the development of two historiographies: one devoted to the study of exemplary Dominican women and feminism; the other focused on the Trujillo dictatorship as a violent, authoritarian regime.[9] Another outcome is contemporary Dominican feminists' discomfort with claiming Trujillo-era feminism as a part of their history. Debates about female activism during the dictatorship—its significance and possible contribution to the evolution of feminist thought in the Dominican Republic—still occur among Dominican feminists, especially those who came of age during the last years of the dictatorship and grew into political consciousness during Juan Bosch's short term as president (1961–1963); among those women who fought against U.S. invasion during the civil war in April of 1965; and among those who went into exile or underground political activity during Joaquín Balaguer's bloody regime (known as "the 12 Years," 1966–1978).[10]

Rather than accept Trujillo's turn to educated, activist women as cynical political farce or erase women as political actors in the early decades of his regime, I argue that feminism was a necessary building block for the regime because, by the 1930s, feminists had provided Dominican political culture with important tools: a nationwide organizational structure (through the AFD); island-wide media through magazines such as *Fémina*; ties to hemispheric and international organizations; a new theory of state, nation, and citizen; and, most important, thousands of women anxious and able to lend a helping hand to modernizing Dominican society.

Official Trujillo feminism did not mean that all activist women were *trujillistas* (supporters of the regime). Making this distinction explicit may address the quite understandable reservations expressed by present-day Dominican feminists about Trujillo-era feminism. Some of the people featured in this chapter, such as Ercilia Pepín and Américo Lugo, for example, adopted anti-Trujillo stances even as some of their writings, letters, and lectures informed the regime's ideological evolution toward *hispanidad* nationalism. Yet, an analysis of Trujillo-era feminism can address important questions whose implications go far beyond the Dominican Republic and Trujillo: Why do women become important in state building efforts? How do ideas and idealizations about men and women shape new policies and new politics in eras of radical change and social transformation?

Like modernizing regimes throughout the Americas in the 1920s through the 1940s, the Trujillo dictatorship drew women into the nationalist project. I contend that by examining the early period of the Trujillato as if gender ideologies and women mattered, we can trace the continuities that link *hispanicismo*, Hostosian social thought, and *latinidad* nationalism with *hispanidad* nationalism. We can also highlight important differences and tensions within these idealizations of the Dominican nation. Securing Dominicans' adherence to a national ideal became crucial, particularly during the first decade of the regime, when, in the wake of the Haitian Massacre in 1937,[11] Trujillo and his intellectual cadres elaborated a virulently anti-Haitian, patriarchal nationalist ideal, *hispanidad*. Trujillo leaned on activist women to transform *hispanidad* from an ideal into daily practice.

. . .

Dominican feminism and female-led social reform were products of ideological currents and transformations in education that spanned the late nineteenth and early twentieth centuries. Eugenio María de Hostos and Gregorio Luperón valued educated women's contributions to Dominican nation building. Secular education prepared women intellectually and also gave them the organizational capacity to mobilize activist networks across the island. Education also played an important role in women identifying as a group invested in social reform. At the same time, though, Hostos's *moral social* emphasized the home as women's main sphere of influence; domestic life was a model of the social world. The *moral social*, as I argue in chapter 3, influenced San Pedro's associational culture and bequeathed a complex, contradictory legacy for female activists.

During the late nineteenth century and into the first decades of the twentieth century, the *normalista*, the teacher, symbolized the virtuous, educated woman committed to social uplift and national progress.[12] Eugenio María de Hostos convinced his Dominican counterparts that "women [were] an integral part of society." The *normalista* ideal became a dominant one thanks to Salomé Ureña Henríquez's early leadership in women's education. She made teaching a respectable form of employment for women in the 1890s and early 1900s, a time of economic depression. Although female employment challenged traditional gender norms, the *normalista* model transformed educated women's domestic labors (including teaching, which often took place in women's homes) into virtuous activities through which elite and upwardly mobile women addressed social problems without questioning the naturalness of sex differences.[13]

One of these committed *normalistas* was Dr. Evangelina Rodríguez. Born the child of unwed parents, she grew up on the streets of San Pedro de Macorís selling sweets with her grandmother. As a streetwise adolescent, Rodríguez should have become one of the many poor women of color hounded by San Pedro's police, but the arduous work she performed for the renowned poets Gastón and Rafael Deligne became her ticket to upward mobility. At the urging of the Deligne brothers, Anacaona Moscoso, a graduate of Salomé Ureña's school and the founding director of the Salomé Ureña Institute in San Pedro, admitted Rodríguez. After graduation in 1903, she attended medical school in Santo Domingo but returned to San Pedro in 1907 to direct the institute after Moscoso died in childbirth (figure 6.1).[14]

While teaching in San Pedro and completing her medical degree in Santo Domingo, Rodríguez wrote *Granos de polen*, a collection of essays that reflect the profound influence of Hostos's *moral social* on her intellectual life and ideas for social reform. Her friend, the prominent intellectual José Ramón López, applauded her effort, as he wrote in the book's prologue, "Our regeneration, I repeat, is not in the law, but in the customs that mothers plant in the tender hearts of future Latin Americans."[15] *Granos* was meant to be a guide for the educated woman in this regenerating work. For example, Rodríguez insisted that educated people were responsible for "curing" the poor of their "indolence." This was possible because "our masses are not instinctively perverse;

Figure 6.1. Evangelina Rodríguez. Archivo General de la Nación.

they are immoral for lack of education." She also argued that nurture, not nature, caused the masses' "moral poverty": "a man's ideas [arise] according to the environment that surrounds him. In miserable [conditions], [one] has little more than small, petty things. . . . An elevated and healthy environment brings forth high and healthy ideas and [men from this class] are civilized and lucid."[16]

These more progressive interventions, however, cannot be separated from the parts of *Granos* in which Rodríguez, following Hostos, stresses the naturalness of the hierarchy between men and women based on their biological differences. For instance, although she encourages women to provide the masses with "conscientious direction," she warns them not to "emasculate" their husbands with their intellect: "Don't even think about it, ever. . . . Do not upbraid him because it would be like robbing him of the only thing he has." The Dominican household under the care of the conscientious mother was the nation's incubator; therefore, women's domestic labors were critical to national development and were serious responsibilities that demanded women's full attention.[17]

Rodríguez's *Granos* treats all Dominican women as potential *normalistas*. As *normalistas*, women educated in secular schools were primed to help their male counterparts cultivate national progress. As such, *Granos* represents the profound influence of Hostosian thought on a select group of economically mobile women who came of age between 1880 and 1916 and who became, as a result of these educational reforms, among the first Dominican women to identify as social reformers and feminists.[18] This occurred because small groups of teachers trained with the same women and then brought their skills to their communities. For example, Anacaona Moscoso studied at Salomé Ureña's Institute for Young Women in Santo Domingo and then established a school in San Pedro where Evangelina Rodríguez studied. Casimira Heureaux Figuereo, daughter of the former dictator, studied at the Young Women's Institute in Santo Domingo, graduated as a *normalista*, and, along with Rodríguez, founded a night school for working women. Mercedes Laura Aguiar was also among the first graduates of the Young Women's Institute, and she taught in San Pedro, primarily Afro-Antillean immigrant children. Ana Teresa Acevedo Camarena studied with Salomé Ureña in Santo Domingo, graduated as a *normalista*, returned to San Pedro, where she taught and, in collaboration with Evangelina Rodríguez, founded the Sociedad Protectora de Niños Escolares Pobres (Protective Society for Poor Schoolchildren). Isabel Rojo Carbuccia, the daughter of Spanish and Italian immigrants and a graduated *nor-*

malista, was also one of the founders of the first women's club in San Pedro, El Abanico.[19] As Lori Ginzberg has observed for the nineteenth-century United States, women's education and activism were important in the transformation of local elites into a nationally integrated and powerful interest group.[20]

Prior to the U.S. invasion and occupation, *normalistas* played an instrumental role in cultivating a political identity for men and women from the dominant political and social class, composed of intellectuals and professionals. Yet the U.S. occupation added another complex layer onto Dominican feminist theory and activism. As I argue in previous chapters, San Pedro's elite embraced an *hispanicismo* that privileged whiteness and European ancestry as wealthy, white immigrants became part of the dominant class in the city. During the occupation, the discursive tone of some male nationalists became even more racially explicit and decidedly patriarchal, affirming the authority of Latin men as the foundation of Dominican society in the postoccupation period. To preserve a space for their activism within the ideological strictures of *latinidad*, Dominican feminists justified their activism in anti-imperialist language and through adherence to a Latin identity.

Women were pivotal in the struggle against the U.S. military occupation of the Dominican Republic from 1916 to 1924, in part as a result of the intervention itself, which had profoundly transformed the political landscape and social norms in women's favor.[21] On the one hand, the arena of acceptable female activity broadened under the occupation as the military government expanded the economic and professional opportunities available for women. Executive Order 201 allowed women to practice law, and Order 338 permitted all women to practice medicine and other health-related occupations without special permission. The occupation government even offered women gainful employment in the state bureaucracy as clerks, typists, and secretaries. Following a precedent established in Puerto Rico, the military government hoped that these measures would be taken as evidence of the progressiveness and benevolence of U.S. rule.[22]

One result of these measures, though, was a fierce reaction among Dominican men. While U.S. officials viewed women entering the professions as progress, some male commentators considered women's visibility in the public sphere and their seemingly high appreciation for U.S. consumer goods, fashion, and hairstyles an affront to Hispanic culture.[23] As did their counterparts in Nicaragua (also under U.S. occupation at this time), male antioccupation activists perceived that Dominican women had uncritically and unpatriotically embraced U.S. cultural norms. As a result, they made the rejection of U.S. values the cornerstone of their antioccupation, anti-imperialist campaign.[24]

During the occupation, anti-imperialist activists embraced transnational *latinidad* as an ideological counterpoint to U.S. hegemony and U.S.-driven Pan-Americanism.

Horacio Blanco, for example, argued that North Americans "[threatened] the traditional modesty of Dominican women" and reproached women for neglecting their traditional duties, such as devotion to domestic labors.[25] An anonymous commentator in Santiago indicted Dominican women for learning the "wrong" lessons from the occupation: "Nine things our women have learned in six years: To show their legs more than they should. To go marketing, playing the role of servants. To become typists and neglect the kitchen. To go out racing in automobiles or in airplanes with whomever they think best. To become chauffeurs. To marry for business. To cross their legs in public places. To wear excessively low-cut dresses and to dance in cafes and restaurants."[26]

As these critiques suggest, male nationalists had specific ideas about how women could contribute to the antioccupation cause by returning to tradition. For instance, the all-male executive committee of the National Dominican Union, founded "for the purpose of saving the Dominican people from the danger of being prostituted," emphasized the "virility and dignity" of the Dominican people and proclaimed, "The day has already arrived when the Dominican people shall grasp the fruit of their manly resistance and . . . the United States shall withdraw."[27] Nationalists also insisted that Dominican men "embrace each other in paternal love."[28] Federico Antonio García, a vocal nationalist, was even more specific. He argued that true patriotism revealed itself in the manner in which men transformed their households into "temples of perfection," protected their manly honor, and sheltered the virtue of their wives and children. Patriotic duty, García insisted, rested in the man "who married, kept his wife saintly, and transformed his children into a *holy family*."[29]

Some male antioccupation activists equated the loss of Dominican sovereignty with the nation being "prostituted" against its will. In the 1920s Dominican Republic, at the height of the campaign against clandestine sexual commerce, the prostitute was a highly charged image, as suggested in the commentary by the anonymous writer from Santiago. His complaint that women were now "playing the role of servants," wearing suggestive clothing, dancing in bars, and taking off "with whomever they think best," implies that the "modern girl" was little more than a prostitute in the minds of some and could easily be confused as one. This suggests that Dominicans thinking critically about U.S. occupation drew a connection between notions of sexual deviance and transgression and intervention. So as not to prostitute the nation any more, male nationalists idealized domesticity and the family as the new foundation of the nation. Women were present as daughters, wives, or mothers but invisible as independent agents or political actors.[30]

While some male nationalists blamed women for behaving badly in the face of foreign occupation, other men and women active in the antioccupation campaign turned to hemispheric organizing to protest U.S. hegemony. Dominican men and women contributed to the creation and spread of Pan-Iberian, pro-Hispanic organizations, and they helped in the formulation of a Latin American response to U.S.-driven Pan-Americanism. During the occupation, nationalist manifestations such as Semanas Patrióticas (Patriotic Weeks) in June and July of 1920 and 1922, and activist-intellectuals such as Américo Lugo, Ercilia Pepín, and Petronila Angélica Gómez, the founding editor of the feminist magazine *Fémina*, emphasized Dominicans' belonging to a Latin race, united in its opposition to U.S. imperialism. *Latinidad* provided an important counternarrative to U.S. hegemony in the region. Most important, in the hands of feminists like Pepín and Gómez, *latinidad* (inter)nationalism preserved a space for female activism. At the time, however, *latinidad*, like Hostosian social thought, was double-edged. While national and transhemispheric activism as Ibero-Americans, Hispanics, and Latin Americans proved immensely popular and meaningful, this ideological turn imposed its own limits on strategy and political imagination.

Américo Lugo was a particularly formidable voice who advocated an Iberian-American response to Pan-Americanism. Lugo was born in 1870 and studied in Hostos's Professional Institute, where he earned a doctorate in law. He rejected U.S. military occupation and encouraged Dominicans to resist all efforts to end the intervention on terms favorable to the United States. Jailed various times for his anti-imperialist writings, Lugo founded the newspaper *Patria*, in which he published editorials critical of both the occupation government and Dominican party politics. In the pages of *Patria* and elsewhere, he drew on nineteenth-century *hispanicismo* to argue that, indeed, Dominicans were the heirs of a noble Spanish tradition that had bequeathed them a religious, spiritual, and political heritage they had maintained since the colonial era. He pushed this thinking a bit further to claim, according to Rafael Darío Herrera, that Dominicans were one nation, one *raza*, "Spanish." Racial mixture with Africans and Jews, however, diminished the purity of this biological inheritance. On the one hand, Lugo insisted, "we are the products of Spaniards mixed with Africans, in which the affixed defects of the night people [Africans] have eclipsed the virtues of the day people [Europeans],"[31] leaving in their wake "miserable and ignorant rural masses." These ignorant masses, Lugo claimed, were not ready for universal suffrage since they existed beyond the "slightest notion of the state." Worse yet, he wrote, "the cause of our per-petual political failures as a nation is primarily because of suffrage accorded to the peasant majority."[32] Unfortunately, according to Lugo, Dominican politi-cal parties were no better prepared for the challenge of rebuilding Dominican sovereignty in the postoccupation period.

According to Lugo, although Dominicans' racial mixture made them nearly incapable of becoming a true nation, like their counterparts elsewhere in the Americas, Dominicans had remained "an exemplar of loyalty to the Mother Country [Spain]" and were "loyal . . . guardians of Spanish and Latin civiliza-tion in the Americas." Well before the occupation, in 1912, Lugo had argued that Pan-Americanism brought together "*iberoamericanismo*" and "*angloameri-canismo.*" At that time, and again in the late 1920s, Lugo argued for the creation of a confederation of Hispanic republics where "consciousness of the Hispanic world would be popularized and mature . . . until . . . it became like a physiologi-cal need . . . second nature."[33] In Lugo's hands, *hispanicismo* was the means for confronting U.S. imperialism in the hemisphere. At the same time, however, its prescriptions were less democratic at home. Lugo's pessimistic *hispanicismo-latinidad* exposed the central tension within Hostosian nation-building ideol-ogy. The belief that the masses were unprepared to govern left open the ques-tion of which came first: helping the nation evolve toward governability, or creating a strong state to impose civilization from above?

Lugo's argument favoring a strong state apparatus to bring about the level of civilization necessary for Dominicans to be a true nation presented reform-minded women with a problem: without the vote or equal civil rights, what role did they play in building the new Dominican nation? In response to this question, female activists drew on another legacy of their mentor, Hostos: his emphasis on transnational and hemispheric activism. International politi-cal mobilization served women particularly well because feminists had long worked in a broader arena to advance changes for women throughout the hemisphere. Petronila Gómez and her magazine, *Fémina,* played a critical role in connecting the antioccupation movement in the Dominican Republic with interhemispheric organizations (figure 6.2).

Petronila Angélica Gómez was a woman of color and a "natural child" who, like Evangelina Rodríguez, also achieved extraordinary social mobility by becoming, in 1910, principal of San Pedro's first coeducational school.[34] That same year, the First International Women's Congress was held in Buenos Aires. There, reform-minded women outlined a number of goals that became the foundational tenets of liberal feminism throughout the continent: juridical status for women; access to education; maternity laws; prostitution reform;

Figure 6.2. Petronila
Angélica Gómez. Archivo
General de la Nación.

equal pay; and suffrage. These goals were further elaborated in 1922 during the Pan-American Association for the Advancement of Women meeting in Baltimore. In April of 1922 Dominican feminists organized their first Women's National Congress and formulated an agenda for social reform that mirrored the goals of feminist organizations throughout the Americas.[35] In July 1922, Gómez founded *Fémina*, organized the Dominican branch of the Liga Internacional de Mujeres Ibéricas e Hispanoamericanas (International League of Iberian and Hispanic American Women), and presided over the Liga Feminista de la República Dominicana (Feminist League of the Dominican Republic).[36]

Gómez's feminist vision was marked by the occupation and blended female social activism with a call to resist foreign rule. As she wrote in the first issue of *Fémina*, "we had conceived the purpose of publishing this magazine so that, working for national unity, [it could] offer a wide berth to Dominican women, so that this powerful agent [*Fémina*] would produce, without even the tiniest hindrance, fruitful and beneficial action."[37] For Gómez, women's activism had two objectives: to create a civilized citizenry, and to assist men in ending the occupation: "The country needs our practical service! In this great hour of moral social unrest, rise up, Dominican woman, and come to help your companion, the man. Today is the day to cooperate with him in that great work of social improvement!"[38] Gómez reiterated that Dominican women were not only moral but also "noble and patriotic." Even as they assumed nontraditional roles, their ultimate loyalty remained to the nation.[39]

Fémina connected the feminist movement in the Dominican Republic with its counterparts throughout the Spanish-speaking world in a way that underscored the centrality of Hispanic identity to anti-imperialist feminism. In one notable edition of *Fémina*, published in August of 1923, Gómez reproduced articles from *Feminismo Internacional* (International Feminism), the official paper of the International League of Iberian and Hispanic American Women. Complementing the establishment of the league's Committee of International Cooperation in the Dominican Republic, articles outlined the group's vision: "the larger work is educational, defensive, and constructive." It is almost certain that the creator of the league, Mexican feminist Elena Arizmendi de Duersch, wrote the anonymously published piece in which was outlined the league's goals: "to maintain constant communication between cultured, altruistic, and progressive Hispanic women and men ["de la raza"][in order] to cultivate and conserve solidarity, cooperation, and fraternity as the foundation of unity."[40]

In another issue, published near Columbus Day in 1923, Gómez devoted quite a number of pages to reflections on Columbus and the dream of a united Latin America. Included in this edition was the poem "La Santa María" by César Nicolás Pensón; a reflection on Columbus's significance by Joaquín María Bobea; and a contrived dialogue, "Los muertos hablan" (the dead speak) between José Martí and Eugenio María de Hostos in which both men reflect on the possibility that the Latin American republics will eventually unite. The author, Francisco Amiama Gómez, ended the piece with Martí proclaiming, "We are 'Twenty Brothers' with forty hands and 200 fingers."[41] As Arizmendi wrote in another article published in *Fémina*, "Spanish-speaking women [were] to help consolidate the Hispanic spirit [espíritu de la Raza]." Their work began in the home and extended from there "to the nation, and then to humanity."[42] In the 1920s, then, Latin/Hispanic feminism flowed naturally from anti-U.S. imperialism activism.

In the pages of her magazine, Gómez salvaged women's agency within a *latinidad* nationalism in which patriarchy, domesticity, and sexual propriety were venerated as central to the antioccupation struggle. One logical outcome was the appearance of "ladies' committees" to raise funds for the antioccupation campaign and to meet with women's groups throughout the hemisphere to formulate plans for resisting U.S. imperialism.[43] Santiago's

Club de Damas (Women's Club) began its celebration of Semana Patriótica with a mass, followed by a horse race, a concert, and a theater production. In Puerto Plata Mercedes H. de Tesson connected her generation's struggle against the occupation with the martyrdom of María Trinidad Sánchez, executed by firing squad in 1845 for refusing to reveal the whereabouts of her nephew and independence leader, Francisco del Rosario Sánchez: "[We are] awake and also struggle for the triumph of the second Restoration. . . . The Dominican woman has come here to also protest the Harding Plan, which is not only an insult to the Dominican people but also a grave dishonor to the North American people."[44] Fifteen hundred women from Santiago signed a petition against Admiral Robinson's announced plans for ending the occupation in June of 1921. In July 400 of Ercilia Pepín's female students joined 13,000 other people in a protest against Robinson and the occupation.[45]

Indeed, Ercilia Pepín, a feminist and educator from Santiago, began a one-woman antioccupation campaign, giving lectures in Santo Domingo, La Vega, Santiago, and Puerto Plata shortly after the invasion.[46] Her commitment to anti-imperialism was reflected in her refusal to accept her selection as the official delegate to the Pan-American Association for the Advancement of Women meeting in Baltimore. "It would be a special honor," she wrote to the military government, "but the abnormality of our true national life has been profoundly altered for the past five years," and her teaching duties forced her to decline the offer. In another gesture of her commitment to anti-imperialist activism, Pepín and her students sent an embroidered Nicaraguan flag to Augusto Sandino in 1928 in "fraternal solidarity" with his struggle to liberate Nicaragua from U.S. control. In response, Sandino demonstrated a deep appreciation for Pepín and her students, calling the flag a "sign . . . that there is unity of thought among the American peoples against Yankee imperialism" (figure 6.3).[47]

As a result of antioccupation activism and participation in Pan-Iberian and Pan–Latin American feminist organizations such as the Liga, activists like Gómez and Pepín made Dominican feminism decidedly anti-imperialist, but through the cultural matrix of *latinidad*. "Latin feminism" drew activists in the Dominican Republic closer to Spain and to the rest of Latin America, Cuba, and Puerto Rico but undermined the older Hostosian ideal of an Antillean confederation that included English-speaking islands.[48] They restored the *normalista* as a political actor by arguing that educated women's domestic labors and natural talents had civic value. At the same time, they tried to reassure nationalist men that female activism did not threaten Hispanic "tradition," the holy family on which it rested, and the significance of Latin culture in Dominican society. As Pepín once wrote, Latin feminists remained feminine "without losing [their]

Figure 6.3. Ercilia Pepín. Archivo General de la Nación.

graces, without scorning [their] beauty, without tempering [their] hearts, or becoming masculine because of [their] ideas, actions, or opinions."[49]

As in Cuba and Puerto Rico, transforming the household inspired social reformers to intervene directly in the domestic spaces of the working classes and reinforce class and race hierarchies. Through the lens of the patriotic household, these intrusions were not only benevolent, but also necessary to the creation of a strong state and civil society.[50] A strong state had been an elusive goal for Dominican elites from the 1860s until the U.S. military occupation. Américo Lugo argued in his doctoral thesis, "the Dominican people do not constitute a nation. It is undoubtedly a spiritual community united by language, customs, and other ties; but its lack of culture impedes the political development necessary for all peoples to become a nation."[51] For Lugo, Dominicans required a strong state apparatus to help them become a nation. Whereas Hostos had focused his attention on civilizing the Dominican nation,

Lugo reversed the order to emphasize, first, the formation of a strong state that would impose its will on the nation.[52]

San Pedro's Evangelina Rodríguez provides an appropriate example of how female activism engendered state formation. After publishing *Granos* in 1915, Dr. Rodríguez spent the years between 1918 and 1921 working as a doctor in San Francisco de Macorís. With a scholarship from San Pedro's city council, she trained in Paris in gynecology and obstetric medicine from 1921 to 1926. Residing in Europe exposed her to radical feminist demands such as safe access to contraception and the right to control reproduction.[53] From 1926 until her death in 1947, Rodríguez was a vocal advocate for San Pedro's poor women and children. She taught informal classes on basic hygiene and instructed midwives on ways to prevent infection during and after childbirth. She also established health clinics, providing free treatment to people suffering from diseases endemic to poor living conditions, such as tuberculosis and leprosy. At a time when female activists in Santo Domingo were focusing on city beautification, Rodríguez acknowledged the needs of poor women and encouraged educated *petromacorisanas* to do the same. For example, she established a center for maternal and infant health from which she distributed milk donated by local farmers to poor women and children. With patient persistence, she and a group of women coaxed—and sometimes prodded and shamed—San Pedro's city council into funding a maternity hospital, which opened in 1929.[54] She even included "fallen women" in her vision of public health, dispensing free contraceptives to prostitutes, whose venereal diseases she also treated, despite criticism from the public-health establishment.[55] That Rodríguez's work influenced local elite women is unquestioned: in 1929, for instance, San Pedro's Feminine League held a trinket sale in the central park to publicize their antisyphilis campaign.[56]

Petromacorisanas under Dr. Rodríguez's guidance transformed the city into an expanded domestic space and its residents into members of a grand household. In meaningful and powerful ways, Rodríguez and her companions challenged moral codes that divided the city into respectable areas and tolerance zones because health-care activism brought affluent and respectable women in contact with poor women of color.[57] At the same time, however, imagining the Dominican nation as a household writ large brought attention to another significant tension within Dominicans' application of Hostosian social thought: how could hierarchical relationships within the home serve as the foundation of a democratic republic?

Additionally, Rodríguez's work built on the interventionist techniques of men like Drs. Tió y Betances and Marchena who, years before, had waged war against women in an effort to stamp out syphilis. Female-led reform, then, contributed to Dominican state formation in important ways. Rodríguez still operated as a Hostosian-minded social reformer for whom domestic hierarchies based on gender, class, and age were part of the natural order, the same nature that provided human beings the rules and obligations necessary for living in an orderly society. As Hostosians their task was to make people aware of this natural law and to encourage their application of it in their everyday lives and in their governing institutions. Living according to the rights and obligations established by nature was supposed to produce social harmony, but, as we have seen here and in chapter 4, it often resulted in social control.

Rodríguez, however, went further. Applying Lugo's theory, she did not wait for the nation to evolve; she brought the power of the state to bear to force change. She made significant strides toward establishing the idea that the state had a significant role to play in addressing public health and beneficence to the poor. Yet, by advocating for maternal and infant clinics, she helped make women's health and children's access to basic needs political questions. In the 1940s this new theory of state, nation, and citizen practiced by Rodríguez and other women in their reform work found its way into the Trujillo regime.

Organized feminism in Santo Domingo, meanwhile, was more woven into that city's associational culture but developed reform-minded, interventionist goals similar to those in San Pedro. The beginnings of the organized feminist movement in Santo Domingo can be traced to the founding of Club Nosotras (Our Club) by Abigaíl Mejía in 1927. The activities of this group included city beautification and advocacy for judicial reform and children's rights. Livia Veloz also recalled that Club Nosotras "was the home of poets, orators, artists . . . and public speakers," essentially a club where educated women gave lectures, exhibited their art, and hosted visiting politicians and intellectuals. Despite this rather nonfeminist start, the club must have provided a unique setting for women, because in 1931, Abigaíl Mejía, from a prominent Santo Domingo family and recently returned from Spain, prodded its members to organize Acción Feminista Dominicana (figure 6.4).[58]

AFD's members wanted to make educated women "relevant to the discussion of policies affecting the family, the school, [and] the workplace." In AFD's manifesto, published in 1931, Mejía and her collaborators outlined feminists' "nonpolitical" goals as well, such as city beautification, educational reforms, juvenile penal reform, and women's suffrage, in that order.[59] Veloz defined the AFD's principal goals as "forming mothers" to participate in social reform (figure 6.5).[60]

Throughout the 1930s, Mejía used the pages of the *Listín Diario*, Santo Do-

Figure 6.4. Acción Feminista Dominicana, 1930s. Archivo General de la Nación.

mingo's premier newspaper, to outline Dominican feminist goals and to explain why feminism was necessary. In one article, she justified feminism because, "in our country, as in many other [parts] of backward Indo-Spanish America, women's civil, political, and juridical rights [are] unheard of."[61] In another article, Dr. Gladys de los Santos, general secretary of the AFD, emphasized that AFD's feminism was one "born in the heart of women truly conscious of their mission . . . to sustain the moral and material equilibrium in the home . . . and in the nation."[62]

The identification of the AFD with the regime became tangible by 1934, such that in her summary of women's participation in a test vote, Abigaíl Mejía affirmed that "96,427 feminist and *trujillista* women voted" (figure 6.6).[63] Why *trujillista*? An editorial published in the *Listín Diario* in November of 1940 made the connection between state building and feminism explicit. Quoting María Cristina Despradel, the editorial noted that revising the civil code to better complement women's changing roles in society acknowledged the most important goal the "Benefactor" had accomplished: "he destroyed once and for all monstrous civil wars whose weight . . . always fell on the weak shoulders of our women." Now that Trujillo had established a strong

Figure 6.5. Abigaíl Mejía. Archivo General de la Nación.

state, that state, in turn, could protect women, providing them the means to "head and sustain the home [and provide] sustenance and education for their children."[64]

During the 1930s, Trujillo and AFD feminists clarified the nature of their relationship, but one tragic consequence of their acquiescence was to transform feminist labor into *trujillista* victories. For example, a photo published in *Fémina* in August 1935 features a poor children's boarding school. Gaunt yet scrubbed faces peer at a camera as the children, some at desks, others standing, appear immobile in orderly rows. The caption credits Trujillo's "new school policy" for the attention paid to poor children when, in fact, feminists such as Evangelina Rodríguez, Casimira Heureaux, and Mercedes Aguiar had spent their professional lives serving the neediest communities.[65]

The late 1930s and early 1940s witnessed the elaboration of *hispanidad* nationalism at the same moment that Trujillo fulfilled his promise to give Dominican women the vote and revise the civil code to make them full citizens.

Figure 6.6. Acción Feminista Dominicana campaigning for women's votes, 1942. Archivo General de la Nación.

Dominican women's suffrage and the Trujillo state's pronatal policies must therefore be understood in the broader context of Dominicanization that began after the Haitian Massacre of 1937.

Also known as El Corte, the Haitian Massacre occurred between October 2 and 4, when the Dominican military executed between 15,000 and 20,000 Haitians, Dominicans, and Dominicans of Haitian ancestry. Richard Turits shows that prior to the massacre, Trujillo "backed policies to foster ethnic Haitians' identities as Dominican citizens and subjects of the regime." This he accomplished by increasing the number of public schools, strengthening the presence of the Catholic Church, and changing the French names of rivers and towns to Spanish ones.[66] Just before and certainly after the massacre, Trujillo initiated a series of programs to secure the borderlands for the state. Concerned that too many Dominicans spoke Haitian Kreyòl, Mario Fermín Cabral, president of the Dominican Senate, "decreed the obligatory teaching of Spanish in all schools." Quoting the writer Ramón Marrero Aristy, linguist Juan Valdez notes that classrooms became "pedagogical laboratories" for accomplishing "the work of Hispanicizing and de-Haitianizing" the borderlands.[67] The massacre, by literally ridding entire communities, colonies, and lands of Haitians and their descendants, secured the border region for Dominicans and assisted the success of efforts to train Dominicans to speak Spanish.

One product of this violent tragedy was the elaboration of anti-Haitian *hispanidad* nationalism. In the late 1930s and early 1940s, *hispanidad* nationalism was inchoate; Manuel Arturo Peña Batlle (1902–1954), who would become one of the main ideologues of *hispanidad* nationalism, began to publish essays to demarcate the "old" from the "new." For example, in sharp contrast to Hostos, Peña Batlle argued that the state's legitimacy derived from Hispanic tradition and that the goal of nation building was not civilization but order. Building on the anti-Haitian sentiments so present in Galván's work, Peña Batlle also insisted that the Hostosian project had failed Dominicans because Hostos "radically diverged from the conservative tradition, from Hispanic and Catholic influence." Dominicans needed to return to their cultural heritage to reinvigorate the nation.[68]

At the same time, however, this national project required women and the modernization of their relationship to the state. In an interesting twist, laws passed in the 1940s regarding women enhanced their access to education while limiting their principal role in Dominican society to motherhood. The Trujillo state adapted feminist-inspired policies and feminist demands to define female citizenship in domestic terms.[69] For example, in 1940 Trujillo created the National Council for the Protection of Maternity and Infancy (Junta Nacional de

Protección de la Maternidad y de la Infancia), authorized to build "institutos y casas de maternidad" (female health clinics and maternity hospitals), and, in honor of his mother, the Julia Molina Maternity Prize (Premio Julia Molina de Maternidad), an award given to Dominican women who had borne and raised at least ten children. Other reforms complemented this striving toward motherhood: those contemplating marriage had to obtain a prenuptial certificate, which involved submitting to a clinical exam (for reasons unknown, women had to submit to a vaginal exam).[70] In November of 1942 the Dominican Congress revised the civil code to grant suffrage to women, give married women civil equality with men, and guarantee women access to university education and the professions.

Some of this legislation actually originated among feminists and reflected the centrality of domesticity to both Hostosian and *latinidad* theories of the nation. Just prior to and during the first decade of Trujillo's dictatorship, feminist social reformers formulated legislative and institutional changes to enhance women's status and provide state services for women and children, as Rodríguez had advocated decades earlier in her work, *Granos*.[71] For instance, thanks to feminist activism, the Dominican Congress passed a law in 1928 requiring fathers and mothers to provide for their children, legitimately or illegitimately born. In 1945, Congress crafted new legislation, also at feminists' behest, protecting the rights of *hijos naturales* (children born out of wedlock) to inherit and to establish paternity (albeit within strict guidelines).[72] As though taking a cue from feminists in San Pedro, the AFD forwarded recommendations for legislation with regard to women's participation in the National Council for the Protection of Maternity and Infancy, home economics courses for girls in secondary schools, a census of homeless children and children of impoverished parents with the goal of placing them in a state facility, and day care centers for working and poor families.[73]

In turn, the "perfect storm" of paternalistic legislation and the ideological framework of *hispanidad* placed constraints on women's political activity and identities. Emergent Hispanic nationalism made it impossible to think in feminist and *normalista* ways about women's roles.[74] The limitations of discourse and the violence that stilled opposition to the regime culminated in the AFD's transformation, in 1942, from an autonomous feminist organization into the Women's Branch of the Partido Dominicano.

By 1942 AFD feminists were faced with the question of how to use the Trujillo state for their purposes and protect the progress they had made during decades of activism. To be sure, the AFD really had no choice about aligning itself with the regime, since the Dominican Party consumed all political activity and mobilization. As in the 1920s under U.S. occupation, the realignment of feminist theory to match new realities was conditioned by violence, political repression, a history of national and transnational activism, and a long engagement with reform-minded regimes. By mobilizing activist women, Trujillo appropriated a nationalist rhetoric centered on harmonious but hierarchical ideals regarding marriage, domesticity, and family life. He amplified this vision, transforming the entire Dominican nation into a single household of which he was the head and in which every citizen had a distinct role. Trujillo in effect consolidated his power over civilian elites by assuming the symbols and political strategies that had defined a generation of nationalists, both men and women.

A telling sign of things to come emerged during the First Feminine (as opposed to "Feminist") Congress, held in Santo Domingo in 1943.[75] Delegates passed a resolution to "reaffirm and increase, within the Dominican nation, the Christian faith, free from strange and retrograde influences . . . and encourage the population in the border regions to preserve the purity of the Spanish language." Enhancing the policy of Dominicanization along the border, female activists at the congress pledged that border residents should use Spanish exclusively "in the family hearth . . . [and] in relations outside the home."[76] Feminine activists now invested in the protection and exaltation of Hispanic womanhood responded enthusiastically; they aimed to work tirelessly to protect the purity of Dominican culture, the Spanish language, and Catholic religiosity. Their efforts must have borne some fruit because Trujillo said to them in 1945, "I know your patriotism, your civic virtues, your spirituality, all those treasures that have spilled [out of your] prodigious hands into the closed sanctuary of our homes. From here on, the Motherland is the big house of all Dominicans [and] I ask that you fill this [vastness] with your virtues."[77] Dominican feminists' role in with the Trujillato was complete.

Even more revealing, Evangelina Rodríguez, whose tireless efforts to ease the suffering of poor women and children and improve the conditions under which women gave birth, suffered the consequences of her independent stance. Despite her brilliance as a doctor, Rodríguez was often ridiculed as a "black" and "ugly" woman because she braided her hair and wore oxfords as opposed to heels. Perhaps Rodríguez's blackness explains why, in contrast to Santo Domingo, San Pedro's feminist activism appears to have developed outside the city's associational culture, characterized by feminine branches of all-male literary societies populated by white and light-skinned Dominicans. She is reported to have said, "Because I don't have a husband, a man to protect me, they accuse me of being a lesbian. I get poison pen letters under my door. Even in the street when I pass by, people hurl insults at me."[78] Her activism, African heritage, and single-mindedness positioned her much like the poor women she tended, as beyond the boundaries of acceptable Dominican womanhood and the emerging Hispanic nation. She was hounded and persecuted by Trujillo's security forces because she failed to pay him proper homage during an acceptance speech for a prize she earned. She suffered a mental breakdown and starved to death on the streets of San Pedro in 1947.[79]

. . .

Gregoria Goins and other women like her who lived between 1880 and 1940 experienced an extraordinary, historic shift in their outlook and life chances. Feminism emerged before Trujillo, was transformed by antioccupation activism during U.S. military governance, and shifted again under the weight of a new political structure, the Trujillato. Feminists' organizational structures, activism in local and hemispheric groups, and theorizations of nation, state, and citizen influenced Dominican state formation. The modern Dominican state and modern feminism, therefore, came of age together. While it may be easy to judge the AFD's transformation from feminist to feminine as a collective failure or to regard it as antithetical to feminist practice, I suggest that this change was, as Philip Cohen has argued regarding white, middle-class feminism in the United States, less "an error of feminist analysis [than] a political strategy reflecting *and creating* privilege."[80] In other words, Dominican feminists found a pragmatic way to use the state for their purposes as well as to be used by the state for Trujillo's.

But why did women matter to Trujillo, and why did gender ideologies become important in the early articulation of Trujillo-era reform and incipient Hispanic nationalism? Robin Derby has argued that the symbolic and literal consumption of women provided the ideological glue that bonded the regime's paternalism with its authoritarian, patriarchal character. Feminine symbolism—sacred and mortal virgins in particular—"functioned as a foil for the dictator's multiple, masculine identities," most notably, "El Jefe" (the Chief), "Padre de la Patría," and "El Benefactor." Like Ulises Heureaux, Trujillo used violence and every mass civic event to reinforce the virility and manliness of his regime. He was the father of a modernizing regime, but this father was both pious and predatory: Trujillo's "father" seduced young elite women and turned them into his mistresses.[81]

Derby's insight is important because Trujillo-era nationalism is most often considered solely in terms of race (for its antiblackness and anti-Haitianism) and class (as an elite ideology used to divide the working classes). Yet the significance of sexual prowess in the symbolic iconography of the regime suggests the need to understand *hispanidad* nationalism as a philosophy firmly rooted in ideologies about gender and sexuality. This was true, in part, because during the occupation, male nationalists forged a consensus on the terrain of masculinity about the evils of U.S. intervention. In antioccupation activism, gender was a powerful discursive and symbolic weapon because the dominant, conceptual language of the occupation posed a virile and civilizing force— U.S. Marines—aiding Dominican men, often described by military authorities in feminine terms, as coy, gentle, vulnerable, and incapable of political leadership.[82]

Perhaps, too, because they were women of the elite, Trujillo might have also thought that an alliance with them would help bring him into a class that rejected his application to high-class status. Or maybe Trujillo needed women, relied on their collective identity to push through his modernizing schemes. As in the 1880s and during the U.S. occupation, women's activism and their networks helped unify an intellectual governing elite—otherwise fractured by the violently divisive practice of Dominican politics—into a coherent ruling group. Female and feminist advocacy accorded the middle class an extensive set of responsibilities that not only strengthened the Dominican family and venerated women's labor within the home but also opened the family to increased state intervention and scrutiny. In this sense, feminism may have helped disseminate new forms of social regulation concerning the family down the class hierarchy.

Yet another possible answer may be found in the interests of Dominican feminism's convergence with those of modernizing regimes. Building on Nancy Fraser's critical analysis of second-wave feminism in the United States, it may be that U.S. imperialism and feminism brought about cultural changes that facilitated deeper transformations in political and economic structures. Fraser has asked the terrifying question: Is it possible that "cultural changes jump-started [by feminists] . . . have served to legitimate a structural transformation of capitalist society that runs counter to feminist visions of a just society"?[83] In the Dominican context, we might ask, did feminists unwittingly prepare the stage for state-driven capitalism in the Dominican Republic, namely, through import-substitution industrialization during the 1930s and 1940s and nationalist development policies in the postwar period?

Helping Hispanic nations confront the onslaught of U.S. economic imperialism meant accepting without debate nationalist development policies. Incorporating women as citizens also meant expanding the ranks of workers needed to feed the growing industrial machine across Latin America. Neici Zeller argues that between 1935 and 1950, a significant number of Dominican women moved into the labor force, working as clerks, salespeople, and in the service sector; others were self-employed.[84] A similar story could be told from Argentina to Mexico. Iberian feminism espoused a way to make women relevant not only to political change in the region but to the region's economic sovereignty as well. Through *hispanidad* nationalism and by incorporating women as (nearly) equal partners, modernizing elites and authoritarian regimes were able to craft unifying ideas of the nation even as economic development and migration to the cities threatened older social patterns and racial/class hierarchies. Women's labors and their ideals became an important bridge uniting the "old" with the "new," providing coherence in a dramatically transformative moment.

CONCLUSION

Sammy Sosa's skin-lightening drama drew attention to questions about race, class, and national identity among Dominicans living in the United States and in the Dominican Republic. His baseball career had socially whitened him, evidenced by his media popularity and wife of European ancestry, so his physical transformation toward whiteness complemented a sociocultural process that had already taken place.

Popular media narratives produced in the United States about Dominicans' denial of blackness make it appear that Sosa's decision to whiten himself is symbolic of a national pathology, of dark-skinned Dominicans' uncritical acceptance of aesthetic norms attached to whiteness and of their overall desire to become white themselves. Recent research on U.S. Dominicans' racial identity, however, suggests that Dominicans' racial preferences are more determined by their experiences with discrimination, which can result from their skin color. As a result, they lean toward whiteness or blackness or even claim yet another ethno-racial identity, such as "hispano/a" or "indio/a," that suggests racial mixture without adhering to blackness or whiteness.[1] In other words, and in sharp contrast to the black denial chorus, not all roads lead blindly to whiteness, and when certain choices are made, there are specific, historically situated reasons that explain why.

I have tried to show here that there existed alternatives to the antiblack, white nationalism that served the interests of the Trujillo dictatorship. I argued that not all expressions of nineteenth-century *hispanicismo* were inherently racist or xenophobic (i.e., anti-Haitian). My examination of Dominican intellectual history in chapter 1 highlights its antiracist, progressive features and builds on a growing body of scholarship by, among others, Silvio Torres-Saillant, Ada Ferrer, James Saunders, and Irmary Reyes-Santos to recuperate the diverse ways Caribbean and Latin American peoples defined race, racial mixture, and their national identity.

The Mulatto Republic agrees with the critical assessment of ideologies such as racial democracy, racial harmony, and *mestizaje* as nationalist discourses that inherently privilege whiteness. At the same time, however, there is a tendency in scholarship produced in the United States to dismiss even progressive thinkers such as Pedro Francisco Bonó, Gregorio Luperón, and Eugenio María de Hostos as fundamentally racist or, even worse, white supremacists. Representations of these intellectuals in the U.S. academy differ significantly from how Dominican scholars regard these important men and their historical legacies. The dismissive way that some U.S. scholars treat Caribbean and Latin American intellectuals who embrace racelessness or racial democracy as only racists and white supremacists presents scholars with a problem: if Caribbean and Latin American intellectuals have only produced racist ideas, then on what literary, historical, or ideological traditions can contemporaries draw to combat racism in the Caribbean and Latin America? This book addresses that concern by presenting these nonracist nationalisms in historical and comparative context.

I have also argued that while twentieth-century *hispanidad* nationalism, especially as it was articulated during General Rafael Trujillo's dictatorship, drew on an intellectual tradition of elevating Spanish cultural norms as the foundation of Dominican identity—*hispanicismo*—it was also the product of a particular historical moment and responded to the needs of a modernizing state in the wake of U.S. military occupation. My analysis of San Pedro's social history demonstrates that formulations of *dominicanidad* became more rigidly racist and sexist as San Pedro's dominant classes shaped their identity as an elite through Hispanic cultural norms. Particularly in the 1880s and 1890s *hispanicismo* facilitated racial unity between wealthy white immigrants and Dominican elites through educational institutions, literary magazines, and an overall consensus about economic and social development.

In the years prior to the occupation, policing urban laborers and sexual vice acquired a racial cast. In San Pedro, the associational culture of clubs, seasonal games, libraries, lectures, and carnival queens affirmed the idea that the city's dominant classes held a monopoly over defining the course of progress and how to bring about civilization. In contrast to this world, and literally pushed farther away from it, were coachmen's stands, laundry areas, tolerance zones, wharves, police stations, and brothels teeming with San Pedro's majority working-class population. I argue that policing the urban poor became a racist practice because the majority of those who were either the victims of abuse or criminalized for their behaviors were African-descended immigrants. Antiblackness also emerged in the policing of deviant female sexuality.

San Pedro's social history forces us, then, to reconsider the relationship of antiblackness, anti-Haitianism, and Dominican nationalism. Rather than "[treating] phenotypical difference as a self-evident biological category," I argue in chapter 4 that policing did the "'ideological work' that has to be done on physical difference to turn it into 'racial' signifiers in the first place."[2]

Moreover, my examination of policing in San Pedro provides historical evidence for Ernesto Sagás's important arguments about anti-Haitianism as a racist discourse. Sagás points out that through anti-Haitianism, Dominican elites construct the fiction that Dominicans and Haitians are separate races. For him, antiblackness is the gateway toward anti-Haitianism because, in addition to how antiblack racism treats Haitians poorly, antiblack racism is also used against poor Dominicans.[3] My study of policing shows that Haitians were not required for police forces to mete out punishment on Afro-Antillean migrants or to enact measures that disproportionally and negatively affected Afro-Antillean migrants.

This work has also showed that the U.S. occupation from 1916 to 1924, as other scholars have argued, profoundly shaped Dominican nationalist discourses. U.S. military governance occasioned yet another debate over Dominicans' race—whether and how as a "mulatto republic" Dominicans could be readied (or, better still, remediated) by their U.S. guardians for self-governance. Resistance to the occupation took many forms, but I focus on two responses: Garveyism and *latinidad* internationalism. San Pedro's Afro-Antillean Garveyites and Dominican nationalists, like their nineteenth-century predecessors, produced powerful analyses that questioned prevailing assumptions about the connection between whiteness, modernity, and nationhood. Both Garveyism and *latinidad*, for instance, resonated with Gregorio Luperón's and Eugenio María de Hostos's acerbic critiques of U.S. imperialism and with their vision of hemispheric unity, beginning with a Pan-Antillean federation. Both Garveyism and *latinidad* internationalism provided their adherents with a new reading of the world order, as racialized and as racist. Garveyism and *latinidad* reinforced patriarchal norms, providing outnumbered and outgunned men with a muscular and militant nationalism without having to pick up arms to fight an invincible enemy.

Yet Garveyism looked toward and drew its strength from an African diasporic community; *latinidad* turned elsewhere, to Europe and to brotherhood among other American republics to add legitimacy to its claims. As Aims McGuinness asked me years ago, Why did Dominican nationalists refuse negritude or Pan-Africanism when their Haitian counterparts would eventually do so? In response, I have suggested that for the country deemed "mulatto" by U.S. authorities and therefore privileged when compared to Haiti, the "black republic," situating Dominicans as a black race became a less viable option.

Rather than opting for Pan-Africanism and Pan-Antilleanism, Dominican nationalists chose *latinidad* because it emphasized their European ties and closeness to whiteness.

Chapter 6 discusses feminism and female activism between 1900 and 1940. I show that the occupation left a complex legacy for a generation of women who, thanks to educational and professional opportunities, were poised to assume more public leadership roles by the end of the occupation. For this reason, in addition to female activists' moral authority, their organizational capacity, years of experience in institution building, particularly in education and health care, and commitment to anti-U.S. imperialist activism, namely, through Iberian/Hispanic international organizations, General Rafael Trujillo incorporated them and their movement into his regime. Trujillo did not invent Dominican feminism; modern feminism and Dominican state formation under Trujillo took place together. Dominican feminism's ties with one of the longest and most violent authoritarian regimes in the hemisphere bequeathed yet another troubling legacy that contemporary and future Dominican feminists will have to address. Here, I have tried to bridge the historiographical abyss between political and feminist history to show Dominican state formation and feminism as mutually constitutive processes.

Most important, my examination of San Pedro helps us situate the Dominican responses to the question of race and nation squarely within Caribbean and Latin American historiography and therefore challenges the narrative of Dominican racial exceptionalism. Even before freedom from Spanish rule was achieved, leaders of independence movements had to deal with the question of national unity. Clearly, colonialism had left a fractured legacy, its enduring strength evidenced by leaders' insistence that, despite slavery and class domination, Latin American republics would be free and equal societies in which merit rather than ancestry would determine one's possibilities. Claims to racial democracy, racial harmony, and racelessness were all assertions that democracy would make race irrelevant in the practice of citizenship.

I argue here that Hispanicism, *mulatismo*, Pan-Antilleanism, *latinidad* and *hispanidad* should be considered among these ideologies. Like their counterparts elsewhere—Cuban racelessness, Colombian racial harmony, Brazilian racial democracy, Mexican *mestizaje*—Dominican renderings of the nation included those that excluded African-descended people from narratives of national progress all the while projecting inclusion. The singularity of *hispanidad* nationalism was not its racism and antiblackness but the clarity with which it explicitly proclaimed the state's investment in whitening and the racial superiority of mixed Dominicans. After 1937 antiblack racism and anti-Haitianism served yet another function: to justify the violent demarcation of Dominican territory along its border with Haiti and to manage the Trujillo state's takeover of sugar enterprises. Anti-Haitianism and antiblack racism, just like the idea of the Mexican *raza cósmica* or *luso-tropicalismo* in Brazil, served the needs of a consolidating, modernizing state. One significant difference between the Dominican Republic, Mexico, and Brazil was that anti-Haitianism complemented the heavy-handed management of the predominantly immigrant workforce that sustained sugar production in regions like San Pedro de Macorís.

. . .

Long identified with sugar and baseball, San Pedro de Macorís has not often been considered central to the story of how Dominicans became ideologically nonblack. Hopefully, this narrative will change this oversight, but it is more likely that Sammy Sosa's dramatic skin bleaching will draw more attention to San Pedro and *hispanidad* nationalism. Sammy Sosa, according to images available online, is remarkably paler than he was in 2009. It remains to be seen if he will go as far as Vybz Kartel, a Jamaican dancehall artist whose skin bleaching caused a similar media storm in the English-speaking Caribbean and in the United Kingdom, home to a significant number of British West Indians. Kartel even launched a men's facial cream line that included bleaching products.[4] A brotherhood in skin bleaching, I suspect, is not quite the fraternity that Luperón and Hostos had in mind when they thought of Jamaica and Santo Domingo as founding members of an Antillean federation.

Yet Sosa's and Kartel's relationship to their skin color, their reasons for whitening, and the global public's response to their personal decisions provide a rare opportunity to bring Anglophone and Spanish-speaking Caribbean peoples into a discussion about blackness and whiteness, race and color. According to recent work in anthropology, contemporary globalization has provoked yet another round of reflection about race, development, and modernity in Caribbean and Latin American societies. Some communities are responding to this by moving toward blackness. In Jamaica, according to Deborah Thomas, migration and a globalized consumer culture have undermined the postcolonial, multiracial, creole nationalism that sustained the independence struggle and defined Jamaican national identity in the postcolonial period. Lower-middle-class Jamaicans, who are the most likely to have migrated, have exchanged multiracialism for a "modern blackness" Thomas defines as "a racialized vision of citizenship" whose roots extend to "urban popular expressions of blackness that had been marginalized" by other visions of creole nationalism proffered by Jamaican elites during the independence struggle.[5] In Colombia, Bettina

Ng'weno argues, globalization has given "a new significance and space . . . to certain kinds of claims to territory, identity, and national belonging," so that Afro-Colombians have gained recognition as a cultural and ethnic group through their struggle to maintain their land.[6]

For the Dominican Republic, Kimberly Simmons argues, thanks to transnational migration, particularly to the United States, "*mulataje* is one of the two emerging racial projects challenging *mestizaje* [in the Dominican Republic]. It articulates a new racial view and reflects a *negro-blanco* (black-white) mixture with assertions of being *mulato*."[7] That is, like Luperón's Antillean transnationalism, contemporary *mulataje* makes whiteness less necessary to national identity and opens a space in which African ancestry becomes more visible.

Whether Dominicans will embrace *mulataje* as a new national identity is still unclear. Nevertheless, the turn to a mulatto identity may have the positive outcome of countering *hispanidad*. In a context where blackness remains a troubled category for many Dominicans, *mulatismo* may represent a good first step in undoing the legacies of the Trujillo regime.

Again, an alternative is available. When Gregoria Goins arrived in Puerto Plata, she asked for a visa; in it her race was described as "*mestizo*," her color, "*mulata*."[8] It appears that Goins was able to stay at least two years in Puerto Plata, and she taught music to make ends meet. However, her quest for citizenship was never fulfilled: since she had married John Goins, a U.S. citizen, Dominican law stipulated that she was no longer a Dominican national. This changed in 1942, but it was too late for Gregoria. In a diary entry dated June 23, 1947, she wrote, "Heard from Celia. No. 32 is being fixed up for rent. Goodbye home." Although not able to live in Puerto Plata, Gregoria continued to lecture about music and Spanish culture in Washington, D.C., at Howard University and local churches. In one lecture about Santo Domingo's country music, she called the country "one of the black republics" and noted the perfect confluence between Spanish and Negro musical traditions in Dominican folk songs: "With the island folk song you have the Spanish rhythm but Negro key relations."[9]

What a perfect metaphor for a *mulata* double-consciousness born at the confluence of U.S. American, Afro-Antillean, and Spanish-speaking worlds.

NOTES

Introduction

1. Enrique Rojas, "Cream Has Bleached His Skin," ESPN Deportes.com, November 10, 2009: http://sports.espn.go.com/mlb/news/story?id=4642952, accessed March 2011. My thanks to Jessica Lewis for bringing this to my attention. Skin bleaching is also common in Jamaica, the United States, and parts of Africa: Christopher Charles, "Skin Bleachers' Representations of Skin Color in Jamaica," *Journal of Black Studies* 40, no. 2 (November 2009): 153–170; Margaret Hunter, "The Persistent Problem of Colorism: Skin Tone, Status, and Inequality," *Sociology Compass* 1, no. 1 (2007): 237–254; Lewis et al., "Investigating Motivations for Women's Skin Bleaching in Tanzania," *Psychology of Women Quarterly* 35, no. 1 (March 2011): 29–37.

2. Rojas, "Cream Has Bleached His Skin."

3. Frances Robles, "Black Denial," *Miami Herald*, June 13, 2007.

4. Andrés Mateo insists, too, that Trujillo-era ideology was more eclectic than coherent. See *Mito y cultura en la era de Trujillo*.

5. Franklin Franco Pichardo, *Sobre racismo y antihaitianismo (y otros ensayos)*; Ernesto Sagás, *Race and Politics in the Dominican Republic*.

6. David Howard, *Coloring the Nation: Race and Ethnicity in the Dominican Republic*; Kimberly Simmons, *Reconstructing Racial Identity and the African Past in the Dominican Republic*; Jim Sidanius, Yesilernis Peña, and Mark Sawyer, "Inclusionary Discrimination: Pigmentocracy and Patriotism in the Dominican Republic"; and Ginetta Candelario, *Black behind the Ears: Dominican Racial Identity from Museums to Beauty Shops*.

7. Manuel Arturo Peña Batlle, *Política de Trujillo*; Joaquín Balaguer, *La isla al revés*.

8. Frank Moya Pons, "Modernización y cambios en la República Dominicana," pp. 243–244.

9. One must also include Juan Bosch as a founding member of the *nueva ola*. Bosch's *Composición social dominicana. Historia e interpretación*, written in 1968 and published in 1970, reoriented Dominican historical analysis around the history of capitalism, resistance to imperialism, and class struggle.

10. Key articles, books, and collections include Franklin Franco Pichardo, *Los negros, los mulatos y la nación dominicana*; Raymundo González, "Notas sobre las concepciones populistas-liberales de Duarte y la independencia dominicana," *Clío* 77, no. 175 (2008): 151–166; idem, "Peña Batlle y su concepto histórico de la nación dominicana," *Anuario de Estudios Americanos* 48 (1991): 585–631; idem, *De esclavos a campesinos. Vida rural en Santo Domingo colonial*; Hugo Tolentino Dipp, *Raza e historia en Santo Domingo. Orígenes del prejuicio en América*; Frank Moya Pons, *Manual de historia dominicana*; Emilio Cordero Michel, "Características de la Guerra Restauradora, 1863–1865"; Rubén Silié, "El hato y el conuco. Contexto para el surgimiento de la cultura criolla."

11. Roberto Cassá and Genaro Rodríguez, "Algunos procesos formativos de la identidad nacional dominicana"; Roberto Cassá, "El racismo en la ideología de la clase dominante dominicana"; Orlando Inoa, *Azúcar, árabes, cocolos y haitianos*; and Michiel Baud, "Sugar and Unfree Labor: Reflections on Labour Control in the Dominican Republic, 1870–1935."

12. Robin Derby and Richard Turits, "Las historias de terror y los terrores de la historia: la masacre haitiana de 1937 en la República Dominicana."

13. Robin Derby, "Haitians, Magic, and Money: *Raza* and Society in the Haitian-Dominican Borderlands, 1900–1937," p. 489; Christian Krohn-Hansen, "Magic, Money and Alterity among Dominicans," p. 130.

14. Candelario, *Black behind the Ears*. See also Derby, "Haitians, Magic, and Money" and idem, "Race, National Identity, and the Idea of Value on the Island of Hispaniola."

15. Silvio Torres-Saillant, "Blackness and Meaning in Studying Hispaniola: A Review Essay," pp. 181–182.

16. Cassá, "El racismo"; Teresita Martínez-Vergne, *Nation and Citizen in the Dominican Republic, 1880–1916*.

17. Important works on the development of the sugar industry include the essays published in Andrés Corten, Mercedes Acosta, and Isis Duarte, eds., *Azúcar y política en la República Dominicana*; Jacqueline Boin and José Serulle Ramia, *El proceso de desarrollo del capitalismo en la República Dominicana (1844–1930)*; Ramonina Brea, *Ensayo sobre la formación del estado capitalista en la República Dominicana y Haití*; Manuel Moreno Fraginals, Frank Moya Pons, and Stanley Engerman, eds., *Between Slavery and Free Labor: The Spanish-Speaking Caribbean in the Nineteenth Century*; Humberto García Muñiz, "The South Porto Rico Sugar Company: The History of a U.S. Multinational Corporation in Puerto Rico and the Dominican Republic, 1900–1921"; Inoa, *Azúcar*; Roberto Marte, *Cuba y la República Dominicana. Transición económica en el Caribe del siglo XIX*; and Juan J. Sánchez, *La caña en Santo Domingo*.

18. Samuel Martínez, "From Hidden Hand to Heavy Hand: Sugar, the State, and Migrant Labor in Haiti and the Dominican Republic," p. 59.

19. Patrick Bryan, "The Question of Labor in the Sugar Industry of the Dominican Republic in the Late Nineteenth and Early Twentieth Centuries," p. 243.

20. Patricia Collins, *Black Feminist Thought: Knowledge, Consciousness, and the Politics of Empowerment*, p. 130.

21. Reed, U.S. Consular Officer, San Pedro de Macorís, to Mr. W. F. Powell, United States Legation in Port au Prince, Haiti, August 3, 1899. Reprinted in "Notas oficiales de los Estados Unidos sobre la muerte de Ulises Heureaux," *Eme Eme: Estudios Dominicanos* 8, no. 48 (1980): 110–111 [105–126].

22. Arístides Incháustegui, "Cronología de gobiernos y gobernantes de la República Dominicana," pp. 8–9; "Notas oficiales de los Estados Unidos sobre la muerte de Ulises Heureaux," p. 110.

23. Frank Moya Pons, *The Dominican Republic: A National History*, pp. 325–326.

24. Bruce Calder, *The Impact of Intervention*, pp. 96–97.

25. Sagás, *Race and Politics*, p. 6.

26. Robin Derby, *The Dictator's Seduction: Politics and the Popular Imagination in the Era of Trujillo*.

27. Candelario, *Black behind the Ears*, chap. 5.

28. Samuel Martínez, "Not a Cockfight: Rethinking Haitian-Dominican Relations," p. 82.

29. Richard Turits, "Par-delà les plantations. Question raciale et identités colectives à Santo Domingo," pp. 58–59.

30. Francisco Moscoso Puello, *Cartas a Evelina*, pp. 9–10.

31. Turits, "Par-delà les plantations," p. 58.

32. Kimberly Simmons addresses these questions in *Reconstructing Racial Identity*.

33. Silvio Torres-Saillant, "Creoleness or Blackness," p. 33.

34. Mimi Sheller, *Consuming the Caribbean: From Arawaks to Zombies*, pp. 115, 118.

35. Moscoso Puello, *Cartas a Evelina*, pp. 48, 52. Unless otherwise noted, all translations are mine.

36. Torres-Saillant, "Blackness and Meaning," p. 181.

Chapter 1. Debating *Dominicanidad* in the Nineteenth Century

1. Gregoria Fraser Goins, "Miss Doc," unpublished manuscript, p. 141, Box 36-4, Folder 52, Moorland-Spingarn Research Center, Howard University (hereafter MSRC).

2. See Corten, Acosta, and Duarte, eds., *Azúcar*; Boin and Serulle Ramia, *El proceso de desarrollo del capitalismo*; Brea, *Ensayo*; Moreno Fraginals, Moya Pons, and Engerman, eds., *Between Slavery and Free Labor*; García Muñiz, "The South Porto Rico Sugar Company; Inoa, *Azúcar*; Marte, *Cuba y la República Dominicana*; and Sánchez, *La caña*.

3. Raymundo González, "El pensamiento de Bonó. Nación y clases trabajadoras," p. 41.

4. Cyrus Veeser, *A World Safe for Capitalism: Dollar Diplomacy and America's Rise to Global Power*, esp. chaps. 1, 2, and 4; Eric Love, *Race over Empire: Racism and U.S. Imperialism*, chap. 2; and Mayes, "Sugar's Metropolis," chap. 2.

5. Emilio Cordero M., "Características de la Guerra Restauradora, 1863–1865," p. 298.

6. Ibid.

7. Julie Franks, "Transforming Property: Landholding and Political Rights in the Dominican Sugar Region, 1880–1930," p. 95.

8. Eugenio Miches to Ministro de Interior, Policía y Agricultura, January 23, 1867, Correspondencia de Gobernación, Secretaría de Interior, Policía y Agricultura, Legajo 5 (1867), Archivo General de la Nación, Santo Domingo (hereafter AGN).

9. Andrés Pérez, Gobernador de la Provincia de El Seibo, a Sr. Ministro de la Secretaría de Estado de Interior, Policía y Agricultura, February 13, 1871, Secretaría del Estado de Interior, Policía y Agricultura, Legajo 13, AGN.

10. Marixa Lasso, *Myths of Harmony: Race and Republicanism during the Age of Revolution, Colombia, 1795–1831*, pp. 11–12, 34–38, 61–63.

11. Aims McGuinness, *Path of Empire: Panama and the California Gold Rush*, pp. 160–161.

12. Ada Ferrer, *Insurgent Cuba: Race, Nation, and Revolution, 1868–1898*, esp. pp. 112–138.

13. "Haiti—Designs on Her Independence," *National Era*, July 4, 1850.

14. Quoted in Love, *Race over Empire*, p. 43. See also Carlos Esteban Deive, *Los dominicanos vistos por extranjeros*, p. 218.

15. Frederick Douglass, "Around the Island of Santo Domingo," Frederick Douglass Papers, Library of Congress, Series: Family Papers, p. 27: http://memory.loc.gov.

16. The author of the manuscript is not known for certain, but I believe it to have been Frederick Douglass, since he traveled to Santo Domingo, and the document appears to be a defense of the commission's work. See unsigned holograph, Frederick Douglass Papers, Box 28-6, Folder 205, MSRC, Howard University.

17. Ibid.

18. Frederick Douglass, "Santo Domingo," Frederick Douglass Papers, Library of Congress, Series: Speech, Article, and Book File-B, Frederick Douglass, undated, Folder 4 of 5, p. 36: http://memory.loc.gov.

19. Quoted in Raymundo González, "Notas sobre las concepciones populistas-liberales de Duarte y la independencia dominicana," p. 156. In Spanish, the quote reads, "Los blancos,

morenos / Cobrizos, Cruzados / Marchando serenos / Unidos y osados. / La patria salvemos / De viles tiranos, / Y al mundo mostremos / Que somos hermanos." See also Fernando Pérez Memén, "El proyecto de Constitución de Duarte," pp. 176–177; Francisco Alberto Henríquez Vásquez, "El pensamiento político y la acción revolucionaria de Juan Pablo Duarte."

20. Manuel de Jesús Galván, "La anexión es la paz," *La Razón* 1, no. 2 (1861), reprinted in Galván, *Manuel de Jesús Galván. Escritos políticos iniciales*, Andrés Blanco Díaz, ed., p. 50.

21. Manuel de Jesús Galván, "Diversas fases de la anexión," *La Razón* 1, no. 8 (1861), in *Escritos políticos*, p. 73. Galván is quoting the Haitian newspaper *L'Opinion Nationale*.

22. Manuel de Jesús Galván, "Santo Domingo, 22 de mayo de 1863," *La Razón* 2, no. 56 (1863), in *Escritos políticos*, p. 254.

23. Manuel de Jesús Galván, "La nueva insurrección," *La Razón* 2, no. 69 (1863), in *Escritos políticos*, p. 271; idem, "Santo Domingo, 12 de septiembre de 1863," *La Razón* 2, no. 71 (1863), in *Escritos políticos*, pp. 281 and 288; idem, "Santo Domingo, 6 de febrero de 1864," *La Razón* 2, no. 92 (1864), in *Escritos políticos*, p. 310.

24. Doris Sommer, *Foundational Fictions: The National Romances of Latin America*, p. 256. See also Meindert Fennema and Toetje Loewenthal, "La construcción de raza y nación en la República Dominicana," pp. 198, 200, 202–203.

25. Pedro Henríquez Ureña, "Enriquillo," *La Nación* (Buenos Aires), January 13, 1935; reprinted as "Prólogo" in *Enriquillo*, p. 12.

26. Sommer, *Foundational Fictions*, p. 256; idem, *One Master for Another: Populism as Patriarchal Rhetoric in Dominican Novels*, p. 16.

27. Candelario, *Black behind the Ears*, p. 59.

28. Raymundo González, "Prefacio," in Raymundo González, *Pedro Francisco Bonó. Textos selectos*, pp. 15–16.

29. Pedro Francisco Bonó, "Apuntes sobre las clases trabajadoras dominicanas," in *Papeles de Pedro Francisco Bonó*, ed. Emilio Rodríguez Demorizi, p. 218.

30. Ibid., pp. 218–219.

31. Ibid.

32. As cited in Carmen Durán, "Alejandro Angulo Guridi (1823–1906)," pp. 20–22.

33. Bonó, "El error de Boyer," undated letter in Emilio Rodríguez Demorizi, ed., *Papeles de Pedro Francisco Bonó*, p. 610.

34. Bonó, "La República Dominicana y la República Haitiana," in Rodríguez Demorizi, ed., *Papeles de Pedro Francisco Bonó*, pp. 343, 344.

35. Bonó, "Apuntes sobre las clases trabajadoras dominicanas," p. 219.

36. Two helpful views on the revisionist scholarship on race in Latin America include Nancy Appelbaum, "Post-Revisionist Scholarship on Race"; and Kwame Dixon, "Beyond Race and Gender: Recent Works on Afro–Latin America." Among the most important works that view racial democracy as white supremacist fiction are Aline Helg, *Our Rightful Share: The Afro-Cuban Struggle for Equality, 1886-1912*; Kia Caldwell, *Negras in Brazil: Re-envisioning Black Women, Citizenship, and the Politics of Identity*; Mark Sawyer, *Racial Politics in Post-Revolutionary Cuba*; Ronald Stutzman, "El Mestizaje: An All-Inclusive Ideology of Exclusion."

37. Pedro San Miguel, *La isla imaginada. Historia, identidad y utopía en La Española*, pp. 80, 81.

38. Pedro Francisco Bonó to Gregorio Luperón, December 30, 1887, reprinted in Rodríguez Demorizi, ed., *Papeles de Pedro Francisco Bonó*, p. 560.

39. Gregorio Luperón to Pedro Francisco Bonó, January 9, 1888, reprinted in Rodríguez Demorizi, ed., *Papeles de Pedro Francisco Bonó*, p. 561.

40. Bonó, "Congreso extraparlamentario. Diario de debates," reprinted in Rodríguez Demorizi, ed., *Papeles de Pedro Francisco Bonó*, pp. 390–392, 393, 394.

41. J. Michael Dash, "Nineteenth-Century Haiti and the Archipelago of the Americas: Anté-

nor Firmin's Letters from St. Thomas," pp. 49, 52, and personal conversation with Marie-Denise Shelton, May 21, 2013.

42. Eugenio María de Hostos to Gregorio Luperón, August 20, 1895, reprinted in Viviana Quiles-Calderín, ed., *República Dominicana y Puerto Rico. Hermandad en la lucha emancipadora. Correspondencia, 1876–1902*, p. 235.

43. José Chez Checo, ed., *Ideario de Gregorio Luperón, 1839–1897*, p. 174.

44. Federico Henríquez y Carvajal to Eugenio María de Hostos, December 18, 1895, in Quiles-Calderín, *República Dominicana y Puerto Rico*, p. 137.

45. Eugenio María de Hostos to Gregorio Luperón, April 16, 1886, in Quiles-Calderín, *República Dominicana y Puerto Rico*, p. 231.

46. Eugenio María de Hostos to Gregorio Luperón, June 11, 1895, in Quiles-Calderín, *República Dominicana y Puerto Rico*, p. 234.

47. Quoted in Emilio Rodríguez Demorizi, "Prefacio," *Informe de la Comisión de Investigación de los Estados Unidos de América en Santo Domingo en 1871*, p. 18.

48. Eugenio María de Hostos to Horacio Vásquez, September 19, 1899, in Emilio Rodríguez Demorizi, ed., *Hostos en Santo Domingo*, vol. 2, p. 289.

49. Gregorio Luperón to Eugenio María de Hostos, November 12, 1895, in Quiles-Calderín, *República Dominicana y Puerto Rico*, p. 238.

50. Gregorio Luperón, *Notas autobiográficas y apuntes históricos*, vol. 3, p. 246.

51. Ibid., vol. 1, p. 34.

52. Irmary Reyes-Santos, "On Pan-Antillean Politics: Ramón Emeterio Betances and Gregorio Luperón Speak to the Present," p. 19.

53. Luperón, *Notas autobiográficas*, vol. 3, p. 51.

54. Ibid., p. 27.

55. Quoted in Sumner Welles, *Naboth's Vineyard: The Dominican Republic, 1844–1924*, p. 369.

56. Reyes-Santos, "On Pan-Antillean Politics," p. 11.

57. As quoted in Sheller, *Consuming the Caribbean*, pp. 132, 135.

58. Quoted in Martínez-Vergne, *Nation and Citizen*, p. 95.

59. Hence fears of a *"pardocracia"* in Nueva Granada and Antonio Maceo's leadership in Cuba. For Colombia, see Lasso, *Myths of Harmony*, and Helg, *Liberty and Equality in Caribbean Colombia, 1770–1835*. For Cuba, see Ferrer, *Insurgent Cuba*, and Aline Helg, *Our Rightful Share*.

60. Hostos, "Quisqueya," in Rodríguez Demorizi, ed., *Hostos en Santo Domingo*, vol. 1, p. 250.

61. Luperón, *Notas autobiográficas*, vol. 2, p. 280.

62. Ibid., vol. 1, p. 354.

63. Thomas C. Holt, *The Problem of Freedom: Race, Labor, and Politics in Jamaica and Britain, 1832–1938*, pp. 213, 215, 217.

64. There is some disagreement over the cause of Charles's death. One biographer claims it was a stroke, but Gregoria wrote that her father contracted consumption. See Eric V. D. Luft, "Sarah Loguen Fraser, M.D., Class of 1876," p. 17. For Gregoria's biography, see Gregoria Fraser Goins, "Miss Doc," unpublished manuscript, Box 36-4, Folder 52, MSRC, Howard University.

65. Goins, "Miss Doc," p. 141.

Chapter 2. The Changing Landscape of Power in the Sugar-Growing East

1. Michiel Baud, "'Constitutionally White': The Forging of a National Identity in the Dominican Republic," pp. 123–124.

2. Miguel Tinker Salas, "Relaciones de poder y raza en los campos petroleros venezolanos, 1920–1940."

3. Miguel Tinker Salas, *In the Shadow of the Eagles: Sonora and the Transformation of the Border during the Porfiriato*, p. 256.

4. Recent examples of this scholarship include Lara Putnam, *The Company They Kept: Migrants and the Politics of Gender in Caribbean Costa Rica*; Aviva Chomsky and Aldo Lauria-Santiago, eds., *Identity and Struggle at the Margins of the Nation-State: The Laboring Peoples of Central America and the Hispanic Caribbean*; Catherine LeGrand, "Living in Macondo: Economy and Culture in a United Fruit Company Banana Enclave in Colombia."

5. And even when U.S. corporations did have a voice in local affairs, the reach of their influence was minimal. See Putnam, *The Company They Kept*.

6. Carol M. Rose, *Property and Persuasion: Essays on the History, Theory, and Rhetoric of Ownership*, p. 277.

7. Bartolomé de las Casas quoted in Fermín Álvarez Santana, *San Pedro de Macorís. Su historia y desarrollo*, p. 27.

8. Richard Turits, *Foundations of Despotism: Peasants, the Trujillo Regime, and Modernity in Dominican History*, pp. 25–27.

9. My thanks to Dr. Fermín Álvarez Santana, who clarified the location of the *yeguadas* for me (personal conversation, July 28, 2010). The name "*yeguada*" appears to derive from "*yegua*," mare, thereby suggesting a connection to horse ranching and pasturing.

10. Melvil Bloncourt, *Le dictionnaire universel du commerce et de la navigation*, reproduced in Roberto Marte, *Estadísticas y documentos históricos sobre Santo Domingo, 1805–1890*, p. 195.

11. Álvarez Santana, *San Pedro de Macorís*, p. 95. A *tarea* is the equivalent of 0.155 acre, 0.628 *hectare*, or 900 square *varas*. According to Frank Moya Pons, 1 *hectare* equals 16 *tareas*.

12. Moya Pons, *The Dominican Republic*, pp. 58–63; Turits, *Foundations of Despotism*, pp. 27–29, 33.

13. Manuel Leopoldo Richiez, "Historia de la provincia i, especialmente de la ciudad de San Pedro de Macorís," pp. 11–12; América Bermúdez, *Manual de historia de San Pedro de Macorís*, p. 13.

14. Moya Pons, *The Dominican Republic*, pp. 117–123.

15. Álvarez Santana, *San Pedro de Macorís*, p. 42. See also Vicente Tolentino Rojas, *Historia de la división territorial*, pp. 9, 63–99, 102–111, 114, 152.

16. Guillermo Atiles Santos, *Guía local y de comercio de la ciudad de San Pedro de Macorís*, p. 15. Elías Camarena to Ministro de Interior, Policía y Agricultura, Santo Domingo, August 10, 1867, Secretaría del Estado de Interior, Policía y Agricultura, Legajo 5, AGN, Santo Domingo. In his report, Camarena lists the following: Sección de Yeguada (new *labranzas* [farms], 17; old *labranzas*, 19); Sección de Punta de Garza (new *labranzas*, 45; old *labranzas*, 51); and Sección de Soco (new *labranzas*, 15; old *labranzas*, 27). Total new *labranzas*, 77; old *labranzas*, 97.

17. Quiterio Berroa Canelo, as cited in Álvarez Santana, *San Pedro de Macorís*, p. 95. Also quoted in Cámara de Comercio, Industria y Agricultura, *Directorio general de San Pedro de Macorís*, p. ii.

18. "Memoria sobre la República Dominicana que presenta el Cónsul Español Ricardo Palomino al Ministro de Estado de la Monarquía en 1883," reproduced in Marte, *Estadísticas y documentos históricos*, p. 248.

19. Ibid., pp. 248–250.

20. Manuel Asunción Richiez to Secretaría de Estado de Interior, Policía y Agricultura, May 17, 1870, Secretaría del Estado de Interior, Policía y Agricultura, Legajo 12, AGN.

21. United States Senate, *Report of the Commission of Inquiry to Santo Domingo*, pp. 469–470.

22. Turits, *Foundations of Despotism*, p. 41. His chapter, "Freedom in *El Monte*," provides an excellent summary of the debate about the origins of *terrenos comuneros*, pp. 25–51.

23. Ibid., p. 43.

24. Ibid. See also Aura Celeste Fernández Rodríguez, "Origen y evolución de la propiedad y de los terrenos comuneros en la República Dominicana."

25. A helpful explanation of these systems can be found in César J. Ayala, *American Sugar Kingdom: The Plantation Economy of the Spanish Caribbean, 1898–1934*, pp. 188–194.

26. Cited in Jaime Domínguez, *La dictadura de Heureaux*, pp. 98–99, and Juan Sánchez, *La caña*, p. 35.

27. José del Castillo, "Consuelo. Biografía de un pequeño gigante," pp. 34–35. See also Juan Sánchez, *La caña*, pp. 36–61.

28. Del Castillo, "Consuelo," p. 35.

29. Protocolo notarial de Silvestre Aybar, vol. 1, Actos 1–77 (May 13, 1898), AGN.

30. Ibid. (March 17 and March 27, 1898), AGN.

31. Álvarez Santana, *San Pedro de Macorís*, pp. 96–106.

32. Arturo Martínez Moya, *La caña da para todo*, p. 236.

33. Marte, *Cuba y la República Dominicana*, p. 427; 6.4 *tareas* equal one acre.

34. Protocolo notarial de Silvestre Aybar, vol. 1, Actos 1–77 (May 13, 1898), AGN.

35. Pedro Francisco Bonó, "Opiniones de un dominicano," in *Papeles de Pedro Francisco Bonó*, ed. Emilio Rodríguez Demorizi, pp. 280, 282.

36. Ibid., p. 300.

37. Eugenio María de Hostos, "Falsa alarma. Crisis agrícola," in Emilio Rodríguez Demorizi, ed., *Hostos en Santo Domingo*, pp. 178–179.

38. Ibid., p. 173.

39. José María Padilla, "Oligarquía y subdesarrollo en Luperón, Región Norte, República Dominicana: 1900–1930," pp. 174–176.

40. Sergio Augusto Beras Morales, Telésforo Zuleta de Soto, and Luis Dalmau Febles, eds., "Gobernadores de San Pedro de Macorís," n.p.

41. Ibid.; Archivo del Ayuntamiento de San Pedro de Macorís Libros de Actas de Sesiones, Libro 5, February 11, 1897; and Libro 8, November 17, 1905 and January 1, 1906 (hereafter cited as Libros).

42. Richiez, "Historia de la provincia."

43. República Dominicana, Secretaría de Estado, *Mensaje y memorias del poder ejecutivo de la República Dominicana*, pp. 15–16, quotation on p. 16.

44. Augusto Vega, *Ulises Heureaux. Ensayo histórico*, p. 39.

45. Domínguez, *La dictadura de Heureaux*, pp. 38–41.

46. General Ulises Heureaux to Charles Wells, February 14, 1897, in Cyrus Veeser, "Cartas escogidas de los copiadores del Presidente Ulises Heureaux correspondientes a los años, 1894–1898," p. 180.

47. President Ulises Heureaux to General Ramón Castillo, March 28, 1895, in ibid., p. 96.

48. Libros de Actas de Sesiones, Libro 6, January 1, 1899, and November 15, 1899; Leonidas García Lluberes, "Historia de la provincia y especialmente de la ciudad de San Pedro de Macorís," p. 27; and Richiez, "Historia de la provincia," pp. 101–102.

49. Quoted in Bosch, *Composición social*, p. 331. Bosch indicates his source as Emilio Rodríguez Demorizi, *Cancionero de Lilís*, p. 347: "Con motivo de un violento altercado entre don Juan [Bautista Vicini] y el joven hostosiano Américo Lugo, Lilís hizo traer a su presencia el escritor, y después de un amable preámbulo le dijo:—Si usted fuera un vagabundo lo pondría en mi estado mayor, porque me gusta la gente de coraje. Pero su camino no es ése. Así es que ya usted sabe, porque yo solo soy el Vice-presidente. El Presidente es don Juan, que es el dueño del dinero."

50. Interview with Santiago Michelena Ariza by Humberto García Muñiz, Santo Domingo, Dominican Republic, May 19, 1991, Box 2, Cassette no. 1.

51. Marte, *Cuba y la República Dominicana*, pp. 403, 419, 424, 427, 428; Domínguez, *La dictadura de Heureaux*, pp. 17–21, 71–74, 211.

52. Veeser, *A World Safe for Capitalism*, pp. 54–55.

53. These efforts seemingly failed because Heureaux did not have the money to pay for a Washington lobbyist. Around 1898 his friend Archibald Grimke, an African American attorney who had served as a U.S. consular representative to Haiti in the 1870s, asked him for employment with his government, but Heureaux denied his application, adding, "Even though I want to [utilize] your efficient services, even if it were only [to make] trips to Washington, and [cover the] costs of representation." In a subsequent letter, he asked for Grimke's help negotiating trade agreements between the two countries. See Ulises Heureaux, Presidente de la República, to Archibald Grimke, c. 1898, in Veeser, "Cartas escogidas," p. 301. If Grimke, a firm supporter of Heureaux, lobbied on his friend's behalf, the tide of international opinion had shifted against the president. See Archibald Grimke, "The Dominican Republic and Her Revolutions."

54. Information culled from Archivo del Ayuntamiento de San Pedro de Macorís, Libros de Actas de Sesiones, Libros 8–10, May 1, 1903–November 21, 1913.

55. General Simon A. Campus to Military Governor, February 24, 1918, Gobierno Militar, Correspondencia con el Ministro de Interior y Policía, Legajo 25, AGN. The first maritime districts (provinces) created after Restoration were Puerto Plata and Samaná, in 1865; Monte Cristi, on the northern tip of the Dominican Republic and on the Haitian border, became a maritime district in 1879, followed by Barahona (1881), San Pedro de Macorís (1882), Espaillat (1885), and Pacificador (1886), the last named in honor of Ulises Heureaux. See also Tolentino Rojas, *Historia de la división territorial*, pp. 152, 160, 168, 170, 180, 188–189.

56. This information was derived by comparing a list of city council members who served between 1880 and 1900 with San Pedro's local commercial guide from 1897. In 1897, for example, Fernando Chalas served as president of the city council; he was also a partner, with his brother, of Chalas Hermanos, a general store (*tienda mixta*); Julio Coiscou, president of the city council in 1900, appears to have been co-owner, with Sylvain Coiscou, of the Dos Hermanos pharmacy. See Álvarez Santana, *San Pedro de Macorís*, pp. 231–236.

57. Alan Trachtenberg, *The Incorporation of America: Culture and Society in the Gilded Age*, pp. 3–4, 7.

58. María Filomena González Canalda, *Los gavilleros, 1904–1916*, pp. 24, 26, 27.

59. Ibid., pp. 34–38, quotation on p. 38. The original source is Del Gobernador de San Pedro de Macorís a Secretaría de Interior y Policia, May 2, 1904, Legajos 195–196, Interior y Policía, AGN.

60. Julie Franks, "The *Gavilleros* of the East: Social Banditry as Political Practice in the Dominican Sugar Region, 1900–1924," pp. 159–160.

61. Juan Pablo Dabove, *Nightmares of the Lettered City: Banditry and Literature in Latin America, 1816–1929*, p. 5.

62. González Canalda, *Los gavilleros*, pp. 166–167.

63. Turits, *Foundations of Despotism*, p. 76.

64. Francisco Peynado to Col. Rufus H. Lane, Encargado de la Secretaría de Estado de Justicia, July 17, 1918. Fondo Peynado, Serie Correspondencia Particular, Cartapacio II, E–L, 1915–1919. Archivo de la Biblioteca del Derecho, Universidad de Puerto Rico at Río Piedras.

65. William O. Rogers, Commanding Officer, 182nd Company, 15th Regiment [U.S. Marine Corps], San Pedro de Macorís, to District Commander, "Report on Concentration at Los Llanos, D.R.," April 25, 1919, RG 45, WA7, Box 757, Folder 4, U.S. National Archives (hereafter USNA).

66. Thomas Snowden, Military Governor of Santo Domingo, to Secretary of the Navy, May 8, 1919, RG 38, E11, Box 2, M62–184, Folder 112–19, USNA.

67. Charles S. Long to the Military Governor of Santo Domingo [H. S. Knapp], "Report of Lorenzo Semple, of the firm of Coudert Brothers," October 8, 1918, RG 45, WA7, Box 761, Folder 4, USNA.

68. Military Governor of Santo Domingo to Chief of Naval Operations, December 3, 1917, RG 45, WA7, Box 747, Document #15–70, USNA.

69. Commander, Cruiser Force, to Secretary of the Navy, "Report of Operations in Haitien [sic] and Dominican Waters from January 7th to January 13th, 1917," May 20, 1917, RG 45, WA7, Box 747, Folder 5, USNA.

70. For example, a report submitted in December 1917 claimed that marines had collected over 32,000 revolvers, 11,000 rifles, 3,000 shotguns, and over 100,000 rounds of ammunition from Dominicans. See "Quarterly Report from the Military Governor Knapp to the Secretary of the Navy," October 1, 1917–December 31, 1917, RG 45, WA7, Box 760, Folder 1, USNA.

71. Brigade Commander [Second Provisional Brigade, U.S. Marines] to Military Governor, "Daily Report, April 1 to 8, 1917," August 8, 1917, RG 80, Box 2302, Folder 27818 (250–99), USNA.

72. G. C. Thorpe, to H. S. Knapp, Military Governor, "Memorandum," dated October 25, 1918, and attached to report from Charles S. Long to H. S. Knapp, "Report of Lorenzo Semple, of the firm of Coudert Brothers," dated October 8, 19198, enclosed with letter from Mr. Lorenzo Semple to Major General George Barnett, Headquarters, USMC, in Washington, D.C., dated October 3, 1918, RG 45, WA7, Box 761, Folder 4, USNA.

73. Ibid.

74. William O. Rogers, Commanding Officer, 182nd Company, 15th Regiment [U.S. Marine Corps], San Pedro de Macorís, to District Commander, "Report on Concentration at Los Llanos, D.R.," April 25, 1919, RG 45, WA7, Box 757, Folder 4, USNA.

75. Bruce Calder, "Caudillos and Gavilleros versus the United States Marines: Guerrilla Insurgency during the Dominican Intervention, 1916–1924," p. 660.

76. Franks, "The Gavilleros," pp. 158, 171.

77. Francisco Peynado, "Deslinde, mensura y partición de terrenos," Revista Jurídica, no. 4 (n.d.), Fondo Peynado, Colección, Archivo de la Biblioteca del Derecho de la Universidad de Puerto Rico at Río Piedras.

78. Correspondencia Interior y Policía, Gobierno Militar, Legajo 40, AGN. This translation was made by a U.S. official.

79. Ibid.

80. Ibid.

81. Félix Servio Ducoudray, Los "gavilleros" del este. Una epopeya calumniada.

82. Calder, The Impact of Intervention, p. 121.

83. Inoa, Azúcar, pp. 19–21.

84. See Gilbert M. Joseph, "On the Trail of Latin American Bandits: A Reexamination of Peasant Resistance," Latin American Research Review 25, no. 3 (1990): 7–53.

85. Dabove, Nightmares, p. 6.

86. Elizabeth Dore, "Property, Households, and Public Regulation of Domestic Life," p. 148.

87. Archivo del Ayuntamiento de San Pedro de Macorís, Libro de Actas de Sesiones, Libro 10, December 4, 1912.

88. González Canalda, Los gavilleros, p. 166, quotation on p. 167.

89. Cited in Raymundo González, "La Guerra de la Restauración vista desde abajo," pp. 160, 162, 163–164.

90. James Sanders, "'Citizens of a Free People'": Popular Liberalism and Race in Nineteenth-Century Southwestern Colombia," p. 278; Ferrer; Insurgent Cuba; and James Sanders, Contentious Republicans: Popular Politics, Race, and Class in Nineteenth-Century Colombia.

Chapter 3. The Culture of Progress in San Pedro de Macorís

1. Baud, "'Constitutionally White,'" p. 124.

2. Barbara Berglund, *Making San Francisco American: Cultural Frontiers in the Urban West, 1846–1906*, pp. 8, quotation on p. 17.

3. A. Ravelo, "Numeración de casas," to Ayuntamiento de San Pedro de Macorís, May 10, 1898, Ayuntamiento de San Pedro de Macorís, Legajo 5,533 (1898), AGN.

4. Álvarez Santana, *San Pedro de Macorís*, pp. 150, 152–153.

5. My heartfelt gratitude to Fermín Álvarez Santana for making *El Cable* available to me: "Todo es progreso," *El Cable*, April 12, 1896; "La Exposición de Chicago," *El Cable*, April 12, 1893; and "Edúquese el pueblo," *El Cable*, September 4, 1893.

6. "Porvenir," *El Cable*, February 12, 1893.

7. Archivo del Ayuntamiento de San Pedro de Macorís, Libros de Actas de Sesiones, Libro 2, January 15, 1891.

8. Census information is given in Álvarez Santana, *San Pedro de Macorís*, p. 383.

9. Archivo del Ayuntamiento de San Pedro de Macorís, Libro de Actas de Sesiones: Request for Mellor telephone line, Libro 1, May 11, 1887; Fereen phone line, Libro 5, May 26, 1898; and permits granted for railway construction and inauguration celebration, Libro 3, October 8, 1891; April 7, 1892; February 22, 1893. Payment for street upkeep, Enrique Valdéz, President of Ayuntamiento of San Pedro de Macorís, to Administrator of Ingenio Santa Fe, May 18, 1911, Ayuntamiento de San Pedro de Macorís, Legajo 5,524, Exp. 37, AGN.

10. Archivo del Ayuntamiento de San Pedro de Macorís, Libro de Actas de Sesiones: Street lighting, Libro 1, July 3 and July 23, 1888, and Libro 2, December 27, 1888 and January 24, 1889. In 1903, 156 bulbs (*faroles*) were lighting thirty streets in addition to the city's downtown. See Álvarez Santana, *San Pedro de Macorís*, p. 381.

11. José Hernández to Ayuntamiento de San Pedro de Macorís, April 29, 1895, Ayuntamiento de San Pedro de Macorís, Legajo 5,517, Expediente 17 (1895) AGN.

12. "Porvenir," *El Cable*, February 12, 1893.

13. Juan Bosch observes that for much of the nineteenth century a national bourgeoisie did not exist in the Dominican Republic, given the generalized impoverishment of the country and the absence of finance capital with which to invest in both trade and manufacturing. See *Composición social dominicana*, p. 286.

14. Protocolos Notariales de Juan Antonio Hernández, February 15, 1922, Libro 1, 1919; July 8, 1922, Libro 2, 1920.

15. M. Leopoldo Richiez, "¿Cúal ha sido el factor principal del progreso de Macorís?" *Renacimiento* 5, no. 53 (December 20, 1916): 910.

16. As in Germany during the nineteenth century; see Geoff Eley, "Nations, Publics, and Political Cultures: Placing Habermas in the Nineteenth Century."

17. José Ramón López, "La Asociación," *Listín Diario*, December 20, 1901. Reprinted in José Ramón López, *Escritos dispersos*, p. 80.

18. José Ramón López, "Reciprocidad," *Listín Diario*, August 9 and 11, 1902. Reprinted in López, *Escritos dispersos*, pp. 98, 99–100.

19. Sr. Lowenski Monzón, "En el Ateneo Macorisano," *Renacimiento* 1, no. 18 (November 15, 1915): 316.

20. M. T. Río, "La velada en Macorís," *Listín Diario*, September 15, 1897. The event took place on September 10.

21. Álvarez Santana, *San Pedro de Macorís*, pp. 412, 418–419.

22. "De Consuelo," *Renacimiento* 4, no. 124 (June 22, 1918): n.p.

23. Bermúdez, *Manual de historia*, pp. 57–58; Álvarez Santana, *San Pedro de Macorís*, p. 349.

24. Sr. Lowenski Monzón, "En el Ateneo Macorisano," *Renacimiento* 1, no. 18 (November 15, 1915): 316. The connection Monzón makes to Hostos is intriguing because I have found no evidence that any of the Amantes' founders attended Hostos's Professional Institute in Santo Domingo, making it difficult to trace precisely how his ideas were disseminated among San Pedro's male intelligentsia. Moreover, although not mentioned as founding members of the Amantes, Antonio Soler and Luis Bermúdez, the editors of *El Cable*, were recognized as early supporters, even though the newspaper's masthead proclaimed them as Lilístas, supporters of Ulises Heureaux, the man who made Hostos's residency in Santo Domingo so unpleasant that he left for Chile. If the Amantes were as Hostosian as Monzón claimed, Soler's and Bermúdez's collaboration suggests they may not have been as loyal as they appeared to have been or that, in San Pedro, Lilísta politics and Hostosian philosophy were somehow reconciled.

25. Eugenio María de Hostos, *Moral social*, p. 25.

26. Ibid., p. 8.

27. Ibid., p. 40.

28. Eugenio María de Hostos, "La que algún día será una gran nacionalidad," in Rodríguez Demorizi, *Hostos en Santo Domingo*, vol. 1, p. 145.

29. Eugenio María de Hostos, "Inmigración y colonización," in Rodríguez Demorizi, *Hostos en Santo Domingo*, vol. 2, pp. 115 , 117.

30. Álvarez Santana, *San Pedro de Macorís*, pp. 315–316.

31. Rafael Deligne, School Superintendent, to Ayuntamiento, "Informe," January 17, 1895, Ayuntamiento de San Pedro de Macorís, Legajo 5,517, Expediente 17 (1895), AGN.

32. Eusebia Rodríguez y Rodríguez to Ayuntamiento de San Pedro de Macorís, April 4, 1894, Ayuntamiento de San Pedro de Macorís, Legajo 5,591 (1894), AGN.

33. Álvarez Santana, *San Pedro de Macorís*, pp. 318–319.

34. Domínguez, *La dictadura de Heureaux*, p. 45: "una labor disociadora en el seno del pueblo," from *El Orden*, July 15, 1887.

35. Manuel de Jesús Galván, "Santo Domingo, 7 de septiembre de 1862," *La Razón* 1, no. 19 (1862), in *Escritos políticos*, p. 154.

36. Gregorio Luperón, "Mensaje del Presidente del Gobierno Provisional de la República," *Notas autobiográficas y apuntes históricos*, p. 72.

37. Archivo del Ayuntamiento de San Pedro de Macorís, Libro de Actas de Sesiones, Libro 2, May 5, 1891.

38. Ibid., Libro 6, January 30, 1900.

39. Ibid. January 29, 1901.

40. Fernando Chalas, Governor General [San Pedro de Macorís] to Ayuntamiento de San Pedro de Macorís, January 12, 1901, Ayuntamiento de San Pedro de Macorís, Legajo 5,580 (1886), AGN.

41. Archivo del Ayuntamiento de San Pedro de Macorís, Libros de Actas de Sesiones, Libro 8, October 22, 1906.

42. Federico Henríquez y Carvajal, "Certamen literario," *Revista Ilustrada* (March 15, 1899): 5.

43. Harry Hoetink, *El pueblo dominicano*, pp. 87–90. See also idem, "Materiales para el estudio de la República Dominicana en la segunda mitad del siglo XX," p. 18. Hoetink does not cite the source of his census information.

44. José Rodríguez, "Censo de 1917," October 15, 1917; idem, "Censo de 1917," October 15, 1917. Legajo 5,527, Ayuntamiento de San Pedro de Macorís, 1917, AGN.

45. República Dominicana. Secretaría de Estado de Interior, Policía y Agricultura, *Censo de la República Dominicana*, pp. 112, 129–130.

46. Manuel García Arévalo, "La presencia española en San Pedro de Macorís," pp. 38–48; Ernesto Armenteros, *Entre las nieblas del recuerdo*, pp. 23–27.

47. Francisco Richiez Acevedo, "Cocolandia, cosmopolitismo e hibridismo. Consideraciones sobre el cambio social que se opera en la ciudad de San Pedro de Macoris," p. 33.

48. Armenteros, *Entre las nieblas del recuerdo*, pp. 68–69, 103–105.

49. "Juegos Florales Antillanos," *Renacimiento* 27, no. 2 (April 1, 1916): 206–207.

50. See *Revista Ilustrada* (October 1, 1898).

51. Mercedes Mota, "Verdad y gratitude," *Revista Ilustrada* (March 15, 1899).

52. Apolinar Perdomo, "Ex-Voto," *Blanco y Negro* (April 18, 1909).

53. "La reina y su corte," *Blanco y Negro* (April 25, 1909).

54. "Crónica," *Blanco y Negro* (May 9, 1909).

55. "Nueva panadería del Sr. J. Parra Alba," *Blanco y Negro* (August 1, 1909). One important exception I found was a picture and morality tale published by Mercedes A. Heureaux, daughter of Ulises Heureaux, published in the September 12, 1909, edition of *Blanco y Negro*.

56. "Asilo de Santa Cruz," *Blanco y Negro* (October 17, 1909); "Colegio Eu. María de Hostos," *Blanco y Negro* (March 20, 1910).

57. "Escuela 'La Caridad' sostenida por los R.R.P.P. Franciscanos," *Blanco y Negro* (January 16, 1910); "Juegos olímpicos," *Blanco y Negro* (c. 1910), no. 82.

58. "Juegos Florales Antillanos," p. 207; "Concurso," *Renacimiento* 2, no. 42 (September 30, 1916): n.p.

59. See Hoetink, *El pueblo dominicano*, p. 66.

60. Archivo del Ayuntamiento de San Pedro de Macorís, Libros de Actas de Sesiones, Libro 8, October 22 and February 23, 1906; name change to Avenida España, Libro 11, May 28, 1915. Historical figures for whom streets were named include Duarte, Sánchez, and Mella, the leaders of the Independence movement in 1844 against Haiti; and General José María Cabral, who led a raid against Spanish forces after the island's annexation to Spain.

Chapter 4. Policing the Urban Poor

1. H. H. Gosling to A. Cohen, April 16, 1901, Public Record Office, Foreign Office 140/7 (hereafter PRO, FO). Gosling translated the Spanish "*vagabundo*" into "vagabond," which does not suggest the gravity of the insult in Dominican Spanish. According to Juan Bosch, a Dominican historian and political opponent of Trujillo, a "*vagabundo*" in the Dominican context means "a restless, irresponsible man, a braggart and non-conformist"; see *Composición social dominicana*, p. 232.

2. Bosch, *Composición social dominicana*, p. 232.

3. Ibid.

4. Dr. Henríquez y Carvajal to Vice Consul Gosling, October 1, 1901, PRO, FO 140/7.

5. Dr. Henríquez y Carvajal to Vice Consul Gosling, April 5, 1902, PRO, FO 140/7.

6. A not-surprising result given the experiences of Afro-Antillean peoples across the Caribbean rimlands, from Panama to Costa Rica, Cuba to Louisiana. See Putnam, *The Company They Kept*; Michael Conniff, *Black Labor on a White Canal*.

7. Following William French, *A Peaceful and Working People: Manners, Morals, and Class Formation in Northern Mexico*, p. 5.

8. República Dominicana, Congreso Nacional Dominicano, *Mensaje y memorias del poder ejecutivo*, p. 70.

9. Ibid.

10. "Ley de Franquicias Agrícolas," *Gaceta Oficial*, no. 2207 [trans. William Bass], p. 23.

11. William Bass, quoted in del Castillo, "Consuelo," p. 37.

12. Entrevista de Humberto García Muñiz a Hugh Kelly IV en su residencia en la Ave. Lincoln, Santo Domingo, República Dominicana, Sunday, April 28, 1991, Colección Hugh Kelly

IV, Caja 2, Cassette 9, Side B, Archivo del Centro de Investigaciones Históricas, Universidad de Puerto Rico at Río Piedras.

13. "Mucho ruido," *El Cable*, April 8, 1897.

14. De la criminalidad," *El Cable*, February 4, 1893.

15. "Mucho ruido," *El Cable*, April 8, 1897.

16. "Comparad i juzgad," *El Cable*, December 21, 1897.

17. For the development of the sugar industry in the Dominican Republic, see José del Castillo, "The Formation of the Dominican Sugar Industry: From Competition to Monopoly, from National Semiproletariat to Foreign Proletariat," pp. 217, 220–224; Juan J. Sánchez, *La caña*, p. 41.

18. Important works on Caribbean migration in the Caribbean region include Bonham Richardson, *Caribbean Migrants: Environment and Human Survival on St. Kitts and Nevis*; Michael Conniff, *Black Labor*.

19. Richardson, *Caribbean Migrants*, pp. 122–131.

20. Patrick Bryan cites a "Petition of British Subjects in San Pedro de Macorís for Consular Representation, May 1, 1895." See "The Question of Labor," p. 240 and n19 on p. 250.

21. José del Castillo, "La inmigración de braceros azucareros en la República Dominicana, 1900–1930"; idem, "The Formation of the Dominican Sugar Industry," pp. 231–232; Andrés Corten, Mercedes Acosta, and Isis Duarte, "Las relaciones de producción en la economía azucarera dominicana," pp. 11–83. See also "Ley de Franquicias Agrícolas," *Gaceta Oficial*, no. 2207: 23.

22. Gobierno Militar, República Dominicana, Secretaría del Estado de Agricultura e Inmigración, "Informe anual de inmigración del 10 del julio 1919 al 30 de junio 1920," 1920, AGN; Ralph Warfield, Secretaría del Estado de Agricultura e Inmigración, to J. C. McCarthy, Subadministrator, Ingenio Angelina, August 3, 1920, Gobierno Militar, República Dominicana, Secretaría de Estado de Agricultura e Inmigración, Solicitudes de Permisos de Permanencia, Legajo 47 (1920), AGN.

23. Archivo del Ayuntamiento de San Pedro de Macorís, Libros de Actas de Sesiones, Libro 4, January 1, 1895–December 30, 1896 (December 20, 1895), and Libro 8, May 1, 1903–July 31, 1908 (February 9, 1906; March 5, 1906; June 15, 1906).

24. Ibid., Libro 8, May 1, 1903–July 31, 1908 (October 8, 1906).

25. Secretaría de Estado de Interior y Policía, *Censo de la República Dominicana*, p. 130.

26. H. H. Gosling to Acting Governor, Leeward Islands, Antigua, October 1900, PRO, FO 140/7.

27. British Vice Consul to Governor of San Pedro de Macorís, January 13, 1916, Gobernación de San Pedro de Macorís, Legajo 6, Year 1916, AGN: "golpes por todas partes de su cuerpo."

28. British Vice Consul to Governor of San Pedro de Macorís, January 16, 1916, Gobernación de San Pedro de Macorís, Legajo 6, Year 1916, AGN.

29. British Vice Consul to Governor of San Pedro de Macorís, January 10, 1916, Gobernación de San Pedro de Macorís, Legajo 6, Year 1916, AGN.

30. John Roberts to Military Governor, n.d., "Presos." Gobierno Militar Norteamericano, 1917–1922, Legajo 57C, AGN.

31. See, for example, del Castillo, "La inmigración;" Bryan, "The Question of Labor," pp. 235–251; Bonham Richardson, *The Caribbean in the Wider World*; and Franco Pichardo, *Sobre racismo y antihaitianismo (y otros ensayos)*, pp. 29, 67.

32. H. H. Gosling to E. A. Cohen [British consul general], Port au Prince, Haiti, January 19, 1900, PRO, FO 140/7.

33. Trevor Purcell, *Banana Fallout: Class, Color, and Culture among West Indians in Costa Rica*, p. 15.

34. Allen Wells and Gilbert M. Joseph, "Modernizing Visions, *Chilango* Blueprints, and Provincial Growing Pains: Mérida at the Turn of the Century," pp. 172–173.

35. Michele Mitchell, *Righteous Propagation: The Politics of Racial Destiny after Reconstruction,* p. 12. For a similar concern raised among Cubans about black migrant workers from Haiti and Jamaica, see Robert B. Hoernel, "Sugar and Social Change in Oriente, Cuba, 1898–1946," pg. 237.

36. President of the Ayuntamiento to Treasurer, October 9, 1891, and Manuel S. Richiez et al. to President of Ayuntamiento [de San Pedro de Macorís], November 23, 1891, in Legajo 5,601 [7], Ayuntamiento de San Pedro de Macorís, Year 1891, AGN.

37. "Mezclilla," *El Cable,* May 13, 1893, p. 1. I have not been able to locate the date when the city council approved this legislation.

38. Archivo del Ayuntamiento de San Pedro de Macorís, Libros de Actas de Sesiones, Libro 8, August 14, 1906.

39. Interview with Bishop Telésforo Isaac, Santo Domingo, October 9, 1999.

40. Archivo del Ayuntamiento de San Pedro de Macorís, Libros de Actas de Sesiones, Libro 8, July 15, 1908. See also Councilman Brower's complaints noted during a council meeting: Libro 8, July 20, 1908.

41. The council secretary references the regulation in his notes from March 1, 1909: Archivo del Ayuntamiento de San Pedro de Macorís, Libros de Actas de Sesiones, Libro 9, March 1, 1909. In 1919 the provincial governor also made reference to the 1909 regulations when he requested that the city council stop the "spread of prostitution in the city." The governor argued that prostitution had spilled beyond boundaries set by law and wanted the city council to modify Article 15 of the Prostitution Regulation to address this event. See Archivo del Ayuntamiento de San Pedro de Macorís, Libros de Actas de Sesiones, Libro 13, October 24, 1919.

42. Archivo del Ayuntamiento de San Pedro de Macorís, Libros de Actas de Sesiones, Libro 8, May 8, 1908, and Libro 10, December 5, 1910. The regulation is mentioned in Libro 9, March 1, 1909.

43. Dr. Joseph Earle Moore et al., "El cuidado de la sífilis en la práctica general," pp. 2–3.

44. Dr. H. J. Marchena to Ayuntamiento de San Pedro de Macorís, January 27, 1911, Ayuntamiento de San Pedro de Macorís, Legajo 5,524, Expediente 37, Year 1911, AGN.

45. Alain Corbin, "Commercial Sexuality in Nineteenth-Century France: A System of Images and Regulations," pp. 211–212.

46. Ibid., p. 211.

47. Hygiene Inspector to Ayuntamiento de San Pedro de Macorís, January 2, 1911, "Informe de la Salud Pública, 1910," Ayuntamiento de San Pedro de Macorís, Legajo 5,524, Expediente 37, Year 1911, AGN; Ayuntamiento de San Pedro de Macorís, Libro de Actas de Sesiones, Libro 10, February 13, 1911.

48. Moore et al., "El cuidado de la sífilis," pp. 2–3.

49. Dr. Emelio Tió y Betances to Ayuntamiento de San Pedro de Macorís, April 20, 1911, AGN; Ayuntamiento de San Pedro de Macorís, Legajo 5,524, Expediente 37, Year 1911. See also Ayuntamiento de San Pedro de Macorís, Libro de Actas de Sesiones, Libro 10, June 14 and 17, 1912.

50. Laura Engelstein, "Morality and the Wooden Spoon: Russian Doctors View Syphilis, Social Class, and Sexual Behavior," p. 176.

51. Kristin Luker has made a similar argument for antiprostitution campaigns in the United States; see "Sex, Social Hygiene, and the State: The Double-Edged Sword of Social Reform," pp. 622–625.

52. April J. Mayes, "Tolerating Sex: Prostitution, Gender, and Governance in the Dominican Republic, 1880s–1924."

53. Archivo del Ayuntamiento de San Pedro de Macorís, Libros de Actas de Sesiones, Libro 11A, May 11, 1917.

54. Calder, *The Impact of Intervention,* pp. 40–50.

55. Archivo del Ayuntamiento de San Pedro de Macorís, Libros de Actas de Sesiones, Libro 12, December 6, 1918.

56. "Record of Proceedings of a Board of Investigation Convened at Marine Barracks in Santo Domingo City," August 6, 1918, unnumbered Legajo, Gobierno Militar Norteamericano, Correspondencia Cruzados con la Secretaría de Estado de Justicia e Instrucción Pública, AGN.

57. Archivo del Ayuntamiento de San Pedro de Macorís, Libros de Actas de Sesiones, Libro 13, October 24, 1919.

58. Ibid. November 19, November 27, December 29, 1919.

59. Alcaldía de San Pedro de Macorís, Libro 40 [June 1–10, 1920, Case #25; June 16–25, 1920, Cases #89–92], Year 1920, AGN. Military government records suggest the participation of U.S. Marines or Dominicans trained by U.S. Marines in these raids. The provost marshal submitted reports to the occupation government regarding prostitution-based arrests. See Archivo del Ayuntamiento de San Pedro de Macorís, Libros de Actas de Sesiones, Libro 13, December 29, 1919; and C. H. Lyman (District Commander) to Commanding General, April 11, 1922, Legajo 122, Gobierno Militar Norteamericano, Interior y Policía (1922), AGN.

60. Brian Patrick Moran, "Prison Reform in the United States Navy and the Dominican Republic: The Military Occupation and Prisons, 1900–1930," pp. 282–285. By the end of the 1920s, prostitution was illegal in many states and further criminalized in Puerto Rico. See Eileen Findlay, *Imposing Decency: The Politics of Sexuality in Puerto Rico, 1870–1920*, pp. 174–176; Luker, "Sex, Social Hygiene, and the State."

61. Findlay, *Imposing Decency*, p. 9.

62. Kevin J. Mumford, *Interzones: Black/White Sex Districts in Chicago and New York in the Early Twentieth Century*, pp. xvii, 20, 48, 54.

63. Holt, *The Problem of Freedom*, p. 402.

Chapter 5. Debating Dominicans' Race during the U.S. Occupation

1. This sequence of events is gleaned from police records and letters. See James Cooks to the Honorable Fernando Escobar, September 12, 1921, RG 38, Box 5, M201–201, E11, USNA; Provost Marshal C. M. Kincade to District Commander, Eastern District, September 21, 1921, "United [sic] Negro Improvement Association at San Pedro de Macoris—Petition of re-imprisonment of members," September 21, 1921, RG 38, E11, M201–201, USNA; letter from Reverend Beer to Dr. Gray, September 12, 1921, quoted in Philip E. Wheaton, *Triunfando sobre las tragedias. Historia centenaria de la Iglesia Episcopal Dominicana, 1897–1997*, p. 128.

2. Manuel Jimenez, "A True and Correct Copy, 'A,'" September 21, 1921, RG 38, E11, Box 5, Folder 202, USNA; Fernando A. Brea to Encargado del Departamento de Justicia—Santo Domingo, "Hermandad de la Sangre Africana (Asociación Secreta). I Asociación Universal para el Mejoramiento de los Negros, i Liga de la Comunidad Africana," San Pedro de Macorís, January 19, 1922, RG 38, E11, Box 5, Folder 202, USNA.

3. C. M. Kincade to District Commander, "United [sic] Negro Improvement Association at San Pedro de Macorís—Petition of re-imprisonment of members"; Manuel Jimenez, "A True and Correct Copy, 'A,'" RG 38, E11, Box 5, Folder 202, USNA.

4. Frank Guridy, "'Enemies of the White Race': The Machadista State and the UNIA in Cuba," pp. 107–138.

5. Luis Martínez-Fernández, *Torn between Empires: Economy, Society, and Patterns of Political Thought in the Hispanic Caribbean, 1840–1878*, p. 579.

6. Dirección General de Inmigración, "Lista de Inmigración," vol. 7, AGN. Similar arguments about the heavily female composition of British West Indian migration to Haiti are discussed

in Peter D. Fraser, "British West Indians in Haiti in the Late Nineteenth and Early Twentieth Centuries."

7. Protocolo Notarial de Juan Antonio Hernández, Libro 3 (entries listed in the order they appear in the text): September 15, 1920; March 2, 1920; December 1, 1920.

8. For information about the Methodist Church, see Archivo del Ayuntamiento de San Pedro de Macorís, Ayuntamiento de San Pedro de Macorís, Libro de Actas de Sesiones, Libro 8, May 14 1904, when the city council received a letter from Father Williams "inviting this body to celebrate, on May 15th, a procession to pronounce the 18th anniversary of his church." For the Episcopal Church, see Wheaton, *Triunfando sobre las tragedias*, pp. 27–30. For a complete description of the various lodges and societies in San Pedro, see Fermín Álvarez Santana, "Histora del desarrollo de la Provincia de San Pedro de Macorís," p. 219.

9. Interview with Don Emille Washington, San Pedro de Macorís, March 28, 2000.

10. Marriage Register, 1921–1922, San Esteban Church, Iglesia Episcopal Dominicana, San Pedro de Macorís. I am grateful to the Reverend Mercedes Julián for making these records available to me. San Esteban remained an English-language church until well into the 1960s. Therefore, records used in this chapter are in English.

11. Baptismal Register, 1920–1964, San Esteban Church, Iglesia Episcopal Dominicana, San Pedro de Macorís, n.p.

12. Interview with Doña Martha Williamson viuda González, San Pedro de Macorís, March 23, 2000.

13. Ibid.

14. Helen A. Regis, "Blackness and the Politics of Memory in the New Orleans Second Line," p. 770.

15. Hart Nelsen and Anne Kusener Nelsen, *Black Church in the Sixties*, pp. 11–13, as cited in C. Eric Lincoln and Lawrence H. Mamiya, *The Black Church in the African American Experience*, p. 11.

16. República Dominicana, Congreso Nacional Dominicano, *Gaceta Oficial del Poder Legislativo*, no. 2207 [copy], July 8, 1911, pp. 11–12. According to the 1911 Agricultural Law, contracted workers were supposed to return to their native lands once the season ended.

17. Godfrey Fisher, British Legation, to His Majesty's Principal Secretary of State for Foreign Affairs, December 8, 1917, "Distressed British Subjects," Consular Reports, PRO, FO 369/999.

18. Laura Tabili, *"We Ask for British Justice": Workers and Racial Difference in Late Imperial Britain*, pp. 16, 29, 32.

19. W. F. Elkins, *Black Power in the Caribbean: The Beginnings of the Modern National Movement*, pp. 5–15.

20. Ibid.

21. Eric D. Duke, "The Diasporic Dimensions of British Caribbean Federation in the Early Twentieth Century," pp. 228–230.

22. Tony Martin, *Race First: The Ideological and Organizational Struggles of Marcus Garvey and the Universal Negro Improvement Association*, p. 370.

23. John Henrik Clarke, "Introduction," pp. 7–12. See also Lawrence Levine, "Marcus Garvey and the Politics of Revitalization," p. 121. The literature on Garveyism is extensive. Works consulted for this chapter include Levine, "Marcus Garvey"; Rupert Lewis, *Marcus Garvey, Anti-Colonial Champion*; Judith Stein, *The World of Marcus Garvey: Race and Class in Modern Society*; Barry Carr, "Identity, Class, and Nation: Black Immigrant Workers, Cuban Communism, and the Sugar Insurgency, 1925–1934"; Marc C. McLeod, "Garveyism in Cuba: 1920–1940"; Pedro Pablo Rodríguez, "Marcus Garvey en Cuba"; Philippe Bourgois, *Ethnicity at Work: Divided Labor on a Central American Banana Plantation*; Aviva Chomsky, *West Indian Workers and the United Fruit Company in Costa Rica, 1870–1940*; and Ronald Harpelle, "Radicalism and Accom-

modation: Garveyism in a United Fruit Company Enclave." Michael Conniff mentions Garvey-ism in the Panama Canal Zone in *Black Labor*, p. 71.

24. Humberto García Muñiz and Jorge L. Giovannetti, "Garveyismo y racismo en el Caribe: El caso de la población cocola en la República Dominicana."

25. Ronald Harpelle, "Cross Currents in the Western Caribbean: Marcus Garvey and the UNIA in Central America," p. 66.

26. Frank Guridy, "'Enemies of the White Race': The Machadista State and the UNIA in Cuba"; Ronald Harpelle, "Cross Currents in the Western Hemisphere: Marcus Garvey and the UNIA in Central America"; and Marc McLeod, "'Sin Dejar de Ser Cubanos': Cuban Blacks and the Challenges of Garveyism in Cuba."

27. Charles Henry, "Report of the U.N.I.A. from Dec. 7, 1919 to Dec. 7, 1920," no date, RG 38, E11, Box 5, Folder 202, USNA.

28. José del Castillo and Walter Cordero, "La economía dominicana durante el primer cuarto del Siglo XX."

29. The Reverend Wyllie witnessed this and wrote about the situation to Dr. Gray. See Whea-ton, *Triunfando sobre las tragedias*, p. 91.

30. Inoa, *Azúcar*, pp. 113–115.

31. Pablo A. Maríñez, *Agroindustria, estado y clases sociales en la era de Trujillo, 1935–1960*, pp. 18–19, 22; and Roberto Cassá, "Reflexiones sobre la estructura de clases entre 1900–1930," pp. 43–63.

32. Great Britain, Commercial Relations and Exports Department, *Economic and Commer-cial Conditions in the Dominican Republic*, p. 16; del Castillo and Cordero, "La economía do-minicana," pp. 110–116; Emelio Betances, *State and Society in the Dominican Republic*, pp. 28–30. Another contemporary writer noticed this process as well; see Melvin Knight, *The Americans in Santo Domingo*, pp. 135–138.

33. Michelle A. Stephens, *Black Empire: The Masculine Global Imaginary of Caribbean Intel-lectuals in the United States, 1914–1962*, pp. 6, 8.

34. Wheaton, *Triunfando sobre las tragedias*, pp. 39–41, 131. Bishop Telésforo Isaac repeated this story to me, one he heard from his father.

35. Reverend Beer to Dr. Gray, August 19, 1921, quoted in Wheaton, *Triunfando sobre las tragedias*, p. 127.

36. Reverend Beer to Dr. Gray, September 12, 1921, quoted in ibid., pp. 127–128.

37. Reverend Beer to Dr. Gray, August 12, 1921, quoted in ibid. p. 126.

38. Reverend William Wyllie to Dr. Gray, December 6, 1920, quoted in ibid, p. 89.

39. James Cooks to Honorable Fernando Escobar, Consul of His Highness the King of the Netherlands, September 12, 1921. RG 38, Box 5, M201–202, E11, USNA. Evidence of the deporta-tion order: Gobierno Militar Norteamericano, "A True and Correct Copy 'D.'"

40. See Harpelle, "Radicalism and Accommodation," pp. 9–11.

41. Provost Marshal C. M. Kincade to District Commander, Eastern District, "United Negro Improvement Association at San Pedro de Macoris—Petition of re-imprisonment of members," September 21, 1921, RG 38, E11, M201–201, USNA; Commanding General to the Military Gov-ernor of Santo Domingo, "Threats of the Alcalde and Marines at San Pedro de Macorís against James Cooks, Dutch Subject," September 30, 1921, RG 38, E11, Box 5, Folder 202, USNA. Inter-estingly, these alleged problems between the city council and the UNIA do not appear in the municipal records, whereas other problem groups and figures are mentioned.

42. For the provost marshal's intent to deport the UNIA leadership, see Provost Marshal C. M. Kincade to District Commander, Eastern District, "United Negro Improvement Association at San Pedro de Macoris—Petition of re-imprisonment of members," September 21, 1921, RG 38, E11, M201–201, USNA; and Commanding General to the Military Governor of Santo Domingo,

"Threats of the Alcalde and Marines at San Pedro de Macorís against James Cooks, Dutch Subject," September 30, 1921, RG 38, E11, Box 5, Folder 202, USNA. For letters and petitions of support for those facing deportation, see Luis Guzmán to Rear Admiral Samuel S. Robison, September 24, 1921, RG 38, E11, Box 5, M 201–202, USNA; Ezel Vanderhorst, José Lucia Martínez, John Kennedy et al. to Rear Admiral Samuel S. Robison, September 26, 1921, RG 38, E11, Box 5, Folder 202, USNA; James Cooks to Fernando Escobar [Dutch consul], September 12, 1921, RG 38, E11, Box 5, M 201–202, USNA; Fernando Escobar to Lieutenant Colonel F. A. Ramsey [head of foreign affairs], September 15, 1921, RG 38, E11, Box 5, Folder 202, USNA.

43. Mary Renda, *Taking Haiti: Military Occupation and the Culture of U.S. Imperialism, 1915–1940*, pp. 149, 155–156 (Wirkus quote).

44. Calder, *The Impact of Intervention*, p. 124.

45. Ana Mitila Lora, "Entrevista con Juan Valdés Sánchez," *Listín Diario*, July 29, 1999.

46. Philip Douglass, "Americanizing Santo Domingo," *The Nation* (May 4, 1921): 663.

47. Ernest Gruening, "The Senators Visit Haiti and Santo Domingo," *The Nation* (January 4, 1922): 10.

48. Max Boot, *The Savage Wars of Peace: Small Wars and the Rise of American Power*, p. 174.

49. Calder, *The Impact of Intervention*, pp. 191, 208–209, 240; Moya Pons, *The Dominican Republic*, p. 327.

50. Military Governor Henry Knapp, "Report," April 8, 1917, RG 45, WA7, Box 747, Folder 7, USNA.

51. Lieutenant Edward A. Fellowes, U.S.M.C., "Training Native Troops in Santo Domingo," *Marine Corps Gazette* 8, no. 4 (December 1923): 215, 218, 219, 230–231. For a description of the Dominican National Police, see Calder, *The Impact of Intervention*, pp. 54–62.

52. Unsigned letter to Major General John A. Lejeune, Commandant, U.S. Marine Corps, October 25, 1921, RG 45, WA7, Box 759, Folder 5, USNA.

53. Eric Roorda, *The Dictator Next Door*, p. 21.

54. Derby, *The Dictator's Seduction*, p. 115.

55. Roorda, *The Dictator Next Door*, pp. 164–165, quotation on p. 177. See also Jesús de Galíndez, *La era de Trujillo*, pp. 26–27.

56. George C. Thorpe, "American Achievements in Santo Domingo, Haiti, and the Virgin Islands," *Journal of International Relations* 11, no. 1 (July 1920): 76; original emphasis.

57. Joshua Lund, *The Mestizo State: Reading Race in Modern Mexico*, p. xiv.

58. Calder, *The Impact of Intervention*, pp. 30–31, 49–54, 84.

59. Quoted in Vicente L. Rafael, "White Love: Surveillance and Nationalist Resistance in the U.S. Colonization of the Philippines," p. 189.

60. Quoting President Woodrow Wilson, cited in ibid., p. 216n8.

61. Jennifer L. Hochschild and Brenna Marea Powell, "Racial Reorganization and the United States Census, 1850–1930: Mulattoes, Half-Breeds, Mixed Parentage, Hindoos, and the Mexican Race," p. 60.

62. Ayuntamiento de Santo Domingo, *Censo de población y otros datos estadísticos de la Ciudad de Santo Domingo*.

63. Hochschild and Powell, "Racial Reorganization," p. 70.

64. República Dominicana, Secretaría de Estado de Interior y Policía, *Censo de la República Dominicana*, pp. 42, 45, 121, 129.

65. Félix Evaristo Mejía, "Raza," in *Prosas polémicas*, vol. 2, p. 261.

66. República Dominicana, Secretaría de Estado de Interior y Policía, *Censo de la República Dominicana*, pp. 128–129, 139.

67. Ibid., pp. 125–126, 130, 139, 145.

68. Lloyd E. Ambrosius, "Woodrow Wilson and *The Birth of a Nation*: American Democracy and International Relations."

69. "Flyer," n.d., RG 38, E11, Box 2-M-62–M184, Folder M141–60, USNA: "Fíjate en el desprecio que tienen por nosotros porque no somos blancos como ellos!"

70. Carta editorial del Don Federico Henríquez y Carvajal a *Las Novedades*, December 31, 1916, quoted in Max Henríquez Ureña, *Los yanquis en Santo Domingo*, pp. 227–228. Alba Josefina Záiter also cites the letter in *La identidad social y nacional en Dominicana. Un análisis psico-social*, p. 171.

71. Matthew Pratt Guterl, "The New Race Consciousness: Race, Nation, and Empire in American Culture, 1910–1925," p. 345.

72. Jacinto López, "The United States and the Nations of the Caribbean," pp. 283–284.

73. Andrés Blanco Díaz, "Apuntes para una cronología de José Ramón López," pp. 29–30.

74. José Ramón López, "El ideal," *Listín Diario*, July 7, 1913, reprinted in José Ramón López, *Escritos dispersos*, vol. 2, p. 206.

75. José Ramón López, "La cuestión américo-dominicana," *Cuba Contemporánea*, September–December, 1921, reprinted in ibid., vol. 3, p. 320.

76. "Un cargo injusto," *Diario Nacional*, October 20, 1921, AGN.

Chapter 6. Gender and *Hispanidad* in the New Era

1. Gregoria Fraser Goins, Diary 1939, Box 36-10, Folder 107, MSRC.

2. Ibid.; quotations from Gregoria Goins to Mrs. Cook, December 3, 1939, Box 32-9, Folder 29, MSRC.

3. Joan W. Scott, "Gender, a Useful Category of Historical Analysis." Recently finished work on Dominican gender history makes significant contributions to our understanding of the uses of gender in state formation, particularly during the Trujillo regime: Melissa Madera, "'Zones of Scandal': Gender, Public Health, and Social Hygiene in the Dominican Republic, 1916–1961"; Elizabeth Manley, "*Poner un Grano de Arena*: Gender and Women's Political Participation under Authoritarian Rule in the Dominican Republic, 1928–1978"; Neici Zeller, *Discursos y espacios femeninos en República Dominicana, 1880–1961*.

4. The scholarship on Dominican feminism is unevenly developed but has experienced growth in recent years: Daisy Cocco de Filippis, ed., *Documents of Dissidence: Selected Writings by Dominican Women*; Teresita Martínez-Vergne, "Bourgeois Women in the Early Twentieth Century Dominican National Discourse"; and Ginetta Candelario, ed., *Miradas desencadenantes. Los estudios de género en la República Dominicana al inicio del tercer milenio.*

5. General Rafael L. Trujillo Molina, "Discurso del Presidente de la República General Rafael L. Trujillo Molina el Ateneo Dominicano, el 14 de Mayo de 1932," reprinted in Ramón Alberto Ferreras, *Historia del feminismo en la República Dominicana*, p. 22.

6. "Aporte de la mujer desde las filas del 'Partido Dominicano' al plan de asistencia social instituido en la república por el Honorable Presidente Rafael Leonidas Trujillo Molina," in ibid., pp. 167–168. See also Elizabeth Manley, "'El Freno Suave': Gender, Politics and Dictatorship in the Dominican Republic, 1928–1942," p. 19.

7. De Galíndez, *La era de Trujillo*, p. 231. Galíndez, an outspoken critic of the regime and, eventually, an exile, was kidnapped on his way home from teaching at Columbia University in New York City, March 12, 1956. His remains have never been found. In his quite reductive assessment of Dominican feminism, Galíndez also reports in a footnote that a certain female Dominican poet, after touring the country giving lectures praising Trujillo, ended up in Carmen viuda Peynado's home: "What happened during that meeting is not very clear, but the poet ended up in the hospital with a broken leg," p. 231, note 15.

8. Robert D. Crassweller, *Trujillo: The Life and Times of a Caribbean Dictator*, pp. 193–194.

9. See note 4 here for works focusing on Dominican women. Emelio Betances, *State and Society*, and Richard Turits, *Foundations of Despotism*, offer particularly trenchant critiques of old debates regarding Trujillo, the regime, and its sociocultural foundations.

10. The understandable hesitation to view contemporary feminism as a product of the Trujillo regime was particularly evident during the conference "Intercambiando Historias: Género y Política en la República Dominicana," held in Santo Domingo, June 30–July 2, 2011.

11. Derby and Turits, "Las historias de terror"; Derby, "Haitians, Magic, and Money."

12. This was true in the United States during the same period; see Paula Baker, "The Domestication of Politics: Women and American Political Society, 1780–1920," pp. 640–642.

13. Cynthia Jeffries Little, "Education, Philanthropy, and Feminism: Components of Argentine Womanhood, 1860–1926," pp. 237–238; Bonnie Frederick, "Harriet Beecher Stowe and the Virtuous Mother: Argentina, 1852–1910," pp. 103–105.

14. Gastón Deligne contracted leprosy in 1913 and killed himself before the disease became too devastating; see Antonio Zaglul, *Despreciada en la vida y olvidada en la muerte. Biografía de Evangelina Rodríguez, la primera médica dominicana*, pp. 19–23, 37, 41–46, 75–78; Fermín Álvarez Santana, *Héroes anónimos: Cien años de magisterio en San Pedro de Macorís*, pp. 44–45. References to funding Dr. Rodríguez's education are found in Archivo del Ayuntamiento de San Pedro de Macorís, Libros de Actas de Sesiones. In 1904 Rodríguez petitioned the city council for 25 pesos to enable her to move to Santo Domingo to continue her medical studies; the city council approved the expenditure: Libro 8, June 17, 1904. Fermín Álvarez suggested to me that Rodríguez might have been romantically involved with one of the Deligne brothers: personal communication, July 30, 2011.

15. Evangelina Rodríguez, *Granos de polen*, p. v.

16. Ibid., pp. 218, 185–187.

17. Ibid., pp. 80–81.

18. Ferreras, *Historia del feminismo*, pp. 100, 113.

19. Álvarez Santana, *Héroes anónimos: Cien años de magisterio en San Pedro de Macorís*, pp. 46–47, 58–59, 65.

20. Lori D. Ginzberg, *Women and the Work of Benevolence: Morality, Politics, and Class in the Nineteenth-Century United States*, pp. 7–8.

21. In the Southern Cone, the expansion of the public sphere and women's emergence in that sphere were encouraged by the increased number of women who were paid for their labor; see Asunción Lavrín, *Women, Feminism, and Social Change in Argentina, Chile and Uruguay, 1890–1940*, pp. 3–4.

22. Calder, *The Impact of Intervention*, pp. 88–89. For Puerto Rico, see Eileen Findlay, "Love in the Tropics: Marriage, Divorce, and the Construction of Benevolent Colonialism in Puerto Rico, 1898–1910," pp. 140–141.

23. Or, as Elizabeth Dore argues, the nation-state was reconceived as hierarchies of patriarchs: "The Holy Family: Imagined Households in Latin American History," p. 106.

24. Michael Gobat, *Confronting the American Dream: Nicaragua under U.S. Imperial Rule*, pp. 175–201.

25. Quoted in Calder, *The Impact of Intervention*, pp. 88–89.

26. "9 Cosas," *El Índice* [Santiago], September 1, 1921, quoted in Robin Derby, "The Magic of Modernity: Dictatorship and Civic Culture in the Dominican Republic, 1916–1962," pp. 97–98.

27. National Dominican Union, "Protest [translation]," December 24, 1920, RG 38, E11, Box 1, Folder 16–47, 2, United States National Archives II, College Park, Md. (hereafter USNA II).

28. Manuel F. Cestero, "La desocupación norteamericana depende de los dominicanos," *Listín Diario*, October 12, 1920. As early as 1917, Federico Henríquez y Carvajal was arguing that

"stubborn resistance, although peaceful . . . was the only solution to the problem of occupation"; see "La resistencia es la clave."

29. Federico Antonio García, "La moral y el patriotismo," *Listín Diario*, November 23, 1920; original emphasis.

30. Anne McClintock, *Imperial Leather: Race, Gender, and Sexuality in the Colonial Contest*, p. 358.

31. Américo Lugo, "La ley electoral," reprinted in Américo Lugo, *Américo Lugo en patria. Selección*, p. 169.

32. Américo Lugo to Dr. Teófilo Hernández, January 25, 1926, in ibid., p. 96.

33. Américo Lugo, "Iberoamericanismo. Oficina paniberoamericana," *Patria*, March 6, 1926; reprinted in ibid., p. 102.

34. Álvarez Santana, *Héroes anónimos*, pp. 64–66, 71–73, 94.

35. Francesca Miller, "Latin American Feminism and the Transnational Arena," pp. 11–14. See also Asunción Lavrín's introduction to *Women, Feminism, and Social Change*, pp. 27–30. Ferreras connects the Baltimore conference to the first women's congress held in the Dominican Republic; see *Historia del feminismo*, p. 143.

36. Various issues of *Fémina*, AGN.

37. Petronila A. Gómez, "Ya es hora," *Fémina*, July 15, 1922.

38. Petronila A. Gómez, "Feminismo," *Fémina*, 1930[?], reprinted in Gómez, *Contribución para la historia del feminismo en la República Dominicana*, p. 86.

39. Ibid., pp. 3–5, quotation on p. 3.

40. "Ideas generales acerca de los fines que inspiran a esta loable institución," *Fémina*, August 31, 1923.

41. Francisco X. Amiama Gómez, "Los muertos hablan," *Fémina*, October 15, 1923.

42. Elena Arizmendi, "Información sobre bases y el plan general de la Organización de la Liga de Mujeres Ibéricas e Hispano Americanas," *Fémina*, November 15, 1923.

43. Calder, *The Impact of Intervention*, pp. 88–89.

44. Mercedes H. de Tesson, "Hermoso gesto de la mujer puertoplateña por la distinguida señora Mercedes H. de Tesson, en la gran manifestación celebrada en Puerto Plata el día 23 de junio de 1921," *Pluma y Espada*, July 10, 1921.

45. Juan Ricardo Hernández, "Participación de la mujer en la resistencia civil (1916–1924)," March 13, 2009: http://historiadominicana.com.do, accessed June 30, 2012.

46. Ibid.

47. Ercilia Pepín to Augusto Sandino, May 15, 1928, and Augusto Sandino to Ercilia Pepín, April 15, 1929, both reprinted in William R. Galván, *Ercilia Pepín. Una mujer ejemplar*, pp. 167, 172.

48. Roxana Lucia Cheschebec makes the point that the turn to Latin feminism "was not so much a rejection of the ideals and ideas promoted by internationalist feminism" as a response to a political context in which nationalists believed it necessary to "restore [the nation's] mythical Latin inheritance." See "The 'Unholy Marriage' of Feminism with Nationalism in Interwar Romania: The Discourse of Princess Alexandrina Cantacuzino": http://www.women.it/cyberarchive/files/cheschebec.htm. Accessed August 2, 2007.

49. Ercilia Pepín, "Diversas consideraciones relativas a la capacidad que tiene la mujer para adquirir una cultura integral en la misma intensidad que el hombre," in William Galván, ed., *Antología de Ercilia Pepín*, pp. 30–32.

50. K. Lynn Stoner discusses the importance of motherhood in the Cuban feminist movement in *From House to Street: The Cuban Women's Movement for Legal Reform*, p. 107. See also Teresita Martínez-Vergne, *Shaping the Discourse on Space: Charity and Its Wards in Nineteenth-Century San Juan, Puerto Rico*, p. 154; Findlay, *Imposing Decency*, p. 54.

51. Américo Lugo, "El estado dominicano ante el derecho público," p. 45.

52. My thanks to Raymundo González for helping me understand the conversation between Lugo and Hostos over Dominican state formation.

53. Zaglul, *Despreciada en la vida*, pp. 19–23, 37, 41–46. The "Pro Evangelina Rodríguez" Committee petitioned for funds on her behalf to help her finish her studies in Paris: Archivo del Ayuntamiento de San Pedro de Macorís, Libros de Actas de Sesiones, Libro 15, November 13, 1924. Dr. Rodríguez requested 200 pesos from the city council to help her move back to San Pedro from Paris.

54. Ibid., Libro 16, May 3, May 6, and June 17, 1926; reference to the Casa de Maternidad is taken from Libro 17, January 25, 1929, and May 6, 1930.

55. Zaglul, *Despreciada en la vida*, pp. 81–84.

56. Archivo del Ayuntamiento de San Pedro de Macorís, Libros de Actas de Sesiones, Libro 17, January 4 and March 8, 1929; March 4 and June 2, 1931.

57. Scholarship on women's lives in the nineteenth-century urban United States speaks directly to the issue of women transforming city space by appearing in public and performing social service. Sarah Deutsch argues that in turn-of-the-century Boston, social reformers, women writers, and female socialites "challenged the dominant, idealized sexual division of urban space and function." See *Women and the City: Gender, Space, and Power in Boston, 1870–1940*, p. 4; also, Glenda Gilmore, *Gender and Jim Crow: Women and the Politics of White* Supremacy *in North Carolina*.

58. Livia Veloz quoted in "Fragment from *Historia del feminismo en la República Dominicana*," p. 61. Other information about Club Nosotras is from Ferreras, *Historia del feminismo*, pp. 143–149.

59. La Junta de la Acción Feminista Dominicana, "Manifiesto de la 'Acción Feminista Dominicana,'" in Arístides Incháustegui and Blanca Delgado Malagán, eds., *Abigaíl Mejía. Obras escogidas*, vol. 2, pp. 541–542.

60. Veloz, "Fragment," pp. 61–62.

61. Abigaíl Mejía de Fernández, "Mensaje de adhesión a la Junta de Acción Feminista de la Sra. Abigaíl Mejía de Fernández," *Listín Diario*, May 20, 1931.

62. "Palabra de la Dra. G[ladys] de los Santos en el acto de la constitución del 'Grupo de Acción Feminista' de Santo Domingo," *Listín Diario*, May 19, 1931.

63. Abigaíl Mejía, "De la Acción Feminista al Honorable Presidente Trujillo," *Listín Diario*, May 31, 1934.

64. Editorial, "La voz de la mujer dominicana," *Listín Diario*, November 29, 1940.

65. "Internado para menores desvalidos," *Fémina* 14, nos. 178–179 (August 1935).

66. Richard Turits, "A World Destroyed, a Nation Imposed: The 1937 Haitian Massacre in the Dominican Republic," pp. 608–609.

67. Maite Celada and Xoán Lagares, "República Dominicana/Haití—Fronteras lingüísticas y políticas en el territorio de la Hispaniola. Entrevista a Juan Valdez," p. 169.

68. Manuel Arturo Peña Batlle, *El Tratado de Basilea y la desnacionalización del Santo Domingo español*, pp. 560, 565.

69. Neici M. Zeller, "El régimen de Trujillo y la fuerza laboral femenina en la República Dominicana, 1945–1951."

70. "Leyes en favor de la mujer," in Carmen Lara Fernández, ed., *Historia del feminismo*, pp. 136–142.

71. Abigaíl Mejía, "Manifiesto de la 'Acción Feminista Dominicana,'" in *Abigaíl Mejía*, vol. 2, p. 542. In August 1940 Dominican Feminist Action sponsored the First Feminist Assembly, inviting women from all over the country to formulate position papers on education, health, women's juridical status, and employment. The assembly recommended that the Dominican Congress pass laws to protect infants, to facilitate marriage, and to negotiate terms of employ-

ment and labor rights for women. See "La Primera Asamblea," reprinted in Fernández, *Historia del feminismo,* pp. 13–17; "Derechos civiles" and "Texto del manifiesto dirigido a la mujer dominicana por el Hon. Pdte. Dr. Rafael L. Trujillo Molina," reprinted in ibid., pp. 47–56 and 63–65; and Ferreras, *Historia del feminismo,* pp. 150–157.

72. "Leyes en favor de la mujer," reprinted in Fernández, *Historia del feminismo,* pp. 126–132. The law stipulated that the status *"natural"* followed from the mother but allowed mothers and children the right to determine paternity.

73. Primer Congreso Femenino Dominicano, "Diario," Ciudad Trujillo, January 9, 1945, pp. 4–28.

74. Sonia Álvarez, *Engendering Democracy in Brazil: Women's Movements in Transition Politics,* p. 20; Sylvia Chant with Nikki Craske, *Gender in Latin America,* p. 25.

75. Roorda, *The Dictator Next Door,* p. 141; Manley, "'El Freno Suave,'" p. 20. The full name of the group was Sección Femenina del Partido Trujillista adscrita al Partido Dominicano. Trujillo created the Trujillo Party in 1940 to further the incorporation of social groups into his regime. According to Manley, before fulfilling his promise to legislate female suffrage, Trujillo held two *"votos de ensayo,"* in 1934 and 1938, to test Dominican women's interest in the vote and the AFD's ability to organize support for the regime. Mejía, for her part, mobilized women's participation in the 1934 electoral process but refused to support the 1938 *voto,* apparently frustrated by Trujillo's foot-dragging on the question of suffrage. Elizabeth Manley emphasizes that domestic and international linkages AFD members made throughout the 1930s, most notably in their work with the IACW (Inter-American Commission of Women), proved critical in turning the tide toward women's suffrage; see "'El Freno Suave,'" pp. 11–14.

76. Primer Congreso Femenino Dominicano, "Homenaje al Generalísimo Dr. Rafael Leonidas Trujillo Molina, Honorable Presidente de la República Dominicana, Benefactor de la Patria y Restaurador de la Independencia Financiera de la Nación. Sesión Plenaria Inaugural, 'Diario,' Ciudad Trujillo, Dominican Republic, January 8, 1945," pp. 21–22.

77. Ibid., p. 46.

78. Huston, "Andrea Evangelina Rodríguez (1879–1947)," p. 16.

79. Zaglul, *Despreciada en la vida,* pp. 101–118. Zaglul speculates that Dr. Rodríguez's emotional decline began when a colleague reproached her for failing to mention General Rafael Trujillo's name during her acceptance speech during an awards ceremony in honor of her paper on social medicine in 1933.

80. Cohen, "Nationalism and Suffrage: Gender Struggle in Nation-Building America," pp. 708–709; original emphasis.

81. Derby, *The Dictator's Seduction,* p. 214.

82. Derby, "The Magic of Modernity," p. 44.

83. Nancy Fraser, "Feminism, Capitalism and the Cunning of History," p. 99.

84. Neici Zeller, "The Appearance of All, the Reality of Nothing," pp. 213–216.

Conclusion

1. Tanya Golash-Boza and William Darity, Jr., "Latino Racial Choices: The Effects of Skin Colour and Discrimination on Latinos' and Latinas' Racial Self-Identifications," pp. 911, 916, 929. See also José Itzigsohn, Silvia Giorguli, and Obed Vázquez, "Immigrant Incorporation and Racial Identity: Racial Self-Identification among Dominican Immigrants," *Ethnic and Racial Studies* 28, no. 1 (2005): 50–78.

2. Cited in Peter Wade, *Blackness and Race Mixture: The Dynamics of Racial Identity in Colombia,* pp. 343, 344. See also Paul Gilroy, *There Ain't No Black in the Union Jack: The Cultural Politics of Race and Nation,* p. 39.

3. Ernesto Sagás, *Race and Politics*, pp. 66, 119.

4. Jessica Lewis, "Dancehall and the Politics of Race and Sexuality in Contemporary Jamaica."

5. Deborah Thomas, *Modern Blackness: Nationalism, Globalization, and the Politics of Culture in Jamaica*, p. 11.

6. Bettina Ng'weno, *Turf Wars: Territory and Citizenship in the Contemporary State*, p. 19.

7. Simmons, *Reconstructing Racial Identity*, p. 117.

8. Gregoria Fraser Goins to Mrs. Mears, August 25, 1946, Box 36-2, Folder 35, MSRC.

9. On selling the Puerto Plata home, see Gregoria Fraser Goins, "Diary, 1945–1947," entry dated June 23, 1947, Box 36-10, Folder 108; Gregoria Fraser Goins, lecture, "Santo Domingo Country Music," presented to the Spanish Club, Howard University, May 1, 1953, Box 36-5, Folder 58; both in MSRC.

WORKS CITED

Primary Sources

ARCHIVO DEL AYUNTAMIENTO DE SAN PEDRO DE MACORÍS
Libros de Actas de Sesiones, vols. 1–17.

SAN ESTEBAN EPISCOPAL CHURCH, SAN PEDRO DE MACORÍS

ARCHIVO GENERAL DE LA NACIÓN, SANTO DOMINGO (AGN)
Alcaldía de San Pedro de Macorís, Copiador de Autos
Alcaldía de San Pedro de Macorís, Libro 1
Ayuntamiento de San Pedro de Macorís
Bartolomé Berroa (1894), Actos 1–227
Correspondencia de Gobernación, Secretaría de Interior, Policía y Agricultura
La Gaceta Oficial
Gobernación de San Pedro de Macorís
Gobernación del Seybo
Gobierno Militar Norteamericano, Ministerio de Interior y Policía
Juan Antonio Hernández (books are divided by years, and each year has multiple volumes. Since there were numerous entries, I selected one, and in the case of 1921 two, volumes for the years cover the *Danza de los millones*: Libro 1 [1919], Libro 2 [1920], Libros 1 and 2 [1921], Libro 3 (1922)
Protocolos Notariales
Silvestre Aybar, vol. 1 (1898), Actos 1–77
Tribunal de San Pedro de Macorís

UNIVERSIDAD DE PUERTO RICO AT RÍO PIEDRAS
Archivo de la Biblioteca del Derecho, Fondo Peynado
Archivo del Centro de Investigaciones Históricas, Universidad de Puerto Rico at Río Piedras
Colección Hugh Kelly IV
Colección Santiago Michelena
Colección Juan José Serrallés
Instituto de Estudios Hostosianos
Interview with Hugh Kelly IV, by Humberto García Muñiz
Interview with Santiago Michelena Ariza by Humberto García Muñiz
Interview with José Juan Serrallés by Humberto García Muñiz

MOORLAND-SPINGARN RESEARCH CENTER, HOWARD UNIVERSITY (MSRC)

Archibald Grimke Papers
Frederick Douglass Papers
Gregoria Fraser Goins Papers

PUBLIC RECORD OFFICE (PRO), KEW GARDENS, LONDON

Colonial Office Records
Foreign Office Records (FO)

U.S. LIBRARY OF CONGRESS

Frederick Douglass Papers, http://memory.loc.gov

MARINE CORPS HISTORY DIVISION, QUANTICO, VA.

U.S. NATIONAL ARCHIVES (USNA II), COLLEGE PARK, MD.

Record Group (RG) 38, Records of the Military Government of Santo Domingo, 1916–1924
Record Group 45, Naval Records Collection of the Office of Naval Records and Library
Record Group 80, General Records of the Department of the Navy

INTERVIEWS

Obispo Telésforo Isaac, Santo Domingo, October 9, 1999
Don Emille Washington, San Pedro de Macorís, March 28, 2000
Doña Martha Williamson viuda González, San Pedro de Macorís, March 23, 2000

Primary Published Sources

Atiles, Guillermo Santos. *Guía local y de comercio de la ciudad de San Pedro de Macorís*. Santo Domingo: N.p., 1902.

Ayuntamiento de Santo Domingo. *Censo de población y otros datos estadísticos de la Ciudad de Santo Domingo*. Santo Domingo: Imp. J. R. viuda García, 1908.

Balaguer, Joaquín. *La isla al revés*. Santo Domingo: Fundación José Antonio Caro, 1983.

Beras Morales, Sergio Augusto, Telésforo Zuleta de Soto, and Luis Dalmau Febles. "Gobernadores de San Pedro de Macorís." In *Álbum del cincuentenario de San Pedro de Macorís, 1882–1932*, ed. Sergio Augusto Beras Morales, Telésforo Zuleta de Soto, and Luis Dalmau Febles. San Pedro de Macorís: N.p., 1932

———, eds. *Álbum del cincuentenario de San Pedro de Macorís, 1882–1932*. San Pedro de Macorís: N.p., 1932.

Bonó, Pedro Francisco. *Papeles de Pedro Francisco Bonó*. Ed. Emilio Rodríguez Demorizi. Barcelona: Gráficas M. Pareja, 1980.

Cámara de Comercio, Industria y Agricultura (San Pedro de Macorís). *Directorio general de San Pedro de Macorís*. San Pedro de Macorís: Cervantes, 1927.

Castillo, Rafael Justino. *Escritos reunidos. Ensayos, 1887–1907*. Vol. 1. Ed. Andrés Blanco Díaz. Santo Domingo: Archivo General de la Nación, 2009.

de Galíndez, Jesús. *La era de Trujillo*. Tucson: University of Arizona Press, 1978.

de Hostos, Eugenio María. *Apuntes de un normalista*. Ed. Andrés Blanco Díaz. Santo Domingo: Archivo General de la Nación, 2010.

———. *Moral social*. San Juan: Editorial Edil, [1884] 2005.

Dirección General de Inmigración. "Lista de Inmigración." Vol. 7. Santo Domingo: Archivo General de la Nación.

Douglass, Philip. "Americanizing Santo Domingo." *The Nation* (May 4, 1921): 663–664.

Evaristo Mejía, Félix. *Prosas polémicas.* Vol. 2. Comp. Andrés Blanco Díaz. Santo Domingo: Archivo General de la Nación, 2008.

Fellowes, Lieutenant Edward A., USMC. "Training Native Troops in Santo Domingo." *Marine Corps Gazette* 8, no. 4 (1923): 215–233.

Fernández, Carmen Lara. *Historia del feminismo en la República Dominicana.* Ciudad Trujillo: Impresa Arte y Cine, 1946.

Fiallo, Fabio. *Fabio Fiallo en La Bandera Libre.* Comp. Rafael Darío Herrera. Santo Domingo: Archivo General de la Nación, 2006.

Galván, Manuel de Jesús. *Enriquillo.* Santo Domingo: Editorial ABC, [1882] 2005.

———. *Manuel de Jesús Galván. Escritos políticos iniciales.* Ed. Andrés Blanco Díaz. Santo Domingo: Archivo General de la Nación, 2008.

García Lluberes, Leonidas. "Historia de la provincia y especialmente de la ciudad de San Pedro de Macorís." In *Álbum del cincuentenario de San Pedro de Macorís, 1882–1932,* ed. Sergio Augusto Beras Morales, Telésforo Zuleta de Soto, and Luis Dalmau Febles. San Pedro de Macorís: N.p., 1932.

Gómez, Petronila Angélica. *Contribución para la historia del feminismo en la República Dominicana.* Ciudad Trujillo: Editora Librería Dominicana, 1952.

Great Britain. Commercial Relations and Exports Department. *Economic and Commercial Conditions in the Dominican Republic.* London: H.M. Stationery Office, 1921–1925, 1928, 1930–1938.

Grimke, Archibald. "The Dominican Republic and Her Revolutions." Unpublished manuscript.

Gruening, Ernest. "The Senators Visit Haiti and Santo Domingo." *The Nation* 64, no. 2948 (January 4, 1922): 7–10.

Henríquez Ureña, Max. *Los yanquis en Santo Domingo.* Barcelona: Gráficas Manuel Pareja, 1929.

Henríquez Ureña, Pedro. *Hostos en Santo Domingo.* Ed. Emilio Demorizi Rodríguez. 2 vols. Ciudad Trujillo: J. R. Vda. García Sucs., 1939.

———. "Prólogo." In *Enriquillo,* ed. Manuel de Jesús Galván. Santo Domingo: Editorial ABC, [1882] 2005. Originally published in *La Nación,* Buenos Aires, January 13, 1935.

Henríquez y Carvajal, Federico. "La resistencia es la clave," Havana, January 26, 1917." In *Nacionalismo.* Santo Domingo: Biblioteca Nacional, [1925] 1986.

Knight, Melvin. *The Americans in Santo Domingo.* New York: Vanguard Press, 1928.

López, Jacinto. "The United States and the Nations of the Caribbean." *Journal of International Relations* (formerly *Journal of Race Development*) 11, no. 2 (October 1920): 276–288.

López, José Ramón. *Escritos dispersos.* Ed. Andrés Blanco Díaz. Santo Domingo: Archivo General de la Nación, 2005.

Lugo, Américo. *Américo Lugo en patria. Selección.* Comp. Rafael Darío Herrera. Santo Domingo: Archivo General de la Nación, 2008.

———. "El estado dominicano ante el derecho público." In *Colección pensamiento dominicano,* vol. 5. Ed. Sociedad Dominicana de Bibliófilos. Santo Domingo: Banreservas, 2009.

Luperón, Gregorio. *Notas autobiográficas y apuntes históricos.* 3 vols. Santo Domingo: Central de Libros, [1939] 1992.

Mejía, Abigaíl. *Obras escogidas.* Vol. 2. Ed. Arístides Incháustegui and Blanca Delgado Malagán. Santo Domingo: Editora Corripio, 1995.

Moore, Dr. Joseph Earle, et al. "El cuidado de la sífilis en la práctica general." *Oficina Sanitaria Panamericana*, no. 22 (December 1929): 1–17.

Moscoso Puello, Francisco Eugenio. *Cartas a Evelina*. Santo Domingo: Editora Manatí, [1941] 2000.

Peña Batlle, Manuel Arturo. *Política de Trujillo*. Santo Domingo: Impresora Dominicana, 1954.

———. *El Tratado de Basilea y la desnacionalización del Santo Domingo español*. Ciudad Trujillo: Impresora Dominicana, 1952.

Pepín, Ercilia. *Antología de Ercilia Pepín*. Ed. William Galván. Santo Domingo: Editora Universitaria, 1986.

Primer Congreso Femenino Dominicano. "Homenaje al Generalísimo Dr. Rafael Leonidas Trujillo Molina, Honorable Presidente de la República Dominicana, Benefactor de la Patria y Restaurador de la Independencia Financiera de la Nación. Sesión Plenaria Inaugural, 'Diario,' Ciudad Trujillo, Dominican Republic, January 8, 1945." Unpublished manuscript.

———. "Sesión Plenaria de Clausura, 'Diario,' Ciudad Trujillo, January 8, 1945." Unpublished manuscript.

———. "Sesión Plenaria de Clausura, 'Diario,' Ciudad Trujillo, January 9, 1945." Unpublished manuscript.

República Dominicana. Congreso Nacional Dominicano. *Mensaje y memorias del poder ejecutivo de la República Dominicana*. Santo Domingo: N.p., 1881, 1882, 1883, 1884, 1888.

República Dominicana. Gobierno Militar Norteamericano. Secretaría de Estado de la Agricultura e Inmigración. *Informe anual de inmigración del 10 del julio 1919 al 30 de junio 1920*. Santo Domingo: N.p., 1920.

———. *Guía comercial de la República Dominicana*. N.p.: N.p., 1927[?].

República Dominicana. Secretaría de Estado. *Mensaje y memorias del poder ejecutivo de la República Dominicana*. Santo Domingo: Imprenta García Hermanos, 1883–1884, 1888.

República Dominicana. Secretaría de Estado de Interior y Policía. *Censo de la República Dominicana*. Santo Domingo: Gobierno Militar de Santo Domingo, 1921.

República Dominicana. Secretaría de Estado de Sanidad y Beneficiencia. *Informe anual del Secretario de Estado de Sanidad y Beneficiencia*. Santo Domingo: J. R. Viuda García, 1920.

Ricart, Elpidio E. "Historia de la sanidad en Santo Domingo." In *Congreso Médico Dominicano del Centenario. Memoria*. Ciudad Trujillo: Congreso Médico Dominicano, 1944.

Richiez, Manuel Leopoldo. "Historia de la provincia i, especialmente de la ciudad de San Pedro de Macorís." In *Álbum del Cincuentenario de San Pedro de Macorís, 1882–1932*, ed. Sergio Augusto Beras Morales, Telésforo Zuleta de Soto, and Luis Dalmau Febles. San Pedro de Macorís: N.p., 1932.

Rodríguez, Evangelina. *Granos de polen*. San Pedro de Macorís: N.p., 1915.

Sánchez, Juan J. *La caña en Santo Domingo*. Santo Domingo: García Hermanos, 1893.

Thorpe, George C. "American Achievements in Santo Domingo, Haiti, and the Virgin Islands." *Journal of International Relations* 11, no. 1 (July 1920): 63–88.

U.S. Senate. *Report of the Commission of Inquiry to Santo Domingo*. Washington, D.C.: Government Printing Office, 1871.

Veeser, Cyrus, ed. and trans. "Cartas escogidas de los copiadores del Presidente Ulises Heureaux correspondientes a los años, 1894–1898." Unpublished manuscript. Private collection.

Welles, Sumner. *Naboth's Vineyard: The Dominican Republic, 1844–1924*. New York: Payson & Clarke, 1928.

Secondary Sources

Álvarez, Sonia. *Engendering Democracy in Brazil: Women's Movements in Transition Politics*. Princeton: Princeton University Press, 1990.

Álvarez Santana, Fermín. *Héroes anónimos: Cien años de magisterio en San Pedro de Macorís*. San Pedro de Macorís: Editorial León, 1997.

———. "Historia del desarrollo de la Provincia de San Pedro de Macorís." Unpublished manuscript, 1999.

———. *San Pedro de Macorís. Su historia y desarrollo*. Santo Domingo: Comisión Presidencial de Apoyo Desarrollo Provincial, 2000.

Ambrosius, Lloyd E. "Woodrow Wilson and *The Birth of a Nation*: American Democracy and International Relations." *Diplomacy and Statecraft* 18 (2007): 689–718.

Appelbaum, Nancy. "Post-Revisionist Scholarship on Race." *Latin American Research Review* 40, no. 3 (2005): 206–217.

Appelbaum, Nancy, Anne S. Macpherson, and Karin Alejandra Rosemblatt. "Introduction." In *Race and Nation in Modern Latin America*, ed. Nancy Appelbaum et al. Chapel Hill: University of North Carolina Press, 2003.

Arévalo García, Manuel. "La presencia española en San Pedro de Macorís." In *Presencia étnica en San Pedro de Macorís*, ed. Miguel Phipps Cueto. Santo Domingo: Editora de Colores, 2000.

Armenteros, Ernesto. *Entre las nieblas del recuerdo*. Santo Domingo: Editorial Rex, 1990.

Ayala, César J. *American Sugar Kingdom: The Plantation Economy of the Spanish Caribbean, 1898–1934*. Chapel Hill: University of North Carolina Press, 1999.

Bacchetta, Paola, and Margaret Power. "Introduction." In *Right-Wing Women: From Conservatives to Extremists around the World*, ed. Paola Bacchetta and Margaret Power. London: Routledge, 2002.

Baker, Paula. "The Domestication of Politics: Women and American Political Society, 1780–1920." *American Historical Review* 89, no. 3 (1984): 620–647.

Baud, Michiel. "'Constitutionally White': The Forging of a National Identity in the Dominican Republic." In *Ethnicity in the Caribbean*, ed. Gert Oostindie. London: Macmillan, 1996.

———. "Sugar and Unfree Labour: Reflections on Labour Control in the Dominican Republic, 1870–1935." *Journal of Peasant Studies* 19, no. 2 (1992): 301–325.

Berglund, Barbara. *Making San Francisco American: Cultural Frontiers in the Urban West, 1846–1906*. Lawrence: University Press of Kansas, 2007.

Bermúdez, América. *Manual de historia de San Pedro de Macorís*. San Pedro de Macorís: Editora Edwin, 1991.

———. *Mosquitisol*. San Pedro de Macorís: Universidad Central del Este, 2009.

Betances, Emelio. *State and Society in the Dominican Republic*. Boulder, Colo.: Westview Press, 1995.

Blanco Díaz, Andrés. "Apuntes para una cronología de José Ramón López." In *Escritos dispersos*, vol. 1, by José Ramón López, ed. Andrés Blanco Díaz. Santo Domingo: Archivo General de la Nación, 2005.

Boin, Jacqueline, and José Serulle Ramia. *El proceso de desarrollo del capitalismo en la República Dominicana (1844–1930)*. Vol. 1. Santo Domingo: Gramil, 1981.

Boot, Max. *The Savage Wars of Peace: Small Wars and the Rise of American Power*. New York: Basic Books, 2002.

Bosch, Juan. *Composición social dominicana. Historia e interpretación.* Santo Domingo: Alfa y Omega, [1970] 1999.

Bourgois, Philippe. *Ethnicity at Work: Divided Labor on a Central American Banana Plantation.* Baltimore: Johns Hopkins University Press, 1989.

Brea, Ramonina. *Ensayo sobre la formación del estado capitalista en la República Dominicana y Haití.* Santo Domingo: Editora Taller, 1983.

Bryan, Patrick. "The Question of Labor in the Sugar Industry of the Dominican Republic in the Late Nineteenth and Early Twentieth Centuries." In *Between Slavery and Free Labor: The Spanish-Speaking Caribbean in the Nineteenth Century,* ed. Manuel Moreno Fraginals, Frank Moya Pons, and Stanley Engerman. Baltimore: Johns Hopkins University Press, 1985.

Calder, Bruce. "Caudillos and Gavilleros versus the United States Marines: Guerrilla Insurgency during the Dominican Intervention, 1916–1924." *Hispanic American Historical Review* 58, no. 4 (1978): 649–675.

———. *The Impact of Intervention.* Austin: University of Texas Press, 1984.

Caldwell, Kia. *Negras in Brazil: Re-envisioning Black Women, Citizenship, and the Politics of Identity.* New Brunswick, N.J.: Rutgers University Press, 2006.

Candelario, Ginetta. *Black behind the Ears: Dominican Racial Identity from Museums to Beauty Shops.* Durham, N.C.: Duke University Press, 2007.

———, ed., *Miradas desencadenantes. Los estudios de género en la República Dominicana al inicio del tercer milenio.* Santo Domingo: Centro de Estudios de Género, INTEC, 2005.

Carr, Barry. "Identity, Class, and Nation: Black Immigrant Workers, Cuban Communism, and the Sugar Insurgency, 1925–1934." *Hispanic American Historical Review* 78, no. 1 (1998): 83–116.

Cassá, Roberto. "El racismo en la ideología de la clase dominante dominicana." *Ciencia* 3 (1976): 61–85.

———. "Reflexiones sobre la estructura de clases entre 1900–1930." In *La sociedad dominicana durante la Segunda República, 1865–1924,* ed. Tirso Mejía-Ricart. Santo Domingo: Editora de la Universidad Autónoma de Santo Domingo, 1982.

Cassá, Roberto, and Genaro Rodríguez. "Algunos procesos formativos de la identidad nacional dominicana." *Estudios Sociales* 25, no. 88 (April–June 1991): 67–88.

Celada, Maite, and Xoán Lagares. "República Dominicana/Haití—Fronteras lingüísticas y políticas en el territorio de la Hispaniola. Entrevista a Juan Valdez." *Abehache* 2, no. 2 (2012): 167–173.

Chant, Sylvia, with Nikki Craske. *Gender in Latin America.* New Brunswick, N.J.: Rutgers University Press, 2002.

Cheschebec, Roxana L. "The 'Unholy Marriage' of Feminism with Nationalism in Interwar Romania: The Discourse of Princess Alexandrina Cantacuzino." http://www.women.it/cyber-archive/files/cheschebec.htm.

Chez Checo, José, ed. *Ideario de Gregorio Luperón, 1839–1897.* Santo Domingo: Taller, 1989.

Chomsky, Aviva. *West Indian Workers and the United Fruit Company in Costa Rica, 1870–1940.* Baton Rouge: Louisiana State University Press, 1996.

Chomsky, Aviva, and Aldo Lauria-Santiago, eds. *Identity and Struggle at the Margins of the Nation-State: The Laboring Peoples of Central America and the Hispanic Caribbean.* Durham, N.C.: Duke University Press, 1998.

Clarke, John Henrik. "Introduction." In *Marcus Garvey and the Vision of Africa,* ed. John Henrik Clarke. New York: Vintage, 1974.

Cocco de Filippis, Daisy, ed. *Documents of Dissidence: Selected Writings by Dominican Women.* New York: City University of New York, Dominican Studies Institute, 2000.

Cohen, Philip N. "Nationalism and Suffrage: Gender Struggle in Nation-Building America." *Signs* 21, no. 3 (2006): 707–727.

Collins, Patricia Hill. *Black Feminist Thought: Knowledge, Consciousness, and the Politics of Empowerment.* London: Routledge, 1991.

Conniff, Michael. *Black Labor on a White Canal.* Pittsburgh: University of Pittsburgh Press, 1985.

Corbin, Alain. "Commercial Sexuality in Nineteenth-Century France: A System of Images and Regulations." In *The Making of the Modern Body: Sexuality and Society in the Nineteenth Century,* ed. Catherine Gallagher and Thomas Laqueur. Berkeley: University of California Press, 1987.

Cordero Michel, Emilio. "Características de la Guerra Restauradora, 1863–1865." *Clío* 70, no. 164 (July–December 2002): 39–78.

Corten, Andrés, Mercedes Acosta, and Isis Duarte. "Las relaciones de producción en la economía azucarera dominicana." In *Azúcar y política en la República Dominicana,* ed. Andrés Corten, Mercedes Acosta, and Isis Duarte. Santo Domingo: Taller, 1981.

———, eds. *Azúcar y política en la República Dominicana.* Santo Domingo: Ediciones Taller, 1981.

Crassweller, Robert D. *Trujillo: The Life and Times of a Caribbean Dictator.* New York: Macmillan, 1966.

Dabove, Juan Pablo. *Nightmares of the Lettered City: Banditry and Literature in Latin America, 1816–1929.* Pittsburgh: University of Pittsburgh Press, 2007.

Dash, J. Michael, "Nineteenth-Century Haiti and the Archipelago of the Americas: Anténor Firmin's Letters from St. Thomas." *Research in African Literatures* 35, no. 2 (Summer 2004): 44–53.

Deive, Carlos Esteban. *Los dominicanos vistos por extranjeros.* Santo Domingo: Banco Central de la República Dominicana, 2008.

del Castillo, José. "Consuelo. Biografía de un pequeño gigante." *Inazúcar* 6, no. 31 (1981): 33–38.

———. "The Formation of the Dominican Sugar Industry: From Competition to Monopoly, from National Semiproletariat to Foreign Proletariat." In *Between Slavery and Free Labor: The Spanish-Speaking Caribbean in the Nineteenth Century,* ed. Manuel Moreno Fraginals, Frank Moya Pons, and Stanley Engerman. Baltimore: Johns Hopkins University Press, 1985.

———. "La inmigración de braceros azucareros en la República Dominicana, 1900–1930." *Cuadernos del CENDIA* 262, no. 7 (1978): 49–54.

del Castillo, José, and Walter Cordero. "La economía dominicana durante el primer cuarto del Siglo XX." In *La sociedad dominicana durante la Segunda República, 1865–1924,* ed. Tirso Mejía-Ricart. Santo Domingo: Editora UASD, 1982.

de los Santos, Danilo. "Referencias sobre la identidad nacional y cultural de los dominicanos." *Eme Eme: Estudios Dominicanos* 8, no. 47 (March–April 1980): 3–16.

Derby, Lauren Robin. *The Dictator's Seduction: Politics and the Popular Imagination in the Era of Trujillo.* Durham, N.C.: Duke University Press, 2009.

———."Haitians, Magic, and Money: *Raza* and Society in the Haitian-Dominican Borderlands, 1900–1937." *Comparative Studies in Society and History* 36 (1994): 488–526.

———. "The Magic of Modernity: Dictatorship and Civic Culture in the Dominican Republic, 1916–1962." PhD diss., University of Chicago, 1998.

———. "Race, National Identity, and the Idea of Value on the Island of Hispaniola." In *Blacks,*

Coloureds, and National Identity in Latin America, ed. Nancy Priscilla Naro. London: Institute of Latin American Studies, 2003.

Derby, Lauren Robin, and Richard Turits. "Las historias de terror y los terrores de la historia: La masacre haitiana de 1937 en la República Dominicana." *Estudios Sociales* 26, no. 92 (1993): 65–76.

Deutsch, Sarah. *Women and the City: Gender, Space, and Power in Boston, 1870–1940.* Oxford: Oxford University Press, 2002.

Dixon, Kwame. "Beyond Race and Gender: Recent Works on Afro-Latin America." *Latin American Research Review* 41, no. 3 (2006): 247–257.

Domínguez, Jaime. *La dictadura de Heureaux.* Santo Domingo: Editora UASD, 1986.

Dore, Elizabeth. "The Holy Family: Imagined Households in Latin American History." In *Gender Politics in Latin America: Debates in Theory and Practice,* ed. Elizabeth Dore. New York: Monthly Review Press, 1997.

———. "Property, Households, and Public Regulation of Domestic Life." In *Hidden Histories of Gender and State in Latin America,* ed. Elizabeth Dore and Maxine Molyneux. Durham, N.C.: Duke University Press, 2000.

Duke, Eric D. "The Diasporic Dimensions of British Caribbean Federation in the Early Twentieth Century." *New West Indian Guide* 83, nos. 3 and 4 (2009): 219–248.

Durán, Carmen. "Alejandro Angulo Guridi (1823–1906)." In *Alejandro Angulo Guridi. Obras escogidas.* Vol. 1: *Artículos,* comp. Andrés Blanco Díaz. Santo Domingo: Archivo General de la Nación, 2006.

Eley, Geoff. "Nations, Publics, and Political Cultures: Placing Habermas in the Nineteenth Century." In *Habermas and the Public Sphere,* ed. Craig Calhoun. Cambridge, Mass.: MIT Press, 1992.

Elkins, W. F. *Black Power in the Caribbean: The Beginnings of the Modern National Movement.* New York: Revisionist Press, 1977.

Enciclopedia Dominicana. *Enciclopedia dominicana.* Vol. 5. Santo Domingo: Enciclopedia Dominicana, 1999.

Engelstein, Laura. "Morality and the Wooden Spoon: Russian Doctors View Syphilis, Social Class, and Sexual Behavior." In *The Making of the Modern Body: Sexuality and Society in the Nineteenth Century,* ed. Catherine Gallagher and Thomas Laqueur. Berkeley: University of California Press, 1987.

Fennema, Meindert, and Toetje Loewenthal. "La construcción de raza y nación en la República Dominicana." *Anales del Caribe* 9 (1989): 191–227.

Fernández Rodríguez, Aura Celeste. "Origen y evolución de la propiedad y de los terrenos comuneros en la República Dominicana." *Eme Eme: Estudios Dominicanos* 9, no. 51 (1980): 1–27.

Ferrer, Ada. *Insurgent Cuba: Race, Nation, and Revolution, 1868–1898.* Chapel Hill: University of North Carolina Press, 1999.

Ferreras, Ramón Alberto. *Historia del feminismo en la República Dominicana.* Santo Domingo: Editorial del Noreste, 1991.

Findlay, Eileen. *Imposing Decency: The Politics of Sexuality in Puerto Rico, 1870–1920.* Durham, N.C.: Duke University Press, 1999.

———. "Love in the Tropics: Marriage, Divorce, and the Construction of Benevolent Colonialism in Puerto Rico, 1898–1910." In *Close Encounters of Empire: Writing the Cultural History of U.S.–Latin American Relations,* ed. Gilbert Joseph, Catherine LeGrand, and Ricardo D. Salvatore. Durham, N.C.: Duke University Press, 1998.

Franco Pichardo, Franklin. *Los negros, los mulatos y la nación dominicana.* Santo Domingo: Editora Nacional, 1984.

———. *Santo Domingo. Cultura, política e ideología.* Santo Domingo: Sociedad Editoral Dominicana, [1975] 1997.

———. *Sobre racismo y antihaitianismo (y otros ensayos).* Santo Domingo: Impresora Librería Vidal, 1997.

Franks, Julie. "The *Gavilleros* of the East: Social Banditry as Political Practice in the Dominican Sugar Region, 1900–1924." *Journal of Historical Sociology* 8, no. 2 (1995): 158–181.

———. "Transforming Property: Landholding and Political Rights in the Dominican Sugar Region, 1880–1930." PhD diss., State University of New York at Stony Brook, 1997.

Fraser, Nancy. "Feminism, Capitalism, and the Cunning of History." *New Left Review* 56 (2009): 97–117.

Fraser, Peter D. "British West Indians in Haiti in the Late Nineteenth and Early Twentieth Centuries." In *After the Crossing: Immigrants and Minorities in Caribbean Creole Society,* ed. Howard Johnson. London: Frank Cass, 1988.

Frederick, Bonnie. "Harriet Beecher Stowe and the Virtuous Mother: Argentina, 1825–1910." *Journal of Women's History* 18, no. 1 (2006): 101–120.

French, William. *A Peaceful and Working People: Manners, Morals, and Class Formation in Northern Mexico.* Albuquerque: University of New Mexico Press, 1996.

Galván, William R., ed. *Antología de Ercilia Pepín.* Santo Domingo: Editora Universitaria, 1986.

———. *Ercilia Pepín. Una mujer ejemplar.* Santo Domingo: Editora Universitaria, 1986.

García Muñiz, Humberto. "The South Porto Rico Sugar Company: The History of a U.S. Multinational Corporation in Puerto Rico and the Dominican Republic, 1900–1921." PhD diss., Columbia University, 1997.

García Muñiz, Humberto, and Jorge L. Giovannetti. "Garveyismo y racismo en el Caribe. El caso de la población cocola en la República Dominicana." *Journal of Caribbean Studies* 31, no. 1 (2003): 139–213.

Gilmore, Glenda Elizabeth. *Gender and Jim Crow: Women and the Politics of White Supremacy in North Carolina, 1896–1920.* Chapel Hill: University of North Carolina Press, 1996.

Gilroy, Paul. *There Ain't No Black in the Union Jack: The Cultural Politics of Race and Nation.* London: Routledge, 1987.

Ginzberg, Lori D. *Women and the Work of Benevolence: Morality, Politics, and Class in the Nineteenth-Century United States.* New Haven: Yale University Press, 1990.

Gobat, Michael. *Confronting the American Dream: Nicaragua under U.S. Imperial Rule.* Durham, N.C.: Duke University Press, 2005.

Golash-Boza, Tanya, and William Darity, Jr. "Latino Racial Choices: The Effects of Skin Colour and Discrimination on Latinos' and Latinas' Racial Self-Identifications." *Ethnic and Racial Studies* 31, no. 5 (2007): 899–934.

González, Raymundo. *De esclavos a campesinos. Vida rural en Santo Domingo colonial.* Santo Domingo: Archivo General de la Nación, 2011.

———. "La Guerra de la Restauración vista desde abajo." *Clío* 79, no. 180 (2010): 147–168.

———. "Notas sobre las concepciones populistas-liberales de Duarte y la independencia dominicana." *Clío* 77, no. 175 (2008): 151–166.

———. "Peña Batlle y su concepto histórico de la nación dominicana." *Anuario de Estudios Americanos* 48 (1991): 585–631.

———. "El pensamiento de Bonó. Nación y clases trabajadoras." In *Política, identidad y pensamiento social en la República Dominicana (Siglos XIX y XX)*, ed. Raymundo González, Michiel Baud, Pedro L. San Miguel, and Roberto Cassá. Madrid: Doce Calles, 1999.

———. "Prefacio." In *Pedro Francisco Bonó. Textos selectos*, ed. Dantes Ortiz. Santo Domingo: Archivo General de la Nación, 2007.

González Canalda, María Filomena. *Los gavilleros, 1904–1916*. Santo Domingo: Archivo General de la Nación, 2008.

Guridy, Frank. "'Enemies of the White Race': The Machadista State and the UNIA in Cuba." *Caribbean Studies* 31, no. 1 (2003): 107–137.

Guterl, Matthew Pratt. "The New Race Consciousness: Race, Nation, and Empire in American Culture, 1910–1925." *Journal of World History* 10, no. 2 (1999): 307–352.

Harpelle, Ronald. "Cross Currents in the Western Caribbean: Marcus Garvey and the UNIA in Central America." *Caribbean Studies* 31, no. 1 (2003): 35–73.

———. "Radicalism and Accommodation: Garveyism in a United Fruit Company Enclave." *Journal of Iberian and Latin American Studies* 6, no. 1 (2000): 1–27.

Henríquez Vásquez, Francisco Alberto. "El pensamiento político y la acción revolucionaria de Juan Pablo Duarte." *Clío* 77, no. 175 (January–June 2008): 49–82.

Hill, Robert. "The First England Years and After, 1912–1916." In *Marcus Garvey and the Vision of Africa*, ed. John Henrik Clarke. New York: Vintage, 1974.

Hochschild, Jennifer L., and Brenna Marea Powell. "Racial Reorganization and the United States Census, 1850–1930: Mulattoes, Half-Breeds, Mixed Parentage, Hindoos, and the Mexican Race." *Studies in American Political Development* 22, no. 1 (2008): 59–96.

Hoernel, Robert B. "Sugar and Social Change in Oriente, Cuba, 1898–1946." *Journal of Latin American Studies* 8, no. 2 (1976): 215–249.

Hoetink, Harry. "Materiales para el estudio de la República Dominicana en la segunda mitad del siglo XX." *Caribbean Studies* 5, no. 3 (1965): 3–21.

———. *El pueblo dominicano*. Santo Domingo: Editora de Colores, 1986.

Holt, Thomas C. *The Problem of Freedom: Race, Labor, and Politics in Jamaica and Britain, 1832–1938*. Baltimore: Johns Hopkins University Press, 1992.

Howard, David. *Coloring the Nation: Race and Ethnicity in the Dominican Republic*. Boulder, Colo.: Lynne Rienner Publishers, 2001.

Huston, Perdita. "Andrea Evangelina Rodríguez (1879–19047)." In *The Right to Choose: Pioneers in Women's Health and Family Planning*, ed. Perdita Huston. London: Earthscan, 1992.

Incháustegui, Arístides. "Cronología de gobiernos y gobernantes de la República Dominicana." *Eme Eme: Estudios Dominicanos*, no. 36 (May–June, 1978): 3–15.

Incháustegui, Arístides, and Blanca Delgado Malagán, eds. *Abigaíl Mejía. Obras escogidas*. Vol. 2. Santo Domingo: Editora Corripio, 1995.

Inoa, Orlando. *Azúcar, árabes, cocolos y haitianos*. Santo Domingo: Editora Cole, 1999.

Inoa, Orlando, and Allen Wells. "Summer of Discontent: Economic Rivalry among Elite Factions during the Late Porfiriato in Yucatán." *Journal of Latin American Studies* 18, no. 2 (1986): 255–282.

Krohn-Hansen, Christian. "Magic, Money, and Alterity among Dominicans." *Social Anthropology* 3, no. 2 (1995): 129–146.

Lasso, Marixa. *Myths of Harmony: Race and Republicanism during the Age of Revolution, Colombia, 1795–1831*. Pittsburgh: University of Pittsburgh Press, 2007.

Lavrín, Asunción. *Women, Feminism, and Social Change in Argentina, Chile and Uruguay, 1890–1940*. Lincoln: University of Nebraska Press, 1995.

LeGrand, Catherine. "Living in Macondo: Economy and Culture in a United Fruit Company Banana Enclave in Colombia." In *Close Encounters of Empire: Writing the Cultural History of U.S.–Latin American Relations*, ed. Gilbert M. Joseph, Catherine LeGrand, and Ricardo Salvatore. Durham, N.C.: Duke University Press, 1998.

Levine, Lawrence. "Marcus Garvey and the Politics of Revitalization." In *Black Leaders of the Twentieth Century*, ed. John Hope Franklin and August Meier. Urbana: University of Illinois Press, 1982.

Lewis, Jessica. "Dancehall and the Politics of Race and Sexuality in Contemporary Jamaica." Unpublished manuscript.

Lewis, Rupert. *Marcus Garvey, Anti-Colonial Champion*. Trenton, N.J.: Africa World Press, 1988.

Lincoln, C. Eric, and Lawrence H. Mamiya. *The Black Church in the African American Experience*. Durham, N.C.: Duke University Press, 1990.

Little, Cynthia Jeffries. "Education, Philanthropy, and Feminism: Components of Argentine Womanhood, 1860–1926." In *Latin American Women: Historical Perspectives*, ed. Francesca Miller. Westport, Conn.: Greenwood Press, 1978.

Lora, Ana Mitila. "Entrevista con Juan Valdés Sánchez." *Listín Diario*, July 29, 1999.

Love, Eric T. *Race over Empire: Racism and U.S. Imperialism*. Chapel Hill: University of North Carolina Press, 2004.

Luft, Eric V. D. "Sarah Loguen Fraser, M.D., Class of 1876." *Alumni Journal* (Syracuse University) (Summer 1998).

Luker, Kristin. "Sex, Social Hygiene, and the State: The Double-Edged Sword of Social Reform." *Theory and Society* 27 (1998): 601–634.

Lund, Joshua. *The Mestizo State: Reading Race in Modern Mexico*. Minneapolis: University of Minnesota Press, 2012.

Madera, Melissa. "'Zones of Scandal': Gender, Public Health, and Social Hygiene in the Dominican Republic, 1916–1961." PhD diss., Binghamton University, 2011.

Manicom, Linzi. "Ruling Relations: Rethinking State and Gender in South African History." *Journal of African History* 33 (1992): 441–465.

Manley, Elizabeth. "'El Freno Suave': Gender, Politics and Dictatorship in the Dominican Republic, 1928–1942." Paper presented at the 2006 Meeting of the Latin American Studies Association, San Juan, Puerto Rico, March 15–18, 2006.

———. "*Poner un Grano de Arena*: Gender and Women's Political Participation under Authoritarian Rule in the Dominican Republic, 1928–1978." PhD diss., Tulane University, 2008.

Maríñez, Pablo A. *Agroindustria, estado y clases sociales en la era de Trujillo, 1935–1960*. Santo Domingo: Fundación Cultural Dominicana, 1993.

Marte, Roberto. *Cuba y la República Dominicana. Transición económica en el Caribe del siglo XIX*. Santo Domingo: Editorial CENAPEC, 1988.

———. *Estadísticas y documentos históricos sobre Santo Domingo, 1805–1890*. Santo Domingo: Amigo del Hogar, 1984.

Martin, Tony. *Race First: The Ideological and Organizational Struggles of Marcus Garvey and the Universal Negro Improvement Association*. Westport, Conn.: Greenwood Press, 1976.

Martínez, Samuel. "From Hidden Hand to Heavy Hand: Sugar, the State, and Migrant Labor in Haiti and the Dominican Republic." *Latin American Research Review* 34, no. 1 (1999): 57–84.

————. "Not a Cockfight: Rethinking Haitian-Dominican Relations." *Latin American* Perspectives 30, no. 3 (2003): 80–101.

Martínez-Fernández, Luis. *Torn between Empires: Economy, Society, and Patterns of Political Thought in the Hispanic Caribbean, 1840–1878.* Athens: University of Georgia Press, 1994.

Martínez Moya, Arturo. *La caña da para todo.* Santo Domingo: Archivo General de la Nación, 2011.

Martínez-Vergne, Teresita. "Bourgeois Women in the Early Twentieth Century Dominican National Discourse." *New West Indian Guide* 75, nos. 1–2 (2001): 65–89.

————. *Nation and Citizen in the Dominican Republic, 1880–1916.* Chapel Hill: University of North Carolina Press, 2005.

————. *Shaping the Discourse on Space: Charity and Its Wards in Nineteenth-Century San Juan, Puerto Rico.* Austin: University of Texas Press, 1999.

Mateo, Andrés. *Mito y cultura en la era de Trujillo.* Santo Domingo: Editora de Colores, 1993.

Mayes, April J. "Sugar's Metropolis: The Politics and Culture of Progress in San Pedro de Macorís, Dominican Republic, 1870–1930." PhD diss., University of Michigan, 2003.

————. "Tolerating Sex: Prostitution, Gender, and Governance in the Dominican Republic, 1880s–1924." In *Health and Medicine in the Circum-Caribbean, 1800–1968,* ed. Juanita De Barros, Steven Palmer, and David Wright. New York: Routledge, 2009.

————. "Why Dominican Feminism Moved to the Right: Class, Colour and Women's Activism in the Dominican Republic, 1880s–1940s." *Gender and History* 20, no. 2 (August 2008): 349–371.

McClintock, Anne. *Imperial Leather: Race, Gender, and Sexuality in the Colonial Contest.* Berkeley: University of California Press, 1995.

McGuinness, Aims. *Path of Empire: Panama and the California Gold Rush.* Ithaca, N.Y.: Cornell University Press, 2007.

McLeod, Marc C. "Garveyism in Cuba: 1920–1940." *Journal of Caribbean History* 30 (1999): 132–168.

————. "'Sin Dejar de Ser Cubanos': Cuban Blacks and the Challenges of Garveyism in Cuba." *Caribbean Studies* 31, no. 1 (January–June 2003): 75–105.

Miller, Francesca. "Latin American Feminism and the Transnational Arena." In *Women, Culture, and Politics in Latin America,* ed. Emilie Bergman et al. Berkeley: University of California Press, 1990.

Mitchell, Michele. *Righteous Propagation: The Politics of Racial Destiny after Reconstruction.* Chapel Hill: University of North Carolina Press, 2004.

Moran, Brian Patrick. "Prison Reform in the United States Navy and the Dominican Republic: The Military Occupation and Prisons, 1900–1930." PhD diss., University of Illinois at Chicago, 2000.

Moreno Fraginals, Manuel, Frank Moya Pons, and Stanley Engerman, eds. *Between Slavery and Free Labor: The Spanish-Speaking Caribbean in the Nineteenth Century.* Baltimore: Johns Hopkins University Press, 1985.

Mota Acosta, José. "El aporte de los cocolos a San Pedro de Macorís." In *Presencia étnica en San Pedro de Macorís,* ed. Miguel Phipps Cueto. San Pedro de Macorís: Universidad Central del Este, 2000.

Moya Pons, Frank. *The Dominican Republic: A National History.* New Rochelle, N.Y.: Hispaniola Books, 1995.

———. "The Land Question in Haiti and Santo Domingo: The Sociopolitical Context of the Transition from Slavery to Free Labor, 1801–1843." In *Between Slavery and Free Labor: The Spanish-Speaking Caribbean in the Nineteenth Century*, ed. Manuel Moreno Fraginals, Frank Moya Pons, and Stanley Engerman. Baltimore: Johns Hopkins University Press, 1985.

———. *Manual de historia dominicana*. Santiago: Universidad Católica Madre y Maestra, 1978.

———. "Modernización y cambios en la República Dominicana." In *Ensayos sobre cultura dominicana*, ed. José Chez Checo. Santo Domingo: Fundación Cultural Dominicana, [1981] 2001.

Mumford, Kevin J. *Interzones: Black/White Sex Districts in Chicago and New York in the Early Twentieth Century*. New York: Columbia University Press, 1997.

Nash, Mary. "Un/Contested Identities: Motherhood, Sex Reform and the Modernization of Gender Identity in Early Twentieth Century Spain." In *Constructing Spanish Womanhood: Female Identity in Modern Spain*, ed. Victoria Larée Enders and Pamela Beth Radcliff. Albany: State University of New York Press, 1999.

Ng'weno, Bettina. *Turf Wars: Territory and Citizenship in the Contemporary State*. Stanford: Stanford University Press, 2007.

"Notas oficiales de los Estados Unidos sobre la muerte de Ulises Heureaux." *Eme Eme: Estudios Dominicanos* 8, no. 48 (May–June 1980): 105–126.

Padilla, José María. "Oligarquía y subdesarrollo en Luperón, Región Norte, República Dominicana: 1900–1930." MA thesis, University of Puerto Rico at Río Piedras, 1995.

Pérez Memén, Fernando. "El proyecto de Constitución de Duarte." *Clío* 77, no. 175 (2008): 167–198.

Purcell, Trevor. *Banana Fallout: Class, Color, and Culture among West Indians in Costa Rica*. Los Angeles: University of California at Los Angeles, Center for Afro-American Studies Publications, 1993.

Putnam, Lara. *The Company They Kept: Migrants and the Politics of Gender in Caribbean Costa Rica*. Chapel Hill: University of North Carolina Press, 2002.

Quiles-Calderín, Viviana, ed. *República Dominicana y Puerto Rico. Hermandad en la lucha emancipadora. Correspondencia, 1876–1902*. Río Piedras, P.R.: Instituto de Estudios Hostosianos, 2001.

Rafael, Vicente L. "White Love: Surveillance and Nationalist Resistance in the U.S. Colonization of the Philippines." In *Cultures of United States Imperialism*, ed. Amy Kaplan and Donald Pease. Durham, N.C.: Duke University Press, 1993.

Regis, Helen A. "Blackness and the Politics of Memory in the New Orleans Second Line." *American Ethnologist* 28, no. 4 (2001): 752–777.

Renda, Mary. *Taking Haiti: Military Occupation and the Culture of U.S. Imperialism, 1915–1940*. Chapel Hill: University of North Carolina Press, 2001.

Reyes-Santos, Irmary. "On Pan-Antillean Politics: Ramón Emeterio Betances and Gregorio Luperón Speak to the Present." *Callaloo* 36, no. 1 (Winter 2013): 142–157.

Richardson, Bonham. *The Caribbean in the Wider World*. Cambridge: Cambridge University Press, 1992.

———. *Caribbean Migrants: Environment and Human Survival on St. Kitts and Nevis*. Knoxville: University of Tennessee Press, 1985.

Richiez Acevedo, Francisco. "Cocolandia, cosmopolitismo e hibridismo. Consideraciones sobre el cambio social que se opera en la ciudad de San Pedro de Macorís." PhD diss., Universidad Autónoma de Santo Domingo, 1967.

Robles, Frances. "Black Denial." *Miami Herald*, June 13, 2007.

Rodríguez, Pedro Pablo. "Marcus Garvey en Cuba." *Anales del Caribe*, nos. 7–8 (1987–1988): 279–301.

Rodríguez Demorizi, Emilio, ed. *Hostos en Santo Domingo*. Vols. 1 and 2. Ciudad Trujillo: J. R. Vda. García Sucs., 1939.

Rojas, Enrique. "Cream Has Bleached His Skin." ESPN Deportes.com, November 10, 2009. http://sports.espn.go.com/mlb/news/story?id=4642952.

Roorda, Eric Paul. *The Dictator Next Door: The Good Neighbor Policy and the Trujillo Regime in the Dominican Republic, 1930–1945*. Durham, N.C.: Duke University Press, 1998.

Rose, Carol M. *Property and Persuasion: Essays on the History, Theory, and Rhetoric of Ownership*. Boulder, Colo.: Westview Press, 1994.

Sagás, Ernesto. *Race and Politics in the Dominican Republic*. Gainesville: University Press of Florida, 2000.

Sanders, James. "'Citizens of a Free People'": Popular Liberalism and Race in Nineteenth-Century Southwestern Colombia." *Hispanic American Historical Review*, vol. 84, no. 2 (May 2004): 277–313.

——. *Contentious Republicans: Popular Politics, Race, and Class in Nineteenth-Century Colombia*. Durham, N.C.: Duke University Press, 2004.

San Miguel, Pedro. *La isla imaginada. Historia, identidad y utopía en La Española*. San Juan: Isla Negra, [1997] 2006.

Sawyer, Mark. *Racial Politics in Post-Revolutionary Cuba*. Cambridge: Cambridge University Press, 2005.

Scott, Joan W. "Gender, a Useful Category of Historical Analysis." *American Historical Review* 91, no. 5 (December 1986): 1053–1075.

Servio Ducoudray, Félix. *Los "gavilleros" del este. Una epopeya calumniada*. Santo Domingo: Editora de la Universidad Autónoma de Santo Domingo, 1974.

Sheller, Mimi. *Consuming the Caribbean: From Arawaks to Zombies*. London: Routledge, 2003.

Sidanius, Jim, Yesilernis Peña, and Mark Sawyer. "Inclusionary Discrimination: Pigmentocracy and Patriotism in the Dominican Republic." *Political Psychology* 22, no. 4 (2001): 827–851.

Silié, Rubén. "El hato y el conuco. Contexto para el surgimiento de la cultura criolla." In *Ensayos sobre cultura dominicana*, ed. Bernardo Vega et al. 2d ed. Santo Domingo: Fundación Cultural Dominicana, 1988.

Simmons, Kimberly. *Reconstructing Racial Identity and the African Past in the Dominican Republic*. Gainesville: University Press of Florida, 2009.

Sommer, Doris. *Foundational Fictions: The National Romances of Latin America*. Berkeley: University of California Press, 1991.

——. *One Master for Another: Populism as Patriarchal Rhetoric in Dominican Novels*. New York: University Press of America, 1983.

Stein, Judith. *The World of Marcus Garvey: Race and Class in Modern Society*. Baton Rouge: Louisiana State University Press, 1991.

Stephens, Michelle A. *Black Empire: The Masculine Global Imaginary of Caribbean Intellectuals in the United States, 1914–1962*. Durham, N.C.: Duke University Press, 2005.

Stoner, K. Lynn. *From House to Street: The Cuban Women's Movement for Legal Reform*. Durham, N.C.: Duke University Press, 1991.

Stutzman, Ronald. "El Mestizaje: An All-Inclusive Ideology of Exclusion." In *Cultural Trans-formations and Ethnicity in Modern Ecuador*, ed. Norman Whitten. Urbana: University of Illinois Press, 1981.

Tabili, Laura. *"We Ask for British Justice": Workers and Racial Difference in Late Imperial Britain.* Ithaca, N.Y.: Cornell University Press, 1994.

Thomas, Deborah. *Modern Blackness: Nationalism, Globalization, and the Politics of Culture in Jamaica.* Durham, N.C.: Duke University Press, 2004.

Tinker Salas, Miguel. *The Enduring Legacy: Oil, Culture, and Society in Venezuela.* Durham, N.C.: Duke University Press, 2009.

———. *In the Shadow of the Eagles: Sonora and the Transformation of the Border during the Por-firiato.* Berkeley: University of California Press, 1997.

———. "Relaciones de poder y raza en los campos petroleros venezolanos, 1920–1940." *Asuntos* [Centro Internacional de Educación y Desarrollo] 5, no. 10 (2001): 77–104.

Tolentino Dipp, Hugo. *Raza e historia en Santo Domingo. Orígenes del prejuicio en América.* Santo Domingo: Fundación Cultural Dominicana, [1974] 1992.

Tolentino Rojas, Vicente. *Historia de la división territorial.* Santiago de los Caballeros, D.R.: Edi-torial El Diario, 1944.

Torres-Saillant, Silvio. "Blackness and Meaning in Studying Hispaniola: A Review Essay." *Small Axe* 10, no. 1 (2006): 180–188.

———. "Creoleness or Blackness: A Dominican Dilemma." *Plantation Society in the Americas* 5, no. 1 (1998): 29–40.

Trachtenberg, Alan. *The Incorporation of America: Culture and Society in the Gilded Age.* New York: Hill and Wang, 1982.

Turits, Richard. *Foundations of Despotism: Peasants, the Trujillo Regime, and Modernity in Domini-can History.* Stanford: Stanford University Press, 2003.

———. "Par-delà les plantations: Question raciale et identités collectives à Santo Domingo." *Genesès* 66 (2007): 51–68.

———. "A World Destroyed, A Nation Imposed: The 1937 Haitian Massacre in the Dominican Republic." *Hispanic American Historical Review* 82, no. 3 (2002): 589–635.

Veeser, Cyrus. *A World Safe for Capitalism: Dollar Diplomacy and America's Rise to Global Power.* New York: Columbia University Press, 2007.

Vega, Augusto. *Ulises Heureaux. Ensayo histórico.* Ciudad Trujillo: Imprenta Arte y Cine, n.d.

Vega, Bernardo, Carlos Dobal, Carlos Esteban Deive, Rubén Silié, José del Castillo, and Frank Moya Pons. *Ensayos sobre cultura dominicana.* Santo Domingo: Fundación Cultural Domini-cana, 1990.

Veloz, Livia. "Fragment from *Historia del feminismo en la República Dominicana*." In *Documents of Dissidence*, ed. Cocco de Filippis. New York: City University of New York Dominican Studies Institute, 2000.

Wade, Peter. *Blackness and Race Mixture: The Dynamics of Racial Identity in Colombia.* Baltimore: Johns Hopkins University Press, 1993.

Wells, Allen, and Gilbert M. Joseph. "Modernizing Visions, *Chilango* Blueprints, and Provincial Growing Pains: Mérida at the Turn of the Century." *Mexican Studies/Estudios Mexicanos* 8, no. 2 (1992): 167–205.

Wheaton, Philip E. *Triunfando sobre las tragedias. Historia centenaria de la Iglesia Episcopal Do-minicana, 1897–1997.* Santo Domingo: Iglesia Episcopal Dominicana, 1997.

Zaglul, Antonio. *Despreciada en la vida y olvidada en la muerte. Biografía de Evangelina Rodríguez, la primera médica dominicana.* Santo Domingo: Editora Taller, 1997.

Záiter, Alba Josefina. *La identidad social y nacional en Dominicana. Un análisis psico-social.* San Pedro de Macorís: Universidad Central del Este, 1996.

Zeller, Neici M. "The Appearance of All, the Reality of Nothing: Politics and Gender in the Dominican Republic, 1880–1961." PhD diss., University of Illinois at Chicago, 2010.

———. *Discursos y espacios femeninos en República Dominicana, 1880–1961.* Santo Domingo: Editorial Letra Gráfica, 2012.

———. "El régimen de Trujillo y la fuerza laboral femenina en la República Dominicana, 1945–1951." In *La República Dominicana en el umbral del Siglo XXI,* ed. Ramonina Brea, Rosario Espinal, and Fernando Valerio-Holguín. Santo Domingo: Editora Centenario, 1999.

INDEX

Page references in *italics* refer to illustrations

Acción Feminista Dominicana (AFD), 117, 118, 132; First Feminist Assembly, 168n71; manifesto of, 131; Mejía's work with, 131–32; suffrage campaign of, *134*; and Trujillato, 132–33, 136–37, 138, 169n75

activism: Afro-Antillean, 96; circum-Caribbean, 96. *See also* Garveyism; United Negro Improvement Association

activism, antioccupation, 96, 115, 143; gender in, 139; Lugo's, 124–25; women's, 122, 123–24, 125–29, 138

activism, Dominican: anticolonial, 17; transnational networks of, 104–5; women's, 11, 28

Afro-Antilleans: activists, 96; of Caribbean rim, 158n1; coachmen, 83–84, 85, 142; Garveyites, 95, 96; identity among, 99; living conditions among, 81–82; misdemeanors by, 84, 86; police violence against, 84–86, 88; policing of, 79–86; in San Pedro, 7, 79–86, 88, 102; tensions with Hispanics, 84–85; in UNIA, 101. *See also* immigrants, Afro-Antillean; West Indians, British

agriculture, Dominican: legislation concerning, 39–40, 162n16; problems of, 41; of San Pedro de Macorís, 39, 63; on *terrenos comuneros*, 46. *See also* sugar estates, Dominican

El Albanico (women's club), 66, 71, 122

Alexander, James: murder of, 78, 83, 84, 86

Amantes de Estudio (San Pedro de Macorís), 65, 71, 157n24

Amechazurra, Juan, 8, 16, 39; financing of, 48; honoring of, 75

antiblack racism: in Caribbean societies, 32; in Jamaica, 33; in Wilsonian democracy, 112–13. *See also* blackness

antiblack racism, Dominican, 1–3; among elites, 2, 3, 4–6, 8–9; among intellectuals, 2, 3; and black mobility, 12; and *dominicanidad*, 17; in Dominican identity, 6–7; against Haitians, 108–9; Hispanophilic, 4; in nationalism, 2–3, 14, 142; relationship to anti-Haitianism, 6; role in modernization, 145; in San Pedro de Macorís, 80, 94; sexualized, 9, 88, 90; of Trujillato, 138, 144–45; by U.S. Marines, 105–6; during U.S. occupation, 10, 95–115; against West Indians, 103–4

anti-Haitianism, 1, 2; of Dominican elites, 143; and *dominicanidad*, 3, 17; in Dominican modernization, 145; in Dominican national identity, 11; in Dominican nationalism, 2–3, 135, 142; of *hispanidad*, 135; in labor management, 8; origins of, 4, 5; outside Santo Domingo, 7; power relations of, 6; as racist discourse, 143; relationship to antiblack racism, 6; role in labor exploitation, 8; in support for annexation, 21; of Trujillato, 5, 135, 138, 144–45. *See also* xenophobia, anti-Haitian

Athenaeum club (San Pedro de Macorís), 65

Báez, Josefa, 72, 73

bagaje (forced labor), 17

Balaguer, Joaquín, 3, 4; violence under, 118

banditry, Dominican, 51–52; causes of, 58; ideological construct of, 51–52, 53, 54–58; in Seibo Province, 54; during U.S. occupation, 53–56

bandits, Dominican: attacks on sugar estates, 53, 57, 95; conflict with U.S. Marines, 53, 95; disarming of, 54, 155n70; extortion by, 56–57; kidnapping by, 114; motives of, 54–55; peasants, 37, 53–60; versus revolutionaries, 58–59; social problem of, 37

baseball teams, West Indian, *105*

Bass, Alejandro, 44, 45

Bass, William, 80

71–72; occupation officials on, 111; U.S. foreign policy elites on, 21

womanhood, Hispanic: feminist advocacy of, 137

women, Dominican: antioccupation activism of, 122, 123–24, 125–29, 138; domestic role of, 119, 121, 123, 135, 139; education of, 68, 119, 120–21, 136; festival queens, 71, 72, 73, 142; historiography of, 118; in labor force, 140; and *latinidad* nationalism, 127; political activity of, 11, 28; relationship to state, 135; role in nationalism, 118, 119, 125, 126–31; of San Pedro de Macorís, 65, 66; suffrage for, 117–19, 132, 133, 135, 136, 169n75; *trujillistas*, 118, 132; Trujillo's programs for, 135–36; during U.S. occupation, 122–29, 138, 144. *See also* feminists, Dominican; prostitutes

Women's National Congress (Dominican Republic), 126

working class, Dominican: domestic spaces of, 129; racialization, 77; threats to, 8; during U.S. occupation, 97. *See also* Afro-Antilleans; labor force, Dominican; West Indians

working class, *petromacorisano*, 77, 78; labor protests by, 95; policing of, 79–86, 142–43

World War I: sugar industry during, 102; West Indians during, 100

xenophobia, anti-Haitian, 1, 3, 4. *See also* anti-Haitianism

yeguadas, of San Pedro de Macorís, 38, 152n9

Young Women's Institute (Santo Domingo), 121

April J. Mayes is associate professor of history at Pomona College and is an affiliated faculty member of the Pedro Francisco Bonó Institute in Santo Domingo. A founding member of the Transnational Hispaniola Collective, she conducts research and writes about the Dominican Republic and has published articles in *Gender & History*, *Radical History Review*, and *Estudios Sociales*.

The University Press of Florida is the scholarly publishing agency for the State University System of Florida, comprising Florida A&M University, Florida Atlantic University, Florida Gulf Coast University, Florida International University, Florida State University, New College of Florida, University of Central Florida, University of Florida, University of North Florida, University of South Florida, and University of West Florida.

Printed in the USA
CPSIA information can be obtained
at www.ICGtesting.com
JSHW020207290124
56037JS00005B/133

9 780813 061962